No Entry

*"No place on earth is
further than 18 hours away from here"*
Heathrow Airport, London.

UNIVERSITY OF
WOLVERHAMPTON

Harrison Learning Centre
City Campus
University of Wolverhampton
St Peter's Square
Wolverhampton WV1 1RH
Telephone: 0845 408 1631
Online Renewals:
www.wlv.ac.uk/lib/myaccount

Telephone Renewals: 01902 321333 or 0845 408 1631
Please RETURN this item on or before the last date shown above.
Fines will be charged if items are returned late.
See tariff of fines displayed at the Counter. (L2)

Hans Kornø Rasmussen

No Entry
Immigration Policy
in Europe

Handelshøjskolens Forlag
Copenhagen Business School Press

© Handelshøjskolens Forlag, *Copenhagen Business School Press*, 1996
English Version, 1997
Printed in Denmark
Set in Plantin by AKA-PRINT A/S, Denmark
Translated by M.D.R. Murphy, M.D.R.M. Transnational
Cover designed by Kontrapunkt
Book designed by Jørn Ekstrøm

ISBN 87-16-13358-7

Series D, no. 28

Distribution

Scandinavia:
Munksgaard/DBK, Siljangade 2-8, P.O. Box 1731,
DK-2300 Copenhagen S, Denmark,
phone: +45 3269 7788, fax: +45 3269 7789

North America:
Global Management, LLC, Book Service, 2564 Branch Street, B2,
Middleton, WI 53562, USA
phone: +1 608 836 0088, fax: +1 608 836 0087
E-mail: 102135.2151@compuserve.com

Rest of the World:
Marston Book Services, P.O. Box 269,
Abingdon, Oxfordshire, OX14 4YN, UK
phone: +44 (0) 1235 465500, fax: +44 (0) 1235 465555
E-mail Direct Customers: direct.order@marston.co.uk
E-mail Booksellers: trade.order@marston.co.uk

Foreword

Emigration, to a great extent, has been a European phenomenon throughout history. Voyages of discovery, colonial ventures and the "dream of America" have for centuries formed an important part of the European outlook on the world. The change came about at the end of the 1980s when, inspite of the official halt on immigration, Europe suddenly became a continent of immigration. Nowadays, the flow of immigration to Western Europe is greater than that to the USA.

This development is taking place at a time when the countries of Western Europe are in the middle of a process of economic and political integration where both the physical and psychological barriers between countries are being broken down. It is at this point that immigrants and refugees find themselves in an awkward predicament.

My book is about all those foreigners who, throughout history, have come to this continent as well as all those who doubtless will come in the future. In the ever more intensive process of internationalization, human beings are often forgotten in its wake. I hope this book will go some way to correcting this state of affairs.

I am grateful for help and encouragement from Dr. Ole Lange, Journalist Alex Frank Larsen, Artist Mie Luf, Professor of Demography, Poul Christian Matthiessen, Henrik Olesen, former IGC Coordinator in Geneva, Thomas Mortensen, MSc. graduate in Demography, also of the IGC. My greatest debt of gratitude is, however, towards my wife, Karin Kornø Rasmussen, for her invaluable support throughout the entire process.

I am also grateful to the Danish Social Science Research Council and the Council for Development Research who have granted funds for this project. Finally, I would like to express my gratitude to the staff of the Institute of International Economics and Management at the Copenhagen Business School who provided me with office space as well as inspiration.

It goes without saying that none of the above are responsible for any mistakes, misunderstandings or errors of judgement that may be found in this work.

August 1997
Hans Kornø Rasmussen

Contents

1. Introduction

1.1 A sea of troubles

All over Europe the ongoing debate about the foreigners in our midst is laden with dilemmas and contradictions; arguments and opinions streak through the air like fireballs in one of the most emotionally complex and ill-documented debates in recent times.

Other topics, too, give rise to controversy. Environmental issues divide people although most people prefer a healthier environment to a less healthy one. The welfare state, although most are in favour of it. Military defence, although most people want it either for their country or for Europe in general.

The great debate about refugees and immigrants is, however, different. The points of reference are barely visible, which makes it extremely hard to keep one's bearings in this all-encompassing debate. For that reason too, an unusually wide range of opinions and attitudes emerges with "foreigners have something positive to contribute to society" at one end, to "refugees and immigrants constitute a dire threat to ordered society" at the other.

It is not so strange that the opinions are so diverse and divergent for it is precisely at this point that individuals find themselves in a dilemma. On the one hand, most people clearly realize that there are limits to how many foreigners a given country can take in and assist. On the other hand, most Europeans are humanists who want to help their fellow human beings in distress to a certain extent.

In Western Europe, our entire set of values is put to a stern test. The traditional political groupings do not provide much guidance as neither the Left nor the Right have any long-term solutions. A religious approach might provide an answer such as, for instance, when a church in Paris provides refuge and shelter for refugees who are going to be returned. However, when seen in a broader context, this kind of effort provides no lasting answer either. Anyway, most of the men and women of the church are just as hesitant and as much in the dark on this issue as the rest of the population.

One of the major problems bedevilling the debate on refugees and immigrants is how to distinguish properly between the multitude of diverse groups of people who travel to Europe. It is of overriding importance to draw the essential distinction between two categories: refugees and immigrants.

In general, immigration into Western Europe takes place primarily through family reunification or through illegal channels. It is clear that the measures needed to influence immigration differ fundamentally from those required when dealing with people fleeing catastrophes.

Nowadays, political refugees constitute only a minor part of total migration, although they are given very prominent media coverage. Fewer than 50,000 people have been granted political asylum in recent years in accordance with the rules of the Geneva Convention, while roughly the same number have been granted asylum on other grounds. Thus, with total migration numbering about two million people, political refugees at the very most constitute about five per cent of the total legal migration to Western Europe.[1]

Although, the number of political refugees to whom asylum has been granted has remained stable for several years, the number of applicants seeking asylum in Western Europe has risen sharply; which means that only a relatively small percentage of asylum seekers have been recognized as refugees.[2]

In the political arena, the established parties have all been forced on to the defensive in an area of great concern to their electorates. Throughout Western Europe, politicians have been performing a tightrope act without the benefit of a safety net, and this particular stunt has become ever harder to pull off since the fall of the Berlin Wall in November 1989.

On the one hand, politicians are obliged to take into account the rise of the extreme-Right, since the experiences of the 1930s still cast a shadow over Europe. On the other hand, Western Europe must uphold and defend democracy and human rights, the observance of which they have been among the foremost to champion since the end of the Second World War. However, it is not just the politicians who face this dilemma; so, too, do all the citizens of Western Europe.

There are no absolutely right or wrong answers to the many questions arising from the issue of refugees and immigrants which will always be a question of weighing up various, and often conflicting, considerations.

It is also possible that immigration will always have conflicts trailing in its wake, whatever the attitude of the host population. These conflicts will be all the more deeply rooted in proportion to the extent that the culture of the immigrants is alien to that of the hosts. One has only to look at the difficulties which have arisen in the West over the Muslim view of gender roles or those difficulties which occur when people from other cultures encounter the western welfare model which displaces the role of the family as the central provider.

However, it is possible that the problems are even more deeply rooted than the above examples show, in that the immigrants are perhaps facing one of our deepest primal driving forces – the need to defend our identity and our territory.

In the summer of 1990, I participated in a series of television programs where we visited remote corners of Denmark. We sailed around the entire kingdom in search of an answer to the question of what being Danish really meant. This question we thought particularly relevant because Denmark was about to enter the Single European Market at the end of 1992, after which everything from people to money was supposed to flow freely from Gibraltar in southern Spain to the Skaw in northern Denmark.

In the small Danish island communities, there was no wavering in the ranks. It was not just a question of being Danish. What really mattered was which part of Denmark you came from and how long you had lived in the locality. Were Copenhageners to move to the little island of Læsø in the Skagerrak, they might as well give up any hopes of being accepted by the locals. No matter how well they learned to speak the local dialect or how eagerly they took up fishing, their grandchildren would be the first to be considered part of the island community. According to the locals, only at that stage would they be integrated into the consciousness of the locality.

The German debater and author, Hans Magnus Enzensberger, was in no doubt when he wrote in his "Die Grosse Wanderung", published in 1992, that "every migration, irrespective of its cause, gives rise to conflicts." A little further on in the same text, he continued, "group egoism and xenophobia are constant factors in anthropology."[3]

If his claims are correct, then there is only one possible course of action which is to close the border crossings throughout Western Europe and allocate so much policing to coast-guard duties that no foreigners could ever hope to get in.

2

But then a new dilemma arises because, in these same years, exactly the opposite trends are in play. Trade and commerce are undergoing a process of internationalization, and ever larger sums of money are moving ever more effortlessly around the globe. We travel more often and further afield, while television, on a daily basis, transmits every disaster, no matter where it happens, into our living rooms. At a local level, we are in the process of creating a united Europe and, if the wishes of the politicians are fulfilled, the internal borders of Western Europe will have disappeared by 1999.

The citizens of Western Europe are in the middle of a process where physical and psychological barriers are being broken down. Among the great leaps forward being taken down the road to Union are the rules of the Single European Market concerning open borders and the powerful political desire for a single currency. However, it is precisely these steps which give rise to strong fears about the loss of national identity; fears further intensified by the presence of foreigners.

In this general climate of insecurity and fear of losing national identities, refugees and immigrants have been made into scapegoats to an extent that their numbers and influence do not warrant. This is the reason why they occupy a position in the media which is out of all proportion with reality.

The award-winning 1990 BBC film, "The March", struck a raw nerve in the major Western European nations. In the film, hordes of starving and exhausted Africans marched on Fortress Europe only to be confronted by ranks of well-armed soldiers with the twelve European stars on their helmets.

The European public was very receptive to this message at that time because mass-migrations were already taking place in the real world – only from an entirely different quarter as endless columns of Trabants and over-filled trains conveyed tens of thousands of East Germans to the West. The Berlin Wall had fallen, Communism was drawing its last breath more or less everywhere and the West was scared out of its wits by the prospect of a mass-influx from the East.

The pace of development was indeed explosive. In 1992 alone, 693,000 people sought political asylum in Western Europe; whereas five years earlier, the equivalent figure had been just over 170,000.[4]

Immigration rose dramatically as well. From 1989 onwards, there was an annual net rate of immigration well over half-a-million;[5] and then there were the illegal immigrants.

Developments in Europe were chaotic at the outset of the 1990s. No one knew what would happen in the ex-Communist countries and, at the same time, there was great uncertainty in Western Europe about the process of integration which was then being hurried along. The currency markets were in chaos and the referenda in Denmark and France, eventually followed by those in Norway and Switzerland, served to illustrate the deep divisions in the populations on the Union issue.

Western Europe looked on helplessly while the biggest post-war catastrophe unfolded in the Balkans as former Yugoslavia dissolved into armed conflict in 1991. In April of the following year, war broke out in Bosnia-Herzegovina and, in the ensuing three months, 2.6 million people were made homeless. All in all, almost four million people were forced to flee, and 700,000 of them came to Western Europe.[6]

1.2 What this book is about

A series of factors seem to indicate that Europe has received a much needed breathing space when it comes to immigration.

The fragile peace process in the former-Yugoslavia gives rise to the hope that the flow of refugees from the Balkans has finally dried up; and, in fact, many refugees are returning home.

The Cold War is over and the ex-Communist states seem to be in a reasonably stable phase of political and economic development, with emigration from these states also at a surprisingly low level.

The total number of people seeking political asylum in Western Europe has fallen sharply from almost 700,000 in 1992 to 240,000 only four years later.[7]

Does this mean that the acrimonious and often openly hostile debate about refugees and immigrants is now over? Have the problems and conflicts engendered by the presence of foreigners in Europe been overcome?

The answer to both of the above questions is that this is highly unlikely.

Over twenty million non-Europeans live in Western Europe today,[8] though what their future role will be is anyone's guess, in a Western Europe which is now in the process of carrying out an historic process of integration.

According to the rules of the Single European Market, labour may travel freely from country to country as long as it is not foreign. The Schengen Convention says that all physical obstacles to journeys between virtually all the Western European nations have been abolished. However, the borders between the countries of Western Europe and their respective legal systems are, by and large, still intact.

What is to be done about all the people who do not belong to any part of an area without borders; in other words, all those who do not have a Western European citizenship? What are we to do about the Egyptian who has a German residence permit, when he or she gets on a bicycle and rides over the former Danish-German border and then crosses the supposedly defunct Danish-Swedish border into Sweden?

In the future, how will the people forced to seek asylum in Western Europe be treated? Will they be able to seek political asylum in Denmark and then travel on to Portugal?

What is to be done about the constantly rising illegal immigration into Western Europe? This particular form of immigration poses an acute problem in many parts, especially in Southern Europe where in Spain, for instance, there were 3,377 officially registered Algerians in 1993 but 8,544 Algerians were detained in the same period.[9]

The most reliable estimates put the yearly entry of illegal immigrants at about half-a-million and, in all, there are approximately three million illegal immigrants in Western Europe at the time of writing.[10] According to the EU Commission, this type of immigration is larger than the legal variety.[11] How is this going to affect the individual countries?

How is a Europe without internal borders going to tackle the problem posed by the potential migratory pressure which will arise as a result of the rapid population growth in many countries in the Third World? Most of those parts of the world where demographic growth is strongest are within a few hours flight-time from Western Europe, and the number of inhabitants of the Muslim countries in the Middle East and North Africa is expected to double towards the year 2025.[12] The population of Western Europe, on the other hand, is set to decline over the same period unless there is a rise in immigration levels over and above those of today.

A wall could be erected around Western Europe that would be virtually impossible to breach. With present developments in the communications and transport sectors, this would require ever increasing amounts of ever more efficient systems of supervision and control in order to prevent unwanted immigration. The question is whether Europeans are prepared to accept such an increase in control and supervision?

The danger in closing the door too firmly towards the outside world is that there is a real risk of suppressing the desirable immigration which comes in the wake of the general process of globalization; a form of immigration which is growing faster than any other type,[13] according to the OECD.

It is anyone's guess how the border-free Europe of the future is going to build up a system capable of distinguishing between the very extensive desirable immigration following in the wake of the internationalization of commerce and trade, cross-border courses of education and the exploding number of tourists coming to Western Europe from every corner of the globe from the not-quite-so desirable immigration of those travelling to Western Europe in search of better prospects.

Instead of building real or virtual walls Western Europe should perhaps welcome future immigration as the continent is on the verge of a grey revolution. Western European women are giving birth to fewer children than ever before. The average fertility rate is 1.43 children per EU woman, which is 30 per cent below the level necessary to prevent a decline in population figures. That this is no passing phenomenon is illustrated by the fact that this process of decline has been under way since the mid 1960s.[14]

If this extremely low birth rate is linked with the entry of the post-war baby-boomers into the pension-arena, and due note is taken of the fact that life-expectancy is still going up, then the scene is set for a constantly ageing and, in the end, extremely-aged pensioners' Western Europe. At the turn of this century, every twentieth European was over the age of 65, today, it is every seventh and, in 25 years time, it will be every fifth.[15]

Perhaps this demographic trap could be avoided if some fresh blood were added to the people of Europe who are already well on their way to forming a small and dwindling exclusive category of an otherwise growing world population. Europeans formed 18.4 per cent of humanity at the outbreak of World War Two; nowadays, they form a little over 8 per cent and, by the year 2025, the Europeans will constitute, at most, 6.5 per cent of the world population.[16]

The debate on foreigners, therefore, whether it focuses on immigrants or refugees, has not been closed; on the contrary, it is possible that the truly serious debate about foreigners is just about to start in a somewhat less tense and uncompromisingly hostile atmosphere than has reigned hitherto. This complicated and multi-faceted set of problems is the subject matter of the remainder of this book.

2. Who are foreigners

2.1 The impossible reckoning

Where do the most foreigners live – in the USA or Western Europe? Most people would answer the USA because all races, nationalities and religions have been well and truly thrown together into the legendary melting pot, and the country still defines itself as an immigrant nation.

Things are different in Europe where there is no melting pot and none of the European countries view themselves as immigrant nations. The continent of Europe consists of several different areas, each with its own historical, cultural and linguistic particularity and, frequently, that particularity and the nation-state coincide – as in the case of Denmark. If an African settles down in Europe, that would not make him or her a European, although he or she might, after some years, become an Italian or a Belgian in accordance with the rules which govern the granting of citizenship.

If the USA is taken to be one end of the immigration spectrum, then Germany represents the other extreme in that, there, the emphasis is placed on citizens either being German or able to prove their German ancestry. German legislation in this field operates on the basis of who is "*deutscher Volkszugehöriger*" or not, this being decided by the individual's consciousness of being German as well as having German blood in their veins.[1]

In practice, this means that someone born and raised in Russia, who knows nothing about Germany and does not speak German, can still automatically obtain German citizenship by satisfying the blood requirement; whereas Moroccan immigrants may never become part of the community through the granting of citizenship no matter how well they might speak the language or can yodel like a South German. This view of the ethnic and cultural community of all Germans is in complete harmony with the Wilhelmine Empire's and the Third Reich's ambitions to bring together all Germans within the area of one nation-state,[2] one of the consequences of which is the emphasis with which Germany points out that it is not an immigrant nation.

Similar blood ties connect Latin America and Southern Europe in that Latin Americans who can prove an ancestral connection to Italy, Spain or Portugal are also eligible to become citizens of those countries.[3]

There are other ways whereby nations define their populations. For instance, all Jews may travel to Israel and automatically obtain citizenship, but what exactly is a Jew in this context? According to the religious definition, Judaism is transmitted through the mother, though the present requirement for immigrants is that just one of either of the applicant's parents or grandparents was Jewish, which means that even if applicants are completely atheist, do not speak Hebrew nor have any knowledge of the state of Israel and its history, the reason for them being accepted and obtaining citizenship in Israel is one based on religion. Thus, of the 500,000 Russian Jews who have emigrated to Israel since 1989, only 2 per cent at the most are believers.[4]

An idea of the great difficulties encountered in the debate about foreigners in Western Europe may be gained from the fact that, according to statistics, there are more foreigners in Germany than there are in the USA. In 1993, 8.5 per cent of the total population of Germany consisted of foreigners while the equivalent percentage in the USA was 7.9.[5] However, these two percentages are not comparable in that foreigners in Germany are those without German citizenship whereas that particular group in the USA consists of those who were born outside the country.

The confusion is not lessened by the fact that, although Germany is not officially an immigrant nation, in 1994 it received more immigrants than the USA. In that year, Germany received over a million immigrants while the figure for the USA was 776,000. However, it should be pointed out that there were far more people leaving Germany than the USA. In 1994, the figure for Germany was 740,000.[6]

The USA does not record how many people leave the country, in any case, this figure is relatively small. This means, in net terms, that immigration to the USA is still larger than immigration to Germany, although this does not alter the fact that in recent years Germany has received more immigrants than the USA. However, as mentioned above, this has been partly compensated for by extensive emigration.

The confusion does not end here as these German figures do not include the many hundreds of thousands of ethnic Germans – the *"Aussiedler"*– who have moved to Germany since the collapse of Communism. If they are included, then immigration to Germany in 1992 was of the order of around one and a half million people. If the emigration figure for that year of 720,000 is also taken into account, this means that, in net terms, Germany received almost as many immigrants as the USA; the figures being 780,000 and 974,000 respectively if one includes the ethnic Germans.[7]

The Western European figures for foreigners are generally based on juridical status, i.e., the number of people resident who do not have national citizenship which, in turn, means that the number of foreigners in a given country depends largely on the regulations governing the granting of citizenship. This explains why Germany has so many foreigners which is because only a tiny fraction of the immigrants who have lived there for many years have been granted German citizenship.

A journey through Britain, for instance, would convince most people that there were at least as many foreigners living there as in Germany. All over the country one can see Indians, Pakistanis, Chinese and West Indians; even though foreigners make up only 3.5 per cent of the population.[8] This percentage, however, does not include the figure of around 2.6 million who are considered to be immigrants from the former empire, but who have obtained full British citizenship.[9] If, however, they are included in the tally, then the British figures come close to German levels.

The same applies to France, where people from North Africa and the former French colonies in West Africa and Asia are quite visible in the streets. Here, the foreign share of the population is 6.3 per cent.[10] If France's relatively liberal policy for granting citizenship is taken into account, and the fact that the latest figures date from 1990, from an emotional or popular point of view it will then seem that there are at least as many foreigners in France as there are in Germany. It is only that, as in Britain, they have been migrating to France over a much longer period of time and, consequently, have become French citizens over that time.

Such tallies are further complicated by the fact that it is sometimes very difficult to place correctly people who have come from former European overseas possessions. For instance, people from French overseas territories such as Martinique or Guadeloupe are not foreigners but as French as the Marseilles dockworker who can trace his French ancestry back through several centuries. However, inhabitants of the former Dutch colony of St Martin, who are Dutch passport holders, are foreigners when they travel to the Netherlands.

There is, therefore, no answer to the question of how many foreigners are living in Western Europe because no-one can properly define a foreigner, an alien or a non-European. At which point does someone cease to be a foreigner? How long does a Somali refugee remain a Somalian? Does that particular person have to fulfil certain criteria, belong to a certain religion; and what about the Belgian in the Netherlands or the Swede in Denmark, are they foreigners?

In addition, to say the very least, the statistics in this area are incomplete not just in terms of determining how many are nationals or not, but also in the area of how many emigrate and migrate.

Some nations do not compile any statistics as such, and figures are reached according to widely differing sets of parametres, while some countries only register immigration but not emigration. Some countries, Germany and Ireland for instance, register every person entering as an immigrant, whereas other countries require a stay of anything between twelve months to three years before they are included in the immigration statistics; a factor which leads to an over-estimate of immigration to Germany by comparison with other European nations.[11] The 1989 edition of the UN's Demographic Yearbook contains the following remark about the statistics of migration: "They are the most difficult of demographic entities to define and quantify correctly."[12]

Because of these statistical discrepancies from nation to nation, the comparable figures for the countries of Western Europe only emerge after a considerable period of time. They are published by Eurostat at the end of each year, by which time they are at least two years old.

Why is it so important to know how many foreigners there are in Western Europe, how many arrive and how many leave? This dearth of knowledge was not an issue a few years ago since it did not give rise to political problems as it does today, and each country dealt with immigrants according to its national regulations. However, for a variety of reasons, this state of affairs has proved to be untenable.

To start with, the continent has never experienced immigration on the scale of recent years when, between 1989 and 1993, net immigration in Western Europe almost reached a figure of six million people.[13]

It was from 1988 onwards that immigration assumed such proportions that it was designated in September 1992 by the then British Foreign Secretary, Douglas Hurd, "one of the most serious, perhaps the most serious problem" faced by Europe.[14]

In addition, it is more than probable that the developments of recent years will continue in the decades to come. A series of factors indicate that Europe in the future will come under considerable migratory pressure, not just because many wish to travel to Europe (Chapter 5) but also because, within the foreseeable future, Western Europe may find itself in a situation where immigration becomes desirable (Chapter 6).

Although immigration has levelled off since 1993, this state of affairs cannot be expected to continue. The OECD, in its usual diplomatic fashion, says in the preamble to the organization's latest report that "this levelling-off is largely a consequence of measures taken by host countries to better control the flows, and not from a fall in migration potential, since economic and demographic imbalances between developed and developing nations have not disappeared."[15]

This flow of people from outside, combined with the serious political problems it has brought about, has given rise to a considerable need to map the size of these groups as well as the consequences their presence would have for the rest of society.

The second point is that immigration and the presence of foreigners in Western Europe has caused several almost insoluble problems in terms of the current process of European integration of the present 15 EU member states as well as Norway, Iceland and Liechtenstein. These three, along with the EU countries, are members of the European Economic Area, the EEA, and are thus committed to the freedom of movement for labour according to the rules of the Single European Market. It is expected that this will also apply to the countries of Eastern and Central Europe when they become participants in the process of European Union.

Are the individual European countries willing and able to relinquish control of immigration to community institutions? The prime duty of the nation-state is to protect its citizens by means of adopting rules which are widely accepted. Within its borders, it seeks to create a feeling of community through, for instance, the national education system along with various symbols and rituals such as the national flag and anthem. Towards the outside world, the nation-state has to ensure the security of its citizens by means of its capacity to defend its borders effectively, which makes immigration control one of its most important tasks.

That this, indeed, is the case has been amply proved by the process of European integration. While the countries cheerfully bring down the obstacles to the free movement of capital, services and goods at a rate hitherto unknown in history, they do not want to hand over the task of immigration and border control to community institutions; which means that immigration is primarily dealt with at national level by the individual member states.

Some common regulation in the area of refugees has been implemented by all 15 EU members (Chapter 7), but this is mainly due to necessity. If there were no cooperation between the states and no harmonization of rules whatsoever, then the result would be completely chaotic conditions in which asylum seekers would be able to apply for asylum in one country after the other.

Nor were the rules implemented to improve the refugees' lot. The opposite is closer to the truth, since European cooperation has meant that countries which were traditionally more open have now tightened their legislation in order to fall in line with the rest of Europe. The reasoning behind this is that the defensive chain around Europe is only as strong as its weakest link. This type of legislative manoeuvre has been characterized as "Euro-opportunism".

Therefore, when it is said that the EU is building up "Fortress Europe" in this particular area, this is incorrect as the EU does not have an actual refugee and immigrant policy. As described in Chapter 7, it is the EU member states themselves, by means of inter-governmental cooperation, who work out a common policy. The EU Commission has always wanted the freedom of movement of labour to apply to immigrants also, but since the member states have never been able to reach agreement on this matter, it has never come about.

The process of creating the so-called "Fortress Europe" has thus not been guided by Brussels. The movement towards ever tighter immigration control has been marked by increasingly restrictive national legislation combined with a flurry of inter-governmental agreements.[16] This pattern, however, is slowly starting to change as a result of the Amsterdam Treaty of June 1997 as described in Chapter 7.

This does not mean that the EU has not, on occasion, taken the initiative or pointed out the necessity of a coordinated policy in this area. However, the disagreements between the member states were too great and the EU Commission has felt a growing unease in recognizing "the paradox which characterizes immigration: despite the move in the majority of member states in the mid-1970s to halt permanent legal immigration, it still continues. The facts contradict policy statements which are becoming increasingly out of step with reality. The reality reflects a certain powerlessness in the face of an immigration not fully under control."[17]

That the individual countries have widely differing systems for the regulation of foreigners is not surprising, considering their various historical backgrounds. This means that the problems in coping with the rising number of immigrants are handled in different ways according to which national legislation is in question.

This does give rise to a series of questions when the countries are carrying out a process of economic and political integration as they are at this time. A key factor in the creation of the Single European Market is the freedom of movement for labour between the member states, a particular precondition which becomes all the more necessary to translate into reality should the European Monetary Union (EMU) become a reality.

As things stand, though, this precondition only applies to the citizens of EU member states who may, without any problems or application requirements, look for work in another member state. It does not apply to 14 million people in the EU area who are citizens of states ouside the EU. This is a large number of people and, were they to form their own state, it would be the seventh-largest in the EU.

In the long-run, this limitation on the free movement of labour will cause insurmountable problems when the internal national borders of the EU are abolished. Already, today, there is a pressing problem posed by the question of which foreigners are not to be allowed to cross borders unlike bona-fide EU citizens.

The Franco-German border, for instance, which is over a thousand kilometres long, may be crossed by labour as long as it is not foreign. Since both countries have widely divergent rules for determining who is or is not a foreigner, systems of intensive checks and controls are necessary.

In Germany, there might be an 18 year-old boy who was born in Germany of Turkish parents who had moved to Germany 30 years ago. He is not a German citizen despite having lived nowhere else and speaking fluent German. He may not cross the border into France. In France, there could well be an 18 year-old Algerian girl who moved to the country with her parents six years previously, who is now a French citizen although she does not speak French fluently. She may cross the border to look for work in Germany.

The EU countries are thus in the situation of having to define which categories of foreigner may or may not freely cross the national borders. Not only do foreigners have a different status in law, but they are not even categorized in the same way; there is great confusion solely in the area of what labels are to be appended to the various groups.

In Western Europe there are many different groups of people who have the status of legitimate residents but who do not have national citizenship. Many of these do not want to give up their connection to their homeland as, in many places, dual citizenship is not an option. Some, many of whom are in Germany, have obtained unlimited residence permits after a period of five years whereas large groups of people from Eastern Europe, for instance contract or seasonal workers and some refugees, have only been granted temporary residence permits.

In return for a given nation-state affording protection to its inhabitants and granting them rights, various requirements have to be met. Citizenship is at the heart of the set of formal rules governing who participates in this process because it is the seal of approval which tells foreigners that they now belong to their adopted country. Once they become citizens, the former-foreigners cannot be sent back for military service in their country of origin, they may vote at all elections and they receive new passports. However, they do lose whatever protection their formal connection to their country of origin might have afforded them.

2.2 Blood ties

Normally, people acquire their citizenship through birth; though which citizenship is acquired depends on the legislation in force in the countries in question. There are two main principles governing this: *Ius sanguinis* – blood bond and *Ius soli* – territorial connection.

Ius sanguinis grants citizenship according to the nationality of the father or, if he cannot be traced, then that of the mother. Generally speaking, this rule applies in those instances where there was a distinct people before the creation of the modern nation-state. This principle applies in most Western and Northern European countries and, during the mass migrations of the previous century, a significant number of people maintained a link with their home countries thus enabling descendants to return and claim citizenship in those countries from which their fore-fathers had emigrated.

This principle has been very significant in the case of Germany in recent years since the *Aussiedler*, mentioned earlier, are ethnic Germans able to prove that they are descendants of the German "*Volk*" and are thus eligible for German citizenship. From 1950 up to the present day, approximately three million ethnic Germans have become German citizens in this way.[18]

Ius soli grants citizenship to persons born within the national borders. This principle has been used in immigrant nations who wanted to afford this security to their immigrant population and where there had been no nation as such before their arrival. The USA, Canada, and Australia, along with most of the Latin American nations, embody this principle which, in one sense, is restrictive in that it does not automatically grant citizenship to a person born in another country.

On the other hand, all children born to immigrants are assured of acquiring citizenship irrespective of how long their parents have been in the country. In itself, this gives rise to other problems. For instance, between the Texan towns of Brownsville and Laredo on the Mexican border there is a series of birth clinics where, for a price of anything between $200 and $700, Mexican women may give birth to their little "Americans".[19]

Most Western European countries have legislation which combines both principles and where blood ties are the decisive factor.

Great Britain has traditionally had the same rules as the major immigrant nations. This, however, became untenable when it was realized that almost a billion inhabitants of colonies and Commonwealth countries could thus demand British citizenship and, in 1981, the law was changed so that only those who were actually born in Britain automatically became British citizens. Later on, the principle of *Ius sanguinis* was used when a further requirement was made that at least one of the parents had to be a British citizen.

In France, the principle is that citizenship is in accordance with blood ties in that children of French parents are automatically French citizens irrespective of where they were born. A different principle is applied to foreigners in that children born of immigrants in France may apply for French citizenship and receive it on their eighteenth birthday provided they have been resident in France for the past five years and do not have a criminal record.

The decisive aspect of this particular question is what happens to those children born to immigrants in Western Europe where the national regulation is based on the nationality of the parents. Were the blood-tie principle to be followed to the letter, no children of immigrants could ever acquire citizenship of the country to which their parents had emigrated.

The closest one gets to this situation is in Germany where, in 1993, the immigrant population was around 6.5 million, of whom 2.5 million had been in the country for over fifteen years. Only a little over 250,000 of these had been granted German citizenship in the years between the halt on immigration of 1973 and 1990.[20]

In Western Europe today, a very slow process of convergence of national legislation on citizenship is under way,[21] even though the rules are still very different and the requirement of prior residence varies from five years in many countries to the mandatory fifteen in Germany and twelve in Switzerland.

The important thing is, though, that Germany is well on its way to softening its restrictive legislation, partly in the area of who is eligible or not and also in the area of very strongly favouring ethnic Germans. As the result of a political settlement reached in December 1992, it was decided that foreigners have a right to seek citizenship after fifteen years residence in Germany. Furthermore, a quota was established which set the yearly intake of ethnic Germans at approximately 220,000 and it was stated that people in this category born after 1993 could not avail themselves of the right to migrate to Germany unless it was a question of family reunification. Had this legislation not been passed, as yet unborn descendants of ethnic Germans would have been able to enter Germany for ever.[22]

Another point of convergence among Western European countries concerning the rights of foreigners, has been influenced by the increasing liberalism of the post-War years on both sides of the Atlantic and the growing emphasis on individual human rights.

The relationship between foreigners and society has more and more been defined as a question of social justice and respect for basic human rights; also for those who do not belong in juridical terms. Legislation and subsequent court decisions combined with a plethora of interest and pressure groups, and also within many political parties, have meant that foreigners have often found a place in society where they were not merely seen as imported labour but as human beings, entitled to protection under the law and to be given due process on an equal footing with national citizens.[23]

In practice, this has often meant that governments have found that measures which discriminated against foreigners were overturned by the courts, instances of which are provided by the events subsequent to various governments attempting to tighten legislation governing family reunification in the wake of the 1973 European halt on labour recruitment. In some countries, attempts were made to confine foreigners to certain geographic areas. In others, what turned out to be illegal attempts were made to send foreigners back home and, in others again, permanent work permits were issued instead of residence permits in order to reduce the scope of family reunification.

Thus it is not unusual for national legislation to put a brake on such discriminatory measures by declaring them null and void in law so as to enforce the protection of the rights of the individual or so as not to violate rules relating to the defence of the rights of minorities.[24]

In other words, universal human rights are being used to defend foreigners. These rules are being applied in the grey area where many foreigners find themselves, which means that area where they still do not benefit from the protection afforded by citizenship yet are obliged to obey the laws and rules of the host country.

Perhaps in this fashion, the traditional European view of the relationship between national identity and citizenship is gradually being broken down. Many foreigners in Germany or Denmark do not feel that their cultural or historical identity is Germanic, despite giving birth to children who are Danish or German, although these do not much resemble the original inhabitants of the host country. These people are also entitled to protection just like the original inhabitants, if only in relation to the human rights declarations to which Western European nations have put their signatures. That the Western World fought long and hard to get others to respect them is another story altogether.

In EU language, human rights apply to all human beings, not just citizens. This means anyone residing legally or illegally in Western Europe. They do not have to be citizens of one of the EU member states.

Thus, obtaining citizenship is not the only important thing for foreigners in Europe, although it does provide them with a contract formally guaranteeing them the same rights as all other citizens.

History is full of examples of groups of people being strongly discriminated against although they formally belonged to a given society.

For instance, blacks in the USA were granted citizenship after the American Civil War of the last century. However, it was only through post-Second World War Civil Rights legislation that they formally acceded to the same rights and conditions as white citizens.

Citizenship is of decisive importance, though, when statistics are drawn up as to who is foreign and who is not, as outlined above, this is an arbitrary factor which does not in reality tell us much about the position of foreigners in Western European countries.

2.3 Who are Danes

As an example of the countless dilemmas which arise when an attempt is made to decide who are immigrants, who are foreigners and who are full members of the state in question, the case of Denmark may be used as an illustration.

Only as an illustration, however, because the country is in many ways a unique case, in that it has an unusually well-developed statistical system for population registration. There are very few foreigners illegally resident in Denmark and immigration as such is a relatively recent phenomenon since the country has only a modest history of colonial enterprise.

On the 9th August 1995, I was sitting in a hotel in Ilulissat in Greenland watching the World Athletic Championships. For the first time in history, Denmark won a gold medal in athletics when the former-Kenyan, Wilson Kipketer, convincingly won the 800 metres final in Gothenburg. An hour later, this coal-black African stood on the top of the victory podium while a Swedish band played the national anthem as the Danish flag was raised.[25]

The Greenlanders took it quite calmly but, then again, they are not Danes. They belong to the Inuit people, even if nearly all of them speak Danish, use Danish currency and many still hoist the Danish flag on Sundays.

Was Kipketer a Dane when he won his medal? There was no doubt that he represented Denmark though, equally, there was little doubt that he looked as unlike a Dane as is possible. In point of fact he was not a Dane at all, formally speaking, as he was not even a Danish citizen. Wilson Kipketer came to Denmark in 1990 and citizenship is only granted after a seven-year period of residence and as long as no laws have been broken.

In terms of the World Athletics Championship he was a Dane but, in Olympic terms, he was still a Kenyan since the rules of the International Olympic Committee, IOC, hold that participants can only represent the country of which they are citizens. For that reason, he did not represent Denmark at the Olympics in Atlanta in the following year. As it happens, Kipketer would not have been a Dane if he had played football, badminton or ice-hockey since the same rules obtain in these sports as for the Olympics.

The question of whether Kipketer is a Dane may be viewed from several angles including his own. For instance, does he feel that he is Danish? Hardly. Even if he were to learn the language, marry a Dane and accept and adhere to all the written and unwritten rules, he would still suffer the fate of all migrants, namely of being trapped between two cultures. He may hope that any children he might have will consider themselves to be Danes.

Formally speaking, is he a Dane? In other words, has the Danish Parliament granted him Danish citizenship with all the rights and duties that it implies. As mentioned above, this was not the case when he competed at Gothenburg.

Do the Danes see him as a Dane? Opinions differ widely. Many will answer with a categorical "no" without a second thought, whereas others would answer "yes" since he has lived in Denmark for so long, been educated in Denmark and wishes to spend his life in these cold climes and under these grey skies.

Questions and dilemmas of this nature are quite common at all levels throughout Europe. It is simply, that in the world of sport, they are thrown into sharp relief as large sums of money and national prestige are involved, along with the interest of large sections of national populations.

If one turns one's attention away from the arena of top sport, then matters look completely different in that the politically sensitive question of who are Danes or not cannot ignore elements of nationalism, racism, religion and historical tradition.

How foreigners in a given country view themselves and how the society of the host country treats immigrants depend largely on what kind of integration policy is being practiced. This book does not cover the various approaches taken in the field of integration and this chapter only looks at the nature of the formal difficulties that arise when the nationality of a foreigner in Europe is to be decided.

Thus deciding whether or not the Kenyan Wilson Kipketer is a Dane or not is far from straightforward, which is why it is just as hard to determine how many foreigners there are in Denmark. Simply using the term "foreigner" gives rise to problems. Although most people know what it means, there are no longer just Danes and "the rest". Nowadays, the term "foreigner" has become fairly meaningless, as well as discriminatory, when used.

Swedes, for instance, are seldom considered foreign, even though they have retained their Swedish citizenship, whereas a girl born of Turkish parents and brought up in Denmark will quite rightly feel discriminated against if labelled a foreigner when she might never have ventured beyond the Danish border and is a Danish citizen into the bargain.

So, how many foreigners are there in Denmark? In 1997, there were 238,000 foreign nationals in the country, which corresponds to approximately 4.5 per cent of the entire population. Of that group, 72,000 were from other EU nations, the Nordic countries and North America, about 80,000 were refugees and the remainder were immigrants from other parts of the globe.[26]

Does this constitute an answer to the question of how many foreigners there are in Denmark? Well, the reply has to be both yes and no. In juridical and formal terms, 238,000 people is the closest we can get to the truth; though we are dealing with human beings and not jurisprudence.

According to a more emotional frame of reference, many might be of the opinion that there are only about 166,000 foreigners in Denmark, since other Europeans resemble Danes and do not have too much trouble in acclimatizing.

The immigrant workers – or "guest workers" as they used to be called – numbered about 15,000 before the immigration stop of November 1973. These were, in the main, men from Turkey, Pakistan and Yugoslavia, some of whom went back home while others stayed and had their families join them in Denmark.

So the immigrants are predominantly the original immigrant workers, their children – the second-generation of immigrants – and those family members who joined them as part of family reunification.

The other large group of foreigners is that of the refugees, even though access is tougher for them than it was previously. Gone are the days when the West unhesitatingly helped the Vietnamese Boat People and political refugees from Chile.

There is much talk of "economic refugees" meaning that they are not so much evading persecution as poverty. There will, of course, always be people who purposely seek to sneak their way through the refugee filters built up in western countries but, in practice, it is often very difficult, or well-nigh impossible, to distinguish these people from the genuine article.

The extremes of this spectrum of people are, at one end, the simple working immigrants in pursuit of better economic prospects and, at the other, the political activists persecuted for their opinions. Should the former show up, because all avenues of economic advancement are closed off in their home country, they are not to be let in, whereas the latter, who might be struggling against this very state of affairs and its development, may be let in.

When evaluating refugees, western countries tend to place the emphasis on the degree of persecution suffered by the individual applicant and not the general level of oppression in the home country. They also examine the political nature of the persecution but ignore the economic and social consequences that result from such general oppression. Both these priorities serve to reduce the number of refugees but they do not necessarily identify potential refugees who are suffering the greatest distress.[27] In the early 1990s, this method of distinguishing between refugees and immigrants was also questioned in the highest places. The then UN High Commissioner for Refugees, Thorvald Stoltenberg, pointed out that many people were forced to move because of impossible living conditions even though they were not refugees in the strictest sense of the Geneva Convention.

Towards the end of the 1980s, 90 per cent of those seeking political asylum in Western Europe were turned down because they did not fulfil the requirements of the Geneva Convention's definition of refugees, though many were granted residence permits on humanitarian grounds and, elsewhere, the expulsion orders were not enforced.[28]

This distinction is not only unclear in the collective consciousness but it also causes great problems in the area of formal decisions, which is an expression of the fact that, in many cases, it is an arbitrary and artificial division. So at official levels, several different concepts are used which are often hard to understand, let alone apply. These include de-facto refugees, Convention refugees, war refugees and temporary asylum seekers, and all this and much more may be found in the complex glossary of refugee terminology.

There are many refugees from the Muslim countries of the Middle East. These are often confused in public debate and the public mind – unwittingly or deliberately – with the immigrants who came to Europe 25 years ago. Thus the discussion and the concepts behind it are completely distorted when, for instance, a Muslim refugee fresh from the carnage in the former-Yugoslavia is equated with the Turk who has worked in Western Europe for 25 years and has Danish children.

Defining foreigners is therefore difficult and only possible if one defines beforehand who is to be included in the count as well as who is not. A more popular view of who foreigners are would also include those whose parents were immigrants. If this is done, then the number of foreigners in Denmark rises by about 77,000 people. However, this increase also includes people who originate from North America and the rest of Europe.

There are consequently between 166,000 and 238,000 people in Denmark today whose origin is not North American or European, and there is a sore temptation to write that "they are not white".

This corresponds to between three and four per cent of the population. Can that really be considered many? Of course it is a matter of personal opinion but, are there really so many that, as a lot of politicians keep telling anyone who will listen, Denmark is really on its way to becoming a multi-cultural or multi-ethnic society? That this is a gross exaggeration becomes apparent when at least 96 per cent of the population are Danes, whatever definitions or parametres are used.

The problem is that in Denmark, the foreigners are often concentrated in certain geographical areas just as they are all over the rest of Europe. The question of whether there are many or few depends on which geographic locations are in question.

When viewed in the light of recent historical research, there are probably many foreigners since, in 1960, there were about 40,000 foreign citizens in Denmark, the vast majority of whom came from the other Nordic countries, England, the USA and West Germany.[29]

Compared to the rest of Western Europe Denmark has, on average, slightly fewer residents with foreign citizenship. According to EU figures in 1993, 2.7 per cent of the population of Denmark consisted of citizens of non-EU countries when the average figure for the rest of the EU was 3.3 per cent. Of the fifteen EU member states, there were seven which had a higher average figure than Denmark and seven with a lower average, which leaves Denmark, in terms of residents from third countries, very close to the middle of the Western European average.[30]

2.4 How many foreigners in Western Europe

Throughout history, millions of Europeans have left the continent as most countries experienced extensive emigration and, even today, about a million Europeans emigrate each year.[31]

It is only at the beginning of the 1950s that this picture begins to change as Western Europe started to import labour for post-War reconstruction. From 1950 until the first oil crisis of 1973, Western Europe experienced, all in one step, a net immigration of 10 million people, though this was a modest development, in view of the fact that it represented a yearly addition to Western Europe's population of the order of less than 0.2 per cent.[32]

Apart from the very considerable net immigration to West Germany, Europe is characterized until 1973 by emigration levels which were roughly the same as those for immigration.

It is only by 1989 that there is any significant net immigration. From 1973, the immigration surplus was 2.3 million people all told – or 137,000 per annum,[33] with "Western Europe" meaning the 15 EU countries along with Norway, Iceland, Liechtenstein and Switzerland.[34]

By 1989, immigration had gathered speed and exceeded emigration by over half-a-million people yearly. Consequently, net immigration into Western Europe, minus Germany, in the years from 1989 to 1993 reached a total of 2.7 million people.[35]

During the post-War period, West Germany stood out from all the other European nations in that the country had, with occasional exceptions, experienced considerable immigration totalling 7.8 million people in the period from 1960 to 1993 inclusive. The German figure far exceeds the net immigration figure for the rest of Western Europe. Again, it was in West Germany that immigration figures rose in the wake of the breakup in Eastern and Central Europe. In the years from 1988 to 1993, German net immigration totalled 3.6 million people of whom the majority came from the former-Communist nations.

So, until 1988, immigration to Western Europe was mainly a West German phenomenon whereas, throughout the whole of the rest of Europe, emigration was at roughly the same low level. This factor, however, does conceal some very great differences between individual nations although, after 1988, there is a considerable rise in immigration all over the continent and the only countries with an emigrant surplus were Portugal, Ireland and Iceland.[36]

With immigration at such levels, it goes without saying that the number of foreigners grew rapidly as European emigration was on a far smaller scale. By the beginning of 1987, there were 8.2 million non-Western European citizens in 19 Western European countries, a figure which corresponds to 2.2 per cent of the Western European population.

Table 2.1 shows that this figure had risen by 55 per cent by 1993, when there were 12.8 million foreigners or 3.4 per cent of the population. The figures for 1994 and 1995 were estimated by adding the net immigration of these two years to the 1993 total, thus giving a figure of almost 15 million resident non-Western European citizens, corresponding to 3.8 per cent of the population.[37]

Table 2.1. Persons without citizenship in Western Europe 1985-1995

	Persons without citizenship in Western Europe* 1000	Share of total population %
1985	7.836	2,1
1986	7.935	2,1
1987	8.017	2,2
1988	8.225	2,2
1989	8.834	2,4
1990	9.916	2,6
1991	10.856	2,9
1992	12.568	3,3
1993	12.774	3,4
1994	13.864	3,7
1995	14.688	3,8

* 15 EU-countries, Norway, Iceland, Liechtenstein and Switzerland.

Source: Migration Statistics 1995, Office for Official Publications of the European Communities, 1995 and 1996.

So, is this figure of 15 million the true representation of how many foreigners there are on Western European soil? Once again, this is probably the closest we can get to a juridically correct figure, although the uncertainty factor is even greater than when an estimate of the same type is made for Denmark alone.

Firstly, these figures do not show how many foreign citizens are living in Western Europe as they only comprise those foreigners who come from countries outside Europe. Thus the figure of a little over five million Western Europeans living in other Western European countries is not included.

Secondly, the figures do not indicate the number of people from different ethnic backgrounds who are in the countries concerned, many of them have obtained citizenship and have thus dropped out of the reckoning. Such a figure would be difficult to confirm with any degree of certainty as the old colonial powers such as Britain, France and the Netherlands have granted citizenship to many people from their former colonies.

All that the statistics show is the number of people who, from 1986 to 1993, have obtained citizenship – some two million all told. This figure includes an unknown number of people from other Western European nations, though they cannot be very significant as most Western Europeans tend to retain their original citizenship.[38]

Thirdly, the estimated number of people residing illegally in Western Europe is around three million.[39]

If due allowance is made for these three factors, along with the great uncertainty that impinges on all the figures, then Table 2.2 gives an impression of the proportion of non-native foreigners in Western Europe at the outset of 1995.

Table 2.2. Foreign population in Westen Europe 1995. In millions.

Without citizenship	15
Illigal in Western Europe	3
Total	18
Per cent of total population	**4,7**
Naturalization since 1986	2
Total	20
Per cent of total population	**5,2**

If the term "foreigner" means those who do not have a Western European citizenship, then there are about 15 million, or 3.9 per cent of the total population, who fit the bill. If one then includes the number of people who have been made citizens since 1986, the figure rises to 17 million, 4.4 per cent of the population, and, were one to add the number of illegal residents, then there is a grand total of 20 million foreigners in Western Europe which corresponds to 5.2 per cent of the population.

In other words, no matter who and how many are included in the count, the maximum number of foreigners in Western Europe amounts to one in every twenty inhabitants. There is, however, one group which has stuck out prominently in the immigration of recent years, not so much because of their numbers but more due to the public and political interest their migration has generated – political refugees.

2.5 Political refugees

The past ten years have been a turbulent period for Western Europe in terms of the number of people seeking political asylum. In 1983, there were 65,000 but, in ensuing years, the number grew, peaking in 1992 when almost 700,000 people sought political asylum in Western Europe.[40]

It was at this point that the Western European governments closed the door and, by 1996, only 240,000 people had sought asylum – the same level as in 1988, and, according to the figures for the first part of 1997, this decline is set to continue as the yearly total for 1997 falls to approximately 230,000 asylum seekers.[41]

In this instance too, West Germany acted as the chief magnet because, of the almost 4.1 million people who sought political asylum in Western Europe between 1983 and 1995, almost half that number, nearly two million, sought asylum in West Germany. The state of affairs which many characterized as being a refugee crisis at the end of the 1980s, must therefore be considered as a closed chapter in the continent's brief history of immigration.

It was precisely that rapid rise in asylum applications illustrated in Diagram 2.1 which, in many places, formed the core of the political disquiet aroused by the potential and actual foreign presence. However, this is also a salutary example of how illogical and emotionally-laden political debate has become in this area since, even at its height, the flow of refugees only constituted a small fraction of the foreign population in Europe – out of approximately 20 million foreigners, only about one million of these, at the very most, were political refugees.[42]

In 1995, this constituted only 3 to 10 per cent – depending on how rigorous a definition of refugees was used – of the refugee component of the total migration to the entire OECD area.[43]

That this particular group should be the one which is most often at the centre of the debate about foreigners is unfortunate for several rea-

Figure 2.1 Asylum Applications in Western Europe 1983–1997 and Decisions on Geneva Convention Status and Other Status 1990–1995.

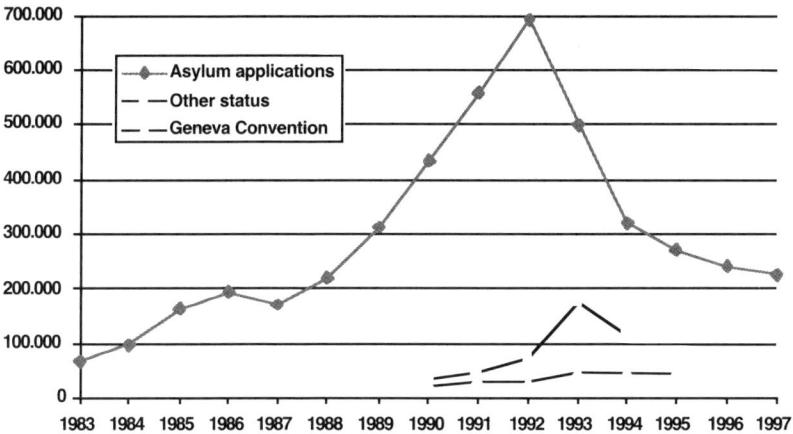

* The number for 1997 is based on the first six months.

Source: Inter-Governmental Consultations on Asylum, Refugee and Migration Policies in Europe, North America and Australia, Geneva 1996 and 1997.

sons; partly because there are so few of them; partly, and more importantly, because the often hostile and uncertain attitude towards strangers comes unreservedly to the fore and affects the weakest of all those who make it to Western Europe – the politically persecuted and victims of war.

A defence of the emphasis placed on asylum seekers at the start of the 1990s rests on the fact that a large proportion of them were clearly not political refugees, but people looking for better living conditions.

This is apparent in Figure 2.1 where the number of people granted asylum according to the terms of the Geneva Convention had only risen slightly throughout the same period; however, a larger number of people were granted asylum on humanitarian and compassionate grounds.

The distinction between political refugees and economic migrants is in many cases impossible to draw or, as the UNHCR puts it in its 1995 report: "Today, more than ever, refugees are part of a complex migratory phenomenon, in which political, ethnic, economic, environmental and human rights factors combine and lead to population movements."[44]

Two other factors increased the panic of those years. One was that ever increasing numbers of refugees were arriving from Third World countries, and the other was the sharp rise in the number of illegal immigrants. Many of those, whose asylum applications had been turned down, did not return home but stayed on illegally in Europe. Both these factors were to intensify the xenophobia towards people who came from completely alien cultures.

Towards the end of the 1980s, the nature of the refugee question changed radically as it became clear that the days of relatively small refugee flows, consisting mainly of hapless victims of dreadful Communism, which served to justify their being granted asylum without further ado, were well and truly over. This change came about before the fall of the Berlin Wall.

3. The Berlin Wall comes down

3.1 Racism and xenophobia

Why did foreigners, towards the end of the 1980s, suddenly come to occupy such a central place as they did in the consciousness of Western Europeans? In some places, the growing debate was accompanied by levels of acrimony and hostility not seen since the rise of Fascism and Nazism in the 1930s.

Dormant forces awoke, which most people believed to be dead and buried. Anti-Semitism, racism, xenophobia and nationalism all became part of the political scene as many countries experienced the rapid rise of right-wing parties, in the main due to party programmes aimed against immigrants.

The progress of the parties of the extreme right could be seen throughout most of Eastern and Western Europe. Levels of support reached their most alarming heights in France and Germany, the two countries with the most immigrants as well as historical traditions of racism and anti-Semitism.

It came as a shock when the *Republikaner Partei* led by Franz Schönhuber won eleven seats at the West Berlin City Council elections in January 1989. Up to that time, the party had languished in obscurity. Another neo-Nazi party, the *Nationaldemokratische Partei Deutschland* was similarly successful when it won seven seats in Frankfurt a few months later. In time, the Republicans were to gain seats in the councils of all the major cities. The extreme right peaked in the elections for the European Parliament in the summer of 1989 when the votes cast by six million Germans won six seats in the Strasbourg Parliament. However, internal disputes and German reunification were to take the steam out of the extreme right-wing parties who only managed to attract a million votes during the German general election held in December 1990.[1]

In France, throughout the 1980s, there had been many violent attacks on foreigners, mainly North Africans. Jean-Marie Le Pen, leader of the *Front National*, as he rode the wave of political success, issued dire warnings against France turning into an "Islamic nation" as well as the "international power and influence of world Jewry". In the first round of the presidential elections in April 1988, his party obtained 14.4 per cent of the votes cast, 4.3 million votes in all, with most support coming from young voters. In the 1989 European Parliament election, the Front National obtained two million votes.

In contrast to developments in Germany, Jean-Marie Le Pen still enjoys considerable popular support, winning one fifth of the votes cast in the first round of the 1995 presidential elections.

In Belgium, the strongly nationalist party, *Vlaams Blok*, enjoyed increased support in the second half of the 1980s. This party, with roots in the Fascist movement of the inter-war period, won almost one-third of the votes cast in Antwerp during the 1991 election. Similar tendencies arose in Austria where the extreme right-wing *Freiheitliche Partei Österreichs* obtained 22 per cent of the votes cast in Vienna the same year. In both countries, these parties were notable for their stance against immigration, *Vlaams Blok's* primary concern was, however, the internal Belgian conflict between Flemings and Walloons.

At this time, Italy had experienced relatively few cases of violent attacks on foreigners. However, in early 1990, a series of events in the big cities indicated that the phenomenon had arrived there too. In April of the same year, the Deputy Prime Minister, C. Martelli, fuelled the flames of growing xenophobia when he announced on television that the police were no longer able to secure the coasts against violation and he went on to say that this meant that the army had to be called in.

Progress for the right wing in party political terms manifested itself through increased support for the *Lega Lombarda*, later absorbed into the *Lega Nord*, which proposed, among other points in its manifesto, the secession of the wealthy north from the rest of the country. The party as such was not racist, though it made much of the specifically northern Italian sense of identity.

Xenophobia and the accompanying violence against foreigners was a pan-European phenomenon. This was demonstrated by the wave of anti-Semitism that, in May 1990, swept across the whole of France in the wake of the serious vandalism perpetrated in a Jewish cemetery near Avignon. This wave was to spread with lightning speed to major cities all over Europe, from Leningrad via East Berlin to Tirgu Mures in Romania, from Lund in Sweden all the way to Naples in Southern Italy.

Everywhere there were parties and organizations that sought and found a popular base upon which xenophobia could grow as well as channelling the general sense of insecurity towards fear of foreigners and the unknown.[2] It later transpired that the attack on the Jewish cemetery in 1990 was probably carried out by people who had no links to any right wing party. The episode did demonstrate, however, that the European extreme right possessed an efficient and effective network.

The political establishment was shaken by these dramatic events and it was soon obvious that these groups and parties had begun to cooperate across national borders. For the first time in the history of the European Community, the twelve member states agreed that they should attempt to reach some degree of cooperation in the area of immigration.

As described in Chapter 7, the Dublin Convention on applications for asylum was signed in 1990. The year after, negotiations were concluded on the External Borders Convention governing procedure at the external borders. In 1992, the London Resolutions, which clarified the rules of asylum, were adopted. All of these were moves that accommodated circles hostile to immigration while all the time demonstrating a growing wish for a common policy in this politically sensitive area.

International organizations began to concern themselves with these issues under the general heading of questions of migration. The Inter-Governmental Consultations on Asylum, Refugee and Migration Policies in Europe, North America and Australia, known as the IGC, an international umbrella organization based in Geneva, has the following to say about these issues:[3]

> "This issue is nevertheless increasingly on the national and international agenda. Specifically the international organizations such as the World Bank, OECD, UNHCR, ILO, IOM are now much more actively involved than before. This is because national politicians and policy makers in OECD countries have become more concerned about international migration and its disruptive consequences in the short-term on national policies, economies and the social climate in their home countries."

How can this popular and political activity be explained? After all, this was not a phenomenon which had arisen overnight. The countries of

Western Europe had experienced a constant flow of immigrants since the 1960s. There had been a roughly equivalent rate of emigration as well. The total number of refugees in the world had been rising sharply over a long period of time. The demographic pressure from North Africa and the Middle East had been a well-known phenomenon for some years. To this could be added that many of the nations of Western Europe had maintained close and intricate connections with foreigners over many decades through colonial ties. For instance, there were already almost three million foreigners in France by the end of the 1920s.[4]

Notwithstanding the above, immigration was only suddenly to become a big issue at the end of the 1980s and the start of the 1990s, and the interest shown in immigrants in the public and political spheres has remained at high and intense levels ever since.

Why did this strong reaction arise at precisely that point in time? Had the situation of the Europeans really changed ? Had so many outsiders come in that they posed a threat to the cultural identity of the countries they had entered, and were they a direct threat to the welfare systems of Western Europe? Or was this sudden upsurge of interest in foreigners in reality the upshot of fundamental changes in society in which the immigrants played no part, other than providing a convenient target?

There are two obvious reasons, one being that the refugee pressure had reached a historical high point in those years. This, however, is only part of the explanation. Although the numbers of people seeking political asylum in Western Europe began to rise sharply in the mid-1980s, when the curve peaked in 1992, the number of applicants was still below 700,000, of whom the majority by far went to Germany. Since then, the number of applicants has more than halved.

The other reason was the collapse of Communism, with the fundamental insecurity this gave rise to. Among other things, it meant that millions of people in the countries bordering Western Europe who, hitherto, could not travel, were now free to do so. All of a sudden, Western Europe was facing immigrant pressure from the East as well as the South.

However, the reasons for immigrants and potential immigrants becoming such a hot topic are by no means restricted to the problems which arose in the wake of the collapse of Communism and the appearance on the scene of many asylum seekers. That this is the case is, in part, shown by the appearance of similar tendencies in the United States, which would not have been affected to the same extent if the inhabitants of the East decided to move West.

Alan Simpson, Republican senator for Wyoming and one of the chief architects of the American Immigration Reform and Control Act of 1986, mainly aimed at illegal immigrants, had warned throughout the 1980s that the U.S. had lost control of its own borders and was suffering from an excessive number of immigrants.[5]

Clearly, several other factors are also involved. The following sections describe how a series of fundamental developmental features interact throughout the 1980s until the early 1990s; different tendencies which share the common trait of fuelling the fire of xenophobia.

3.2 The torches burn out

On 9th November 1989, the wall protecting the East fell. Under a deluge of fireworks and speeches, the Berlin Wall was demolished. Since its erection in 1961 it had been the tangible symbol, more than anything else, of the division of the world which had been a reality for almost half a century.

The pace of events in the ex-Communist countries was rapid in the ensuing years. On 1st April 1991, the military cooperation of the Warsaw Pact came to an end. On 1st July of the same year, political cooperation did so as well. The economic community COMECON lapsed on 29th June and the coup, in August, against General Secretary Mikhail Gorbatchev marked the end of Communism.

The Iron Curtain had never provided a completely hermetic seal between East and West. Since the end of the Second World War, Western Europe had been the recipient of a constant flow of immigrants and refugees from the Communist countries. The main target of this flow throughout the years was West Germany which, from 1945 to 1989, received fifteen million people, the equivalent of a quarter of the West German population.[6]

This immigration from the East was not only welcomed in the West, it was positively encouraged and assisted by all possible means. Any refugee from a Communist country was living proof of western superiority in the Cold War, and they were all granted political asylum in Europe should they not travel on to the USA, Canada or Australia.

The policy all over the western world was to support and assimilate the new arrivals. The key word was resettlement, and the question of sending the refugees back to where they had come from seldom arose. This tendency was not limited to Europe alone, but applied anywhere in the world affected by East-West confrontation.

The western democracies were in an enviable position. The Communist countries themselves ensured that the number of refugees was kept down to an acceptable level. Those who, in spite of everything, did reach the West, never gave rise to serious political or economic tensions.

The after-shocks of the fall of the Berlin Wall were not only felt in the neighbouring countries, they spread like rings in the water to the remotest corners of the globe. The conflicts in Afghanistan, Southern Africa, the Horn of Africa, Central America, the Middle East and Indo-China had all dragged on as a result of the Cold War. Everywhere, millions of people were stuck in miserable and overcrowded refugee camps.

Right up to the mid-1970s, the total number of refugees throughout the world was still below three million. Only four years later, in 1980, the figure had grown to over eight million. By the time the Wall came down, the total figure for refugees had mushroomed to over seventeen million people. This six-fold increase in the number of refugees in less than fifteen years was a clear portent of new times.[7]

During this explosive development throughout the 1980s, it became increasingly clear that the myriad political refugees were no longer the living torches of western superiority as they had been earlier. As long as it had been relatively few Hungarians or Czechs fleeing from cruel and heavily media-covered Russian invasions, there were no limits to the hospitality and generosity.

However, the three million Afghan refugees living in Iran and Pakistan, or the Mozambican refugees in Malawi who numbered almost a million, did not have anything like the same propaganda effect, while rehousing them in the industrialized countries gave rise to acute internal problems since the culture, language and religion of the refugees made it hard for them to adapt to western reality.[8]

The effort made on behalf of the victims of the Cold War's hot spots was signally changed as a consequence of diminishing superpower interest. Now the flows of refugees had to be stopped, partly by tightening asylum procedures which were to prevent them ever reaching the affluent part of the world; and partly through the creation of better environments which would enable the refugees to go home.

For that reason, the 1990s have been dubbed the "decade of repatriation". Impressive measures have been taken to strengthen peace negotiations in all the places where the superpowers previously had ideological, military or strategic reasons for prolonging conflicts.[9]

There have been several instances of the international community directly intervening in a given conflict with the express purpose of ensuring the return of refugees; Cambodia and Mozambique are examples of this.

According to the UN High Commissioner for Refugees, Sadako Ogata, almost nine million refugees returned to their homeland in the period from 1990 to 1994. These movements comprise 2.6 million Afghans, 1.6 million Mozambicans, 600,000 Ethiopians and 400,000 Cambodians[10].

The most remarkable expression of the new view of refugee policy came about on 5th April 1991 when the Security Council adopted a resolution allowing the United Nations the right of intervention in the territory of a sovereign state.

The occasion for this measure was provided by the Iraqi army's persecution of the Kurdish minority in Northern Iraq, while the neighbouring states of Turkey and Iran refused to admit the large mass of refugees within their borders. It was now possible for the international community to intervene directly in the internal affairs of a country and afford relief to the flows of refugees that did or could result from a conflict.[11]

As mentioned in earlier sections, there were ever more refugees from remote places all over the world arriving in Western Europe, in spite of the desire to solve refugee problems on the spot. They were no longer welcome since their role as pawns in the Cold War had ended.

3.3 The Russians are coming

Not surprisingly, the most panic caused by the collapse of Communism was felt in Europe. The migrations from East Germany of the summer and autumn of 1989 slowly eroded the base of the Wall, leading eventually to its complete collapse.

Endless queues of Trabants and overcrowded trains conveyed the East Germans to the West via Czechoslovakia and Hungary. Soon after, tens of thousands of Germans would stream to the West and, with what was to be historic speed, the divided Germany was re-united on the night of 2nd and 3rd October 1990.

In the ensuing period, the western countries were scared out of their wits at the prospect of a mass exodus from the East. During the December 1990 EC summit in Rome, the Italian foreign minister, Gianni de Michelis, put it thus: "We must be careful that these two or three million are not suddenly multiplied by ten, as this sort of invasion would be terribly destabilizing."[12]

In the early 1990s, fear of mass migration from the former Soviet Union was the principal cause of worry. This fear was fed by forces in Russia who saw it as a good card to play in their machinations for more western aid.

Vladimir Chemyatenkov, the Soviet ambassador to the EC from 1989 until 1991, expressed it in the following way: "I do not doubt that millions of Soviet citizens will look for work in the West the moment it becomes possible to do so." He expected the emigration of two to three million Soviet citizens because "the Soviet people have a tradition of mobility. Every year one and a half million people move to the northern and eastern regions of the country because of wage differences. A major factor might be that the people have no property to lose should they emigrate to the West."[13]

The fear of mass immigration was understandable when the unstable situation is taken into account. Emigration in 1989 was on a large scale. All in all, 1.3 million people left the ex-Communist countries. The majority of these consisted of members of ethnic minorities who suddenly took the opportunity to leave; Soviet Jews, Bulgarian Turks and ethnic Germans from Rumania and the Soviet Union. 150,000 people left the Soviet Union in all, most of them were Jewish. The ethnic Germans were, however, the largest single emigrant group in that there were 720,000 of them all told, of whom 354,000 came from East Germany, the remainder coming from Poland and other Eastern European countries.[14] Only 80,000, mainly from Poland and Yugoslavia, sought political asylum in Western Europe.

The fear of westward mass migration was latent. The 3.3 million ethnic Germans living outside Germany were the most immediate threat. They could avail themselves of a right of return enshrined in the German Constitution, though they were feared by a Germany who already dreaded the prospect of the multitudes who wanted to leave the former GDR in order to settle in the far more prosperous West.[15]

The fear of the potentially huge numbers yet to come from Eastern and Central Europe was also widespread. Just by moving, most of them could increase their income ten times over. However, this outside pressure never materialized. The largest groups of asylum seekers in 1990 consisted of 60,000 Romanians, 16,000 Poles and 27,000 Yugoslavs.[16]

The scare was further fed by migratory experiences in recent times. Approximately three per cent of the population of Southern Europe had, in the 1950s and 1960s, migrated to Northern and Western Europe. That meant about five million people, while a similar number migrated to the USA during the same period. Furthermore, in the seventies and eighties, roughly four per cent of the population of Mexico emigrated to the USA. These provide two examples of migration primarily due to vastly different living standards. If this pattern were to be followed, it would have meant ten million immigrants from the ex-Communist countries.[17]

Nowadays it is obvious that the worst case scenarios of the period around 1990 never came to pass. There were no ensuing waves of ethnic German emigration after the first one and, generally, the inhabitants of Eastern European countries can travel without visas to the EU countries and without causing any serious problems. However, the potential threat of waves of migration did exist and could still happen should the Eastern economies fail to thrive or if regional conflicts escalate.

The fact that the collapse of Communism coincided with a sudden and serious increase in the flow of refugees goes some way towards explaining why the question of emigrants and refugees should move to the top of the list of unresolved questions in a Western Europe that, otherwise, was well on its way towards historic political and economic union.

3.4 Euro-euphoria under pressure

At 11.12 a.m., on 19th April, 1990, a fax arrived at the Danish Ministry for Foreign Affairs. It contained a suggestion from the President of France, Francois Mitterrand, and the German Federal Chancellor, Helmut Kohl, that the twelve EC countries should initiate discussions about political union proper.[18]

As luck would have it, the Danish Parliament had held a debate on Europe the day before where there had been broad agreement on Denmark's relationship to the EC. This agreement had only been reached because European political union was deemed to be an issue so far away in the future that no-one had bothered to discuss it.

The Franco-German initiative, which caught Danish politicians completely unawares, was evidence of the utter insecurity then prevalent in Europe. The two Germanies faced reunification as the Soviet Empire was facing its demise. In order to counter this, the twelve EC countries prepared a great leap forward towards even closer cooperation. This was to be known as "in-depth integration".

The then Secretary General of the Council of Ministers, Niels Ersbøll, who was thus privy to the central decision makers, now says that "The reason behind the decision to proceed with integration was the great unpredictability caused by the collapse of Communism."[19]

At that very point in time, the twelve EC members were in the process of creating the Single European Market, often referred to as "Europe 1992". The euphoria of the European business community had gone through the roof. The time was coming when European political and economic integration was to be put to the test and Europe would stand up to the USA and Japan on the world stage.

In the economic area, four freedoms were on the agenda; the free movement of goods and services, capital and labour across borders which were to gradually disappear. This process was not restricted to the twelve EC states, it also comprised the seven members of EFTA, Sweden, Norway, Finland, Austria, Switzerland, Iceland and Liechtenstein. All of these, by virtue of the European Economic Area (EEA) agreement, were to be full participants in this project where the factors of production were to enjoy the same freedom of movement as if they were within the borders of any one country.

The plans in the monetary field were no less ambitious. At the time, a Western European common currency was believed to be just around the corner. European currency cooperation, the European Monetary System (EMS), had been more effective than any of the economists or politicians had dreamt of. In a five year period from 12th January 1987, not one of the rates of exchange was modified. European currencies had not been so stable since the good old days before the late 1960s.[20]

Another project, equally ambitious in scope, was also being drawn up. On 14th June 1985, the leaders of West Germany, France and the three Benelux countries met on a boat on the River Rhone just off the little town of Schengen in Luxembourg. There, they signed the Schen-

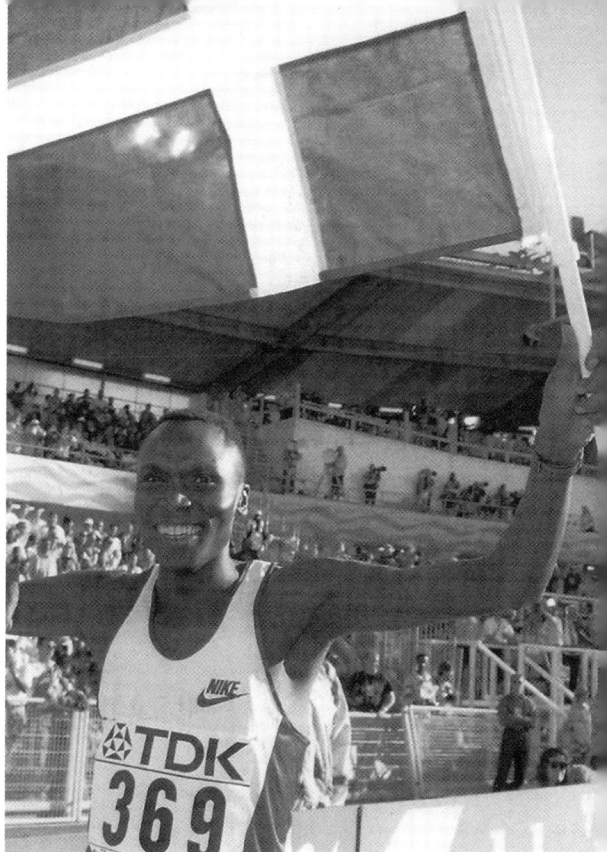

RIGHT: *The real figure for foreigners resident in Europe is unknown. Various countries have different rules on how to obtain citizenship. Wilson Kipketer, a Kenyan-born runner, won the world championship for Denmark in 1995. He was barred from participating in the Olympic games the next year. He was not a Danish citizen after six years of residence. A Kenyan Dane. (Polfoto)*

BOTTOM: *In 1985, just under eight million people with foreign citizenship lived in Western Europe; ten years on, that figure had doubled. They have made their definite mark on the street picture as well as in the grocery business. (Michael Daugård/2maj)*

LEFT: *Already before the fall of the Berlin Wall, endless columns of Trabants, the East German "people's car", were streaming westward. Germany was reunited on the night of 2nd and 3rd October 1990. (Polfoto)*

BOTTOM: *Hand in hand. On 9th November 1989, the Berlin Wall came down. Since 1961, more than anything else, it had been the tangible symbol of the division of the world between East and West. (Polfoto)*

gen Agreement according to which border controls between the five sig-natories were to be abolished on 1st January 1990. The experience gained from this venture was to be used when border controls through-out the entire EU area were to disappear with the introduction of the Single Market on 1st January 1993. When the Berlin Wall fell in 1989, this project was put on hold for the time being. After all, no-one could tell where the many East Germans would travel to.

In the middle of this period of radical transformation, the twelve EC countries adopted the Maastricht Treaty at the end of 1991. On this oc-casion, topics which were far more controversial than those the twelve members had hitherto dealt with concerning the Single European Mar-ket emerged for discussion. These topics were to bring the underlying insecurity right up to the surface.

Besides the set plans for transition to monetary union with a com-mon currency, the Treaty contained several sections which directly or indirectly referred to foreigners and how they were to be handled. The sections in question pertained mainly to national domestic security, ranging from common police jurisdiction to border control and policies for granting asylum. To this was added a section on Union citizenship, the range and consequences of which were hard to fathom.

All these measures, along with the Single Market's requirement for open borders, gave rise to considerable and understandable uncertainty which, in turn, gave extra nourishment to the racism and neo-national-ism which were the causes furthered by the extreme right. The fear of the loss of national identity spread over the whole of Western Europe.

This anxiety manifested itself in two ways. One was at the practical level, where there was a widespread view among large sections of the general public, as well as the financial markets, that the EC countries were nowhere near to being ready to carry out a common economic po-licy at such a high level as that required by the creation of a European Monetary Union. This would naturally require a common currency and exchange rate policies and a far higher degree of harmonization of na-tional financial policies.

Then, in a more diffuse manner, there was marked popular resistance to the gradual surrender of national sovereignty and to the creation of an equivalent European identity which did not yet exist. There was a widespread fear of Brussels "running the show". The subsidiarity prin-ciple was wheeled out to reassure the sceptics. According to this principle, decisions were to be made at as local a level as possible. The snag was, however, that many did not understand the principle, just as it was rarely translated into reality through application and operative use.

In the course of this often confused debate about national sovereignty and identity, it was not surprising that foreigners ended up being made into scapegoats. Not only was there widespread unease at the prospect of losing national independence to the supranational governing authorities in Brussels, but the threat to national identity had come much closer. It existed within the national boundaries and, with the sudden upsurge in the numbers of asylum seekers, this threat became ever more visible.

To this could be added a genuine uncertainty which further exacerbated the position of the foreigners. While the ambitious project of building a united Europe was under way, no-one had decided what to do about the fifteen million foreigners who did not have a European passport. The Single European Market had the completely untenable arrangement whereby labour could move around freely as long as it consisted of European citizens.

This state of affairs gave rise to all sorts of arguments with varying degrees of validity. Perhaps the foreigners would be attracted by the generous Danish welfare system, or they would be enticed by exotic Paris. These arguments did not stand up to proper examination as foreigners could not move around freely throughout the EC member states. The question remained, how was one going to enforce this exception without border controls? This problem was a definite restraint on the realization of the Single European Market.

The fall of the Berlin Wall also demonstrated that the Western European nations were incapable of working together on the refugee question. As the pressure mounted, especially on West Germany, the other EC states did not want to share the burden by introducing, for example, a quota system. Each country was busily defending its own borders at the time.

Although there are many instances of faith moving mountains, especially in the economic sphere, this was not the case for this particular European project. Slowly, but surely, faith began to crumble; first in Denmark, then in the financial markets and, later on, among the peoples elsewhere in Europe.

Before the Danish referendum on the ratification of Maastricht held on 2nd June 1992, the general opinion of the financial markets was that the process towards the European Monetary Union would proceed pretty much as planned. When the Danes voted against ratification, however, it gave rise to considerable uncertainty as to whether the timetable could be adhered to or whether the project was at all feasible.

In order to allay popular discontent, President Mitterrand called a referendum the day after the Danish result. He sought to show that the Danish view was an exception, but the French view, as revealed on 20th September, was largely similar to that of the Danes. However, albeit by a very slender majority, the French did vote for the ratification of the Maastricht Treaty. Nevertheless, the message was clear enough, the peoples of Europe were deeply divided on this issue.

The money markets reacted violently. Until then, the view had been that the political will towards closer cooperation would compensate for any initial basic economic difficulties arising from fixed exchange rates and an eventual common currency. However, with popular resistance and delays in the ratification process, the financial markets went on the offensive against the weaker currencies.

National economic imbalances, first and foremost the large public budget deficits, all of a sudden became decisive factors in the markets' evaluations. From the summer of 1992 till the summer of 1993, the currency markets were in a state of chaos. One national currency after the other had to leave the EMS. Then, on the night of 2nd August 1993, the EU finance and economy ministers and national bank chiefs threw in the towel. They introduced a deviation limit of 15 per cent either way which meant that the EMS had, in fact, irretrievably collapsed.

In the space of two years, Euro-euphoria had turned into huge frustration and uncertainty about the future of this part of the world. The referenda in Denmark and France and opinion polls in Germany and Britain all clearly showed that the peoples of Europe were deeply sceptical. Also, the international money markets did not hesitate to show that, in their opinion, the rapid integration of the Western European economies was more of a political pipe-dream than a reflection of hard economic facts.

This atmosphere of doubt and uncertainty did nothing to help the situation of the foreigners. The debate about them raged everywhere. Was their very presence a threat to national identity, already under pressure from other quarters? Was the traditional nation-state going to be replaced by a multi-ethnic or multi-cultural society? Did they really take jobs away from the locals? These questions, all relevant in themselves, were hard to distinguish amongst all the other factors of uncertainty then extant in Europe. Therefore, foreigners not only came under political pressure but soon found themselves under economic pressure as well.

3.5 Jobless growth

Towards the end of the 1980s, the new phenomenon of jobless growth was observed. For many years, economic growth had outpaced employment, though it had first become a serious problem during the 1980s. Even a strong economic upturn did not affect Western European unemployment which remained stuck at a level of approximately 10 per cent.[21] The young were the hardest hit. In 1989, every fourth person in the 18 to 25 age group was unemployed in the twelve EC countries.[22]

Two years on, this dilemma was acknowledged at the highest level. At the G-7 Detroit summit on employment in March 1994, Henning Christophersen, the EU delegation leader, said: "The new challenge facing all nations is that the connection between economic growth and employment, which has been taken for granted for decades, can no longer be held to be axiomatic. The one does not automatically lead to the other."[23]

By 1991, a slump affected Western Europe and unemployment rose rapidly. Only reunified Germany managed to maintain a reasonable level of demand, whereas Western Europe experienced actual recession in 1993.

When unemployment, already at a high level, began to rise again, foreigners proved to be in serious competition for scarce jobs. A cocktail made up of the fears of mass unemployment and mass immigration pervaded the atmosphere in many parts of Western Europe. In France, the election posters for Jean-Marie Le Pen's *Front National* put it thus: "Two million immigrants equals two million unemployed."

That Le Pen had put his finger on a sore point was obvious. From 1980 to 1993, the number of unemployed in Western Europe more than doubled, rising from 10 to 20.4 million.[24] However, real unemployement was far more extensive in that, according to the OECD, there were also up to 15 million people who were "underemployed". This category comprised people forced to find part-time work, taking job training courses or those who took early retirement since they had given up their careers.[25]

During these years, a new and painful realization dawned that was to have serious repercussions for foreigners. Western European unemployment had come to stay. At the 1993 Copenhagen EC summit, the Commission submitted a proposal for a strategy to reduce unemployment. The proposal document showed that whereas 70 per cent of the working-age population were employed in the USA, and the percentage for Japan was 75, the percentage for the EC countries was 60.

In other words, even under very favourable circumstances, it would have been impossible to reduce unemployment rates to any significant extent as the labour reserve was enormous and, were there to be an upturn, these people would return to the labour market. Denmark was the exception as its employment percentage was the same as that of Japan.[26] In this overall situation, the position of the foreigners on the labour market worsened as the argument that they took work away from the locals was further strengthened by events.

Another structural feature of the Western economies was a hallmark of the eighties. Although countries experienced one of the longest economic upturns of the post-war period, public budget deficits did not fall. On the contrary, public debt grew at an alarming rate. Public debt represented 43 per cent of GNP for the entire OECD membership in 1980; it reached 60 per cent a decade later. The OECD's comment on this is as follows: "...the mistakes made in the late 1980s when some of the unexpected buoyancy of public revenues associated with above average growth was used to reduce tax rates rather than to ensure greater fiscal consolidation and reduce debt."[27]

Once again foreigners were fair game, since rising unemployment largely affected those in low-paid jobs and unskilled labour, groups where foreigners were well represented. As the recession began to bite, a relatively high proportion of foreigners had to claim some form of welfare benefit, just when the pressure for cuts in public spending was at its height.[28]

The number of asylum seekers peaked at around 700,000 in 1992, while the European economies were on their way down. This was the first time since 1974 that the overall growth rate was negative.[29]

The American sociologist James Davies has examined the link between the presence of foreigners and general economic development. His working concept is the "crisis gap" which arises when prevailing economic conditions do not develop as well as had been expected. This situation gives rise to violent social tensions, which was precisely what happened with rising unemployment throughout the 1980s. This process was exacerbated with the onset of recession. The persistently high level of unemployment caused social tension which was aimed principally at foreigners who were arriving in increasing numbers.[30]

To put it another way, the upsurge of xenophobia and racism that occurred was not solely due to the increase in the numbers of asylum seekers. It has to be seen in connection with the general economic trends, high unemployment with its consequent deterioration of the economic situation and the uncertain future prospects of large groups in society.

The combination of high refugee pressure, fear of the collapsed Soviet Union, rising unemployment and cuts in public spending made a dangerous blend, not just for the foreigners, but also for the Western European democracies which were under strong pressure from other quarters.

3.6 Democracies under pressure

The collapse of Communism was a victory for the western democracies and market economics. But the victors of the Cold War were themselves in a situation where many of their basic values and rules were challenged. Development throughout the 1980s had been shaped by three trends which put western democracies to a serious test and were crucially important as to how the nations put themselves across to the outside world.

To start with, globalization began to speed up. A violent process of liberalization and deregulation swept over the globe, supported by the development of information technology. This development reached and affected all levels of society as international relations were subjected to a tidal wave of deregulation. The result of this process is best described as a global revolution and will be discussed in detail in Chapter 5.

In this situation, it is futile to imagine that only human beings avoid being globalized. Although there are those who may not like it, this process is an expression of the fact that most forms of human activity cross national borders. The rise in the number of asylum seekers, of immigrants and illegal aliens in Western Europe was in no way more extensive than the rise of several other indicators which are also an expression of globalization. By itself, this process leads to considerable migrations, not according to the usual patterns, but more in the form of extensive

"professional migrations". Increasing international trade and investment gives rise to a greater need for people to travel to and work or
study in the partner countries.[31]

Through this process of economic globalization, national economies
are tied together ever more closely. Indeed, the very notion of the "national economy" is becoming correspondingly harder to sustain. There
is a growing and increasingly open conflict between the fact of reduced
economic independence and the idea of an homogeneous nation able to
maintain its sovereignty and particular identity built up in the course of
a particular people's long tradition and history.

As a result, another trend which emerged during the 1980s was the
recognition of the dwindling importance of the nation-state. In the case
of Denmark, the then Prime Minister, Poul Schlüter, took the plunge in
a speech he gave in autumn 1988 at the famous Reform Club in Pall
Mall from where the famous fictional character, Phileas Fogg, had started his journey round the world in eighty days over a century before.

In his speech, Poul Schlüter said that the role of the nation-state was
coming to an end, that the large global corporations would have a correspondingly greater say in the running of affairs and that responsibility, in
the future would increasingly devolve to smaller units and the family.[32]

The reactions in Denmark to Poul Schlüter's speech were so strong
that he felt it necessary to issue a communique in which, among other
things, he said: "I maintain that, in the decades to come, we will see a
world where the significance of the nation-state is reduced". In order to
assuage feelings in Euro-sceptic Denmark, the communique went on to
say that: "International cooperation will still take place between
sovereign states. Nations will work together as independent countries
and I am still opposed to any further Danish renunciation of powers to
the EC or any other organ".

At that point in time, the Danes were not at all prepared to accept
this message. It was plain however that, in flying this kite, the Prime
Minister had broached a trend which was to increasingly translate itself
into reality. It was only his timing that might be considered unfortunate.

The next time this message came to the fore was through the medium of a senior civil servant. One of the heads of department of the Ministry of Foreign Affairs, J. Ørstrøm Møller, said the following:

"The nation-state is not being entrusted with new tasks and is with-
ering away. The option of carrying out a national policy in the spheres
of economy, exchange rates and technology is now non-existent. Those

tasks will be carried out exclusively at a European level. The nation-state will be superseded by the regions which will specifically handle such areas as culture, education and social affairs."

There was no clearer way of saying that the dwindling importance of the nation-state was a realization that reached all the way to the top of the national political establishment. No politician contradicted this statement.[33]

The recognition of the fact that the individual nation-states were inexorably losing control over their own development in many places had the illogical yet understandable effect of strengthening the strongly nationalist parties. Furthermore, growing nationalism went hand in hand with xenophobia.

A third trend which could be observed through the 1980s was the experience of a series of fundamental changes in the traditional political systems. Especially since the collapse of Communism, there has been universal agreement on what economic policy any given country should implement. This is not just restricted to Europe, North America and Japan; it applies equally to the many developing countries which are participating to an ever greater extent in the global economy. The same applies to the former Communist countries which, on their way to becoming market driven economies, are known as economies in transition.

This agreement on market economic policy crosses national boundaries and political parties. For decades, the political systems of Western Europe operated between left and right, among different professional groups and employers and employees. These points of reference are ever more difficult to discern and navigate by.

Instead, a concerted effort is being made to build a stable macro-economic climate that will not change, irrespective of which political parties might gain office. The development of the EC, subsequently the EU, is the best example extant of a union of countries wishing to create such an area of economic stability in the midst of globalization.

However, this stable economic area is in sharp contrast to the political climate which is becoming increasingly uncertain and unpredictable. According to the British research-based newsletter, Oxford Analytica, this means that the political dividing lines of the future will be based on non-economic criteria to a far greater extent than today. In future, with the fading out of the ideological differences in the economic sphere, single issues and the general performance and skill of politicians will determine who will accede to political power.[34]

These trends have been visible for many years. In comparison to earlier times, the switching of electoral loyalty from one party to another has become a far more common phenomenon. The power of the traditional parties has been eroded as new parties and movements have appeared on the scene with messages which are focussed on single issues such as the environment or emigration, or even personalities.

In this process of change, refugees and immigrants have found themselves between the Devil and the deep blue sea, partly because, as a group, they have become victims of the tendency of many parties to forsake an overall view of societal evolution so as to be able to concentrate on single issues instead. As described at the start of this chapter, many countries have experienced parties gaining popular support due to their campaigns against immigrants. Often, these parties have had an influence far greater than their number of voters could justify because many parties actually in office felt it necessary to accommodate them in order to stop the growing support for these often extremely right-wing movements.

The immigrants and refugees were further put in jeopardy by the fact that they, as a group, were not a constituency for any of the parties in the midst of all the change.

In the years around 1990, liberalism had triumphed - almost to the extent of being "ruined by success" as the Danish trades union movement would have put it a few years earlier. Ronald Reagan in the US, Margaret Thatcher in Britain and Helmut Kohl in West Germany had liberalized the world economy and deregulated at home and abroad to an extent unparalleled in post-war history. Communism had collapsed and the Western European Single Market had been built up on basic liberalistic tenets.

But what was the triumphant liberal ideology to do about the foreigners? According to the economic tenets of liberalism, there was no doubt. Just like all other factors of production, labour was to be free to move to wherever the return was greatest. Such a policy was, of course, completely unrealistic in view of the potential threats from the East and South. Furthermore, such a policy would be costly in terms of votes, not least because the liberal parties were often fighting to gain the same categories of voter as were the anti-immigration parties.

The European Social-Democratic parties faced a similar dilemma. As their voters were often those who felt themselves to be most threatened in the labour market by the foreigners, consequently there were clear limits to how far they could go in supporting asylum seekers and immigrants. Had the Communist parties of Western Europe not been dragged down by the collapse of the Soviet Union and the Eastern Socialist Republics, they would have faced a dilemma similar to that of the Social-Democrats. It was the very decline of the western Communist parties or their splitting up, as in Spain and Italy, that left many voters in a vacuum which was to be filled by the new parties, including those of the extreme right.

A series of complicated and confused processes were impinging on each other and reinforcing each other throughout the 1980s. The terrific pace of development in the areas of information technology, communications and transport, combined with strongly liberal governments in the leading nations, led to increased transnational cooperation and mutual dependence. It strengthened the nationalist parties who derived a considerable part of their strength through focussing on the presence of foreigners. To this could be added the hesitancy and general groping in the dark of the established parties on the issue of the "new Europeans" due to their having misjudged the situation in the area of immigration over many years. Recent historical developments had provided ample proof of that.

3.7 The historical developments

The number of foreigners in Western Europe did not reflect the wishes or the plans of its politicians. Until 1973, several countries had welcomed guest workers from abroad in order to make up for their own shortage of labour. At the same time, several European countries had no restrictions at all on immigration, while the border controls were minimal. It was only after the economic turmoil in the wake of the first oil crisis of 1973 that an official halt was imposed on all immigration.

However, immigration continued unabated, at first on compassionate grounds where families were reunited and, later on, when an increasing amount of asylum seekers and illegal immigrants arrived. A consequence of this was a large increase in the numbers of women and children among the foreigners who, now, were no longer just a labour reserve which could be called on as and where needed. Hitherto, if there had been a shortage of work, this reserve could be dismissed and sent back home.

After the halt on labour recruitment, the foreigners began increasingly to resemble the society around them. From being a group of predominantly young, single and dynamic men with a great capacity for work, the foreigners, in the main, became families who wanted good housing and health care and whose children entered the common education system.

That the countries had no control over immigration can be seen from the following:

When the moratorium on immigration was imposed in 1973 to 1974, there were ten million foreigners of whom five million were guest workers on the labour market. In 1990, while immigrant labour still consisted of five million people, the total number of foreigners had grown to almost fourteen million. In fact, the number of aliens in Western Europe was higher as this figure does not include some important categories, asylum seekers in particular.[35]

This development caused considerable unease in political circles as they recognized that this was a problem they had not been able to tackle. This situation was worsened by the fact that the politicians, out of fear of the extreme right-wing parties, had not prepared their populations for the necessity of political action in this sensitive area.

3.8 The many children

The collapse of Communism brought an entirely different dilemma to the surface the terrific demographic expansion in the poorer parts of the world. Nowadays, the world population is increasing by almost one hundred million a year, the strongest growth rates being in areas which are fairly close to Europe, the African continent and the Middle East.[36]

Seen from a European perspective, it is especially worrying that the populations of the Muslim countries bordering on the Mediterranean are growing explosively and will continue to rise for many decades to come. From an overall population of 186 million in 1990, the figure will increase to over 340 million by the year 2025. This almost constitutes a doubling within the foreseeable future, whereas the population of Europe is expected to remain more or less at its present level.[37]

In terms of immigration to Europe, further concern is raised by the fact that such a demographic development means that a disproportionately large segment of the population will be young, dynamic people who might nurture the ambition of emigrating to a wealthy Europe.

Traditionally, both the left and the right of the political spectrum have had difficulty in facing up to the fact that an increasing world population would present a problem. The left-wing were afraid that, in the public domain, attention would wander from the crucial point of debate about society concerning social inequality and those mechanisms which made it possible. This view influenced the Communist countries right up till the 1980s until General Secretary Mikhail Gorbatchev recognized that rapid population growth could, on its own, pose a problem for any society. He was the first Soviet Communist to do so. China, with its extremely effective birth control campaign, differed from the other Socialist states, though Mao Zedong had caused problems over many years through his emphasis on the Chinese population being the most important factor in national production.

The right-wing has had an equally hard time knowing which leg to stand on in the population debate. The problem has not been broached at all in these circles in many western countries, primarily out of fear of reviving the abortion issue. There has also been a wish to avoid provoking various religious movements. In the mid-1980s, President Ronald Reagan went so far as to withdraw all American support for international family planning programmes. According to Reagan, market forces were not only capable of regulating production and capital, they were also capable of regulating human procreation. His successor, George Bush, was not much better as there were far too many anti-abortionists among his core voters.[38]

This debate started in earnest after the fall of Communism in the early 1990s as the discussion focused on how to bring down birth rates. A historic level of activity was initiated on the international level in 1994 when a UN Conference on Population was held in Cairo, a Social Summit the next year in Copenhagen and a Women's Conference in Beijing. The purpose of all this activity was to improve people's social condition, principally that of women, in order to reduce the high rates of birth.

This entire debate gave rise to understandable unease and disquiet in Europe as the continent suddenly faced the threat of emigration from the East as well as the South. Evidence of this threat was provided by the large numbers of people seeking asylum, mainly in Northern Europe, whereas Southern Europe had to deal with a significant increase in the number of illegal immigrants, particularly from North Africa.

A new factor arose in 1989, which was to extend itself in the years ahead, though little notice was taken of it initially. This was the fact that for the first time in history, immigration was the single most important factor in Western European demographic growth. Table 3.1 shows the composition of demographic growth in what were the twelve EC countries throughout the period 1980 to 1992.

Table 3.1. The composition of population growth in the 12 EC-countries. 1980-1992

Year	Per. 1000		
	Natural growth	Net immigration	Total population growth
1980	2,6	1,7	4,3
1985	1,5	0,8	2,3
1988	1,9	1,8	3,7
1989	1,7	2,5	3,1
1990	1,7	2,8	4,5
1991	1,4	2,9	4,2
1992	1,4	2,1	3,5

Source: Population, Institut National d'Études Démographiques, vol. 5, Paris 1993.

During most of the 1980s, natural demographic growth accounted for most of the rise in the national populations. By 1988, this growth is matched by immigration and by 1989, immigration had overtaken natural demographic growth. This trend was to become even more marked in the next three years.[39]

As illustrated by the table, this development is an expression of the rise in immigration as well as the falling birthrate in the twelve EC countries, a phenomenon prevalent throughout the whole of Western Europe.

This development fuelled many of the widely-held prejudices about immigrants, the chief one being that immigrants have more children than native Europeans do, a prejudice which is both true and false.

It is true that, on average, immigrants do have more children than Europeans, especially at a time when birthrates in Europe have taken a nosedive. However, it is important to stress that, according to a number of surveys, this applies by and large only to the first generation of immigrants. The second generation tends to adopt, to a large extent, the *mores* and ways of the host population.

Although there are differences in how the various groups of immigrants react to their new surroundings, the claim that immigrants have more children is incorrect when viewed in a long-term perspective. An OECD report puts it thus:

"The arrival of more fertile population groups has not led to an explosion in foreign births that some segments of public opinion allege or fear. In fact foreign natality as a proportion of total births has remained quite moderate in most countries and is even tending to decline."[40]

It is also true that the foreigners in Europe have had more children than the European average. An important reason for this is that the immigrants were younger than the average age of the population when they came to Europe. So, even if the foreigners were to have no more children than the Europeans, to all appearances, it would seem as though they were having more.

That the largest single factor in demographic growth was immigration was like throwing petrol on a bonfire. With a little imagination and some extrapolations based on the false premise that the foreigners would maintain their fertility rates, some dreadful future scenarios could be conjured up - and they were.

The other problem of the Europeans having so few children which, in the fullness of time, would lead to problems on an entirely different scale, was barely touched on. However, it is clear that Germany would not have been the strongest European economy without the help of foreign labour. Every year from 1972 until the fall of the Wall, there were more deaths in West Germany than births.[41]

4. The history

4.1 The European legacy

One of the reasons for the difficulty experienced by Europeans in adjusting to the presence of foreigners may lie in the historic legacy of their continent. In the larger perspective, emigration has been, first and foremost, a European phenomenon. Apart from the special relationships of France, Britain and the Netherlands with their old colonies, there are no European countries which perceive themselves to be immigrant nations as such, unlike the USA, Canada and Australia.

On the contrary, the "dream of the New World" is an important part of the European world view. Although emigration to America has been fraught with difficulties ever since the outbreak of the First World War in 1914, emigration has been a solution for millions of Europeans seeking their fortunes abroad over many generations.

Europeans provided the bulk of the worlds emigrants until the 1960s. From 1945 to 1960, there were twice as many European emigrants as all others from the rest of the world combined, and it was only in 1965 that the USA abolished the quotas which had hitherto favoured European emigrants.[1]

Historically speaking Europe is, therefore, the home of the emigrant. Just as Europeans occupied the New World, so too they subjugated much of the rest of the world in their race for new colonies. They also carried out the exportation of slaves from West Africa to America. They built up sophisticated transport and communication networks and finally encompassed the whole world into a global commercial community.

This also meant that the Europeans had assembled all the world's peoples into a gigantic migratory system where emigration or immigration were possible if the conditions were right and the opportunity arose. The English social scientist, Sarah Collinson has this to say about the early trans-Atlantic migrations: "For the first time, the world began to be one migratory network dominated by a single group of technologically advanced and culturally similar states."[2]

From the discovery of America until 1800, over two million Europeans emigrated to the New World,[3] though this was not a lot in view of future developments. However, from 1820 to 1920, sixty million Europeans emigrated, 60 per cent of these going to America.[4]

The initial wave of Europeans was dwarfed even further by another wave of continental mass migration engineered by Europeans, a movement of people that in terms of size overshadowed the white conquest of America. This was the trade in black slaves from Africa.

4.2 Slaves and coolies

In the two centuries from 1550 onwards, it is estimated that around 15 million Africans were forcibly removed from their native lands to the West Indies and America. The English were the most active in this transportation of humans and were responsible for almost half of the slave trade during the eighteenth century. The other major slave trading nations were, in order of importance, Portugal, France and Holland. Denmark was responsible for about one per cent of the slave trade.

What we have here is one of the largest mass migrations of labour in history. Nowadays, there are about forty million descendants of African slaves in the USA and the West Indies.[5] It was only by 1880 that the total number of European emigrants exceeded that of the Africans forced across the Atlantic in the course of history.[6]

The slave trade was a direct consequence of the growing European colonization of the world. During the initial period of colonization, in the seventeenth and eighteenth centuries, labour was needed to exploit the opportunities offered by the new acquisitions. However, back in Europe the rulers were still under the sway of mercantilism, albeit in its death throes, and so it was still holy writ that a large population denoted economic and military power. Consequently, the labour shortage overseas was solved by using Africans.

Slavery was abolished at the beginning of the nineteenth century and after 1833 slaves were forbidden throughout the British Empire. This gave rise to another form of migration, the extent of which is not so well known though some of its forms were strongly reminiscent of the slave trade.

Indentured labourers – also known as coolies – signed up for several years of work abroad, or they travelled on their own and then signed a

TOP: *During the late 1980s and early 1990s, Western European countries were frightened at the prospect of mass migrations from the ex-Communist countries. Their fears were justified. In 1989 alone, 1.3 million people arrived from the ex-Communist countries. (Polfoto)*

RIGHT: *Overcrowded ships crossing the Adriatic from Albania to Italy. The expression "the Italian solution" was coined at the time. The many would-be refugees were immediately sent back. (Nordfoto)*

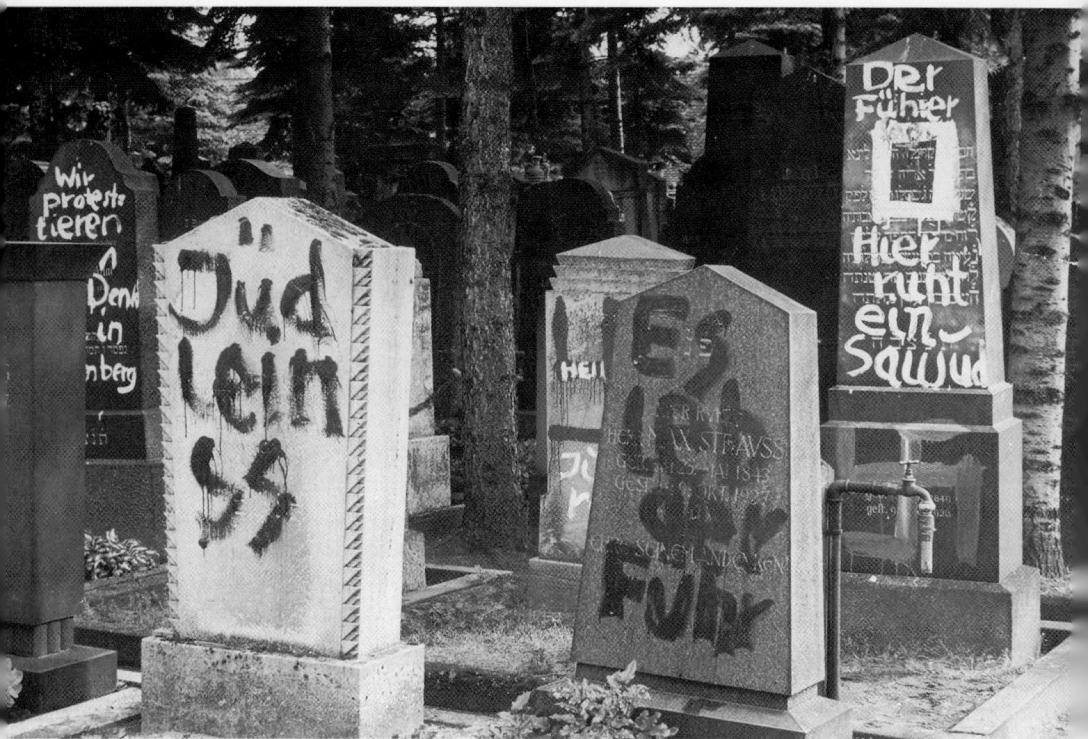

TOP: *The advance of the extreme right during the late 1980s was experienced over most of Europe. Anti-Semitism, racism, xenophobia and nationalism suddenly re-emerged as important features of the political scene. (Polfoto)*

BOTTOM: *The leader of the Front National, Jean-Marie Le Pen, enjoys broad popular support in France. Le Pen issues strongly worded warnings against both Jews and Muslims. In the first round of the 1995 presidential elections, he won almost every fifth vote cast, most of which came from those parts of Southern France with large immigrant communities. (Nordfoto)*[42]

contract with a local employer. Contract labourers were not slaves as many of them travelled of their own free will, and the majority did return to their native country. However, the rights of the employer were not dissimilar to those of a slave owner once the contract had been signed, willingly or unwillingly, by the labourer.

Throughout the nineteenth century, China and India were the prime sources of indentured labour. From 1830 onwards, they could be found all over the globe, though mainly in the European colonies in North America, Asia and Africa.

The total number of people who worked under contract is extremely difficult to determine. According to the International Labour Office (ILO) there were at least twelve million and perhaps as many as thirty-seven million in all.[7]

Most indentured workers came from China. They were peasants who went to the cities where they were often kidnapped and then forced to work in European colonies. These Chinese would go to Shanghai, for instance, where middlemen would seize them and send them on their way by ship, hence the expression to be "shanghaied".

Initially, the indentured workers were primarily used in South-East Asia, though in time they would spread to all the other colonies. The Chinese labourers arrived in the USA after the great gold discoveries in California of 1849, and were later to become a vital labour component in the building of the American transcontinental railways and in Panama.

Indian indentured labourers were the second large group of coolies. The first ship sailed from India in 1834, bound for the British colony of Mauritius where they were to work in the sugar plantations.

In the century after the abolition of slavery, millions of Indians ventured forth to work in the European colonies. Unlike the African slaves, most of them did return home, though the descendants of the six million Indians who did not may be found in the large Indian communities of East Africa and the West Indies.[8]

This type of contract labour was gradually prohibited before 1900, and was abandoned in its original form on Mauritius in 1915. However, a more moderate form of this system was to persist in the Dutch East Indies until the Japanese invasion in 1941.[9]

European emigration was in stark contrast to the non-European migrations where people, by and large, were forced to leave their home country to work under what were usually vilely inhumane conditions.

Emigration from Europe consisted predominantly of people and families who willingly left their homeland in the hope of a better future for themselves and their children. The initial migrations aside, it was seldom that people emigrated in order to escape political or religious persecution. There were even fewer instances of governments assisting or forcing Europeans to emigrate. The dream of a better life was, first and foremost, the source of motivation behind European migration.

Emigration is, therefore, a phenomenon associated with hope and optimism for Europeans, whereas emigration in history for most of humanity is associated with deportation, coercion and an abject existence.

4.3 The demographic transition

European global dominance in the nineteenth century was the outcome of the industrial and bourgeois revolutions. But a third revolution was also significant – the demographic revolution. This revolution is not talked about as much as the two others since it rarely gave rise to problems as the Europeans had the option of emigration.

The consequence of these revolutions was a fundamental change in the European condition. Humanity began to control Nature. The economic progress that followed in the wake of the industrial revolution meant, among other things, an increase in food production and, later on, giant strides in medical science.

Both these factors had an immediate impact on European mortality rates which fell dramatically. In England, mortality fell from 35 per 1000 inhabitants in 1740 to 15 per 1000 in 1900 – in other words, mortality was more than halved over 160 years.

However, the birth rate declined at a much slower rate although the death rate was decreasing, Europeans continued, as before, to have many children. Prior to the industrial revolution, a high birth rate was common, as was an almost equal death rate among infants. To this could be added the impact of epidemics, famine and wars, all of which ensured that the population did not increase.

The birth rate in England was still 35 per 1000 inhabitants in 1870 and it was only by 1930 that it had reached a level of 16 per 1000, thus ending the demographic transition. Throughout the entire nineteenth century, there were far more births per 1000 inhabitants than there were deaths.[10]

Thus, European population figures exploded during the industrial revolution from 194 million in 1840 to 463 million in 1930.[11] Emigration exploded in a similar fashion, albeit with a delay. During the first decade of the nineteenth century, 120,000 Europeans emigrated to the USA, a figure which had risen to 8,5 million by the last decade.

All in all, almost sixty million Europeans emigrated in the years between 1846 and 1939. Most of them, thirty-eight million, went to the USA while seven million went to Canada, another seven million, mainly Spaniards, emigrated to Argentina. Brazil received 4.6 million emigrants, many of whom came from Portugal while Australia, New Zealand and South Africa each received 2.5 million emigrants. In this way the steam was released from the population pressure cooker.[12]

The existence of a link between demographic growth and emigration from Europe during the nineteenth century has subsequently been proved. For instance, an analysis in 1961 showed that one of the reasons for the relatively low rate of French emigration was the low rate of demographic growth in comparison with the rest of Europe. Norway was at the opposite end of the scale with high rates of demographic growth and emigration. The analysis showed that there was a close connection between a rise in population and emigration twenty years later, a period which corresponds with the time it took for the new generation to reach the age when they could emigrate.[13]

It is important to understand this demographic evolution and the decisive influence that emigration had on it, for it is precisely this process that most of the developing nations of the world are undergoing today. In their case, this process started in the years after 1945, although the difference is that emigration from the Third world is minimal since there is no New World to which to emigrate.

4.4 The European emigrant

It is of interest to compare contemporary immigration to Europe with what characterized the many Europeans who migrated during the nineteenth century. The profile of the typical European emigrant had the following elements.[14]

To start with they were young, only eight per cent of those who went to the USA between 1868 and 1910 were over the age of forty whereas 16 per cent were under the age of fifteen. Males predominated, constituting 64 per cent of the total, and there was a marked tendency for Europeans to emigrate singly as opposed to going in family groups, which meant that the majority did not have to support a family from the outset. Close ties were maintained between those who emigrated and those they left behind. A large majority of emigrants were helped on their way by relatives or friends who had emigrated before them. Many Europeans received money or prepaid tickets for the passage from earlier migrants who, to a large extent, also helped them upon arrival. Most of the emigrants were unskilled which was explained by the fact that they were too young to have been trained in a trade.

There are thus similarities and differences between the European emigrants of the past and those who, for various reasons, have migrated to Europe over the last few decades.

Formerly, the main motivation for emigration was economic. The migrants were young, uneducated and, as a rule, had no family to support. They had most of their lives ahead of them where they stood to gain economically by taking their chances.

Post-War emigration to Western Europe presents a different and fuzzier picture. The guest workers of the 1950s and 1960s bore some resemblance to the migrants of the past in that most of them were unskilled young men. The network between the first migrants and the later arrivals is also a widespread present-day phenomenon. However, that is as far as the resemblance goes. Later on, this picture was to be radically altered as immigration to Western Europe became primarily a matter of reuniting families and the quest for asylum, of which more below.

4.5 The clouds begin to gather

The period up to the outbreak of the First World War was notable for the unrestricted entry to and exit from European countries. It was possible to travel throughout Europe and often overseas without even having to produce a passport. Not only were the large immigrant nations such as the USA and Canada accessible, but so were most of the nations of Europe. At the same time, most of the restrictions placed on emigration had been lifted by national governments which, in the face of terrific population growth, had come round to viewing emigration as politically and economically advantageous.

Transatlantic migration peaked in the years before the outbreak of war in 1914 at over a million people per annum of whom 400,000 emigrated from Italy alone.[15]

There were, however, other migrations than those from overseas. Inside Europe itself populations were on the move, primarily to where work could be found. In 1931, there were 300,000 Irish living in Britain, a large number in view of the fact that the population of Ireland was only three million. The Italians went to Switzerland and France, where there were 900,000 of them in the latter country in the same year. The Poles went to Germany and Belgians and Spaniards went to France. As the prominent English demographer, Russell King, noted: "Some of these early patterns of migration were to repeat themselves after 1945, just on a greater scale."[16]

The Europeans could draw three lessons from the history of earlier migrations, the first one being that, nowadays, most of the world is undergoing the demographic revolution that Europe experienced in the previous century. So, the fact that Europe is now facing migratory pressure from the Third world should, in historical terms, not come as a great surprise.

The second lesson is that the large migrations of the latter half of the nineteenth century until the outbreak of the First World War only provide a very limited basis for the analysis of contemporary migratory patterns. This is due to the fact that during that period there were both "push" and "pull" factors. The "push" factors in the home country could be shortage of land, poverty and a growing population and at the other end, in the receiving country, there could be an equal amount of "pull" factors which attracted immigrants. These could be plentiful arable land, rapid economic growth and political and economic freedom. When a comparison is drawn between the situation then and that of the present day, it becomes clear that there are still various factors that compel people to emigrate, though nowadays there are no factors attracting legal immigrants to Europe.

The third lesson is that emigration does not necessarily lead to permanent settlement. Up until the beginning of the nineteenth century it was common for immigrants to live and die in their country of adoption. However, when railways and modern ships appeared and reduced the cost and duration of travel, it became increasingly common for migrants to venture forth and work over shorter periods. This is an important factor to remember in the light of the fact that entry into Western Europe is now a near-impossibility. This means that those who have already entered will stay since they know that they would not be let in a second time.

The outbreak of the First World War in August 1914 marked the end of the period of unrestricted European emigration. That European emigration should reach its peak when the European share of the world population was at its greatest provides food for thought.[17] During the previous century when the Europeans had taken over most of the globe, their share of the world population had been increasing. This share has been diminishing ever since. The consequences of this shrinkage of the European portion of the world population are reflected in migratory patterns throughout the world.

4.6 The borders are closed

At the very beginning of the history of migration, the immigrants originally came from Great Britain, which was also the cradle of the industrial revolution. By the mid-nineteenth century, Germans constituted the largest group of emigrants to the USA. By the 1870s, the large migratory waves were arriving from Eastern and Southern Europe. Henceforth, these peoples were to provide the bulk of emigration to the USA.[18]

In the years leading up to the outbreak of the First World War, there were strong forces in America that sought to restrict the great migration of Eastern and Southern Europeans. They were deemed to be unwilling and incapable of becoming true Americans.[19]

There were other factors around the turn of the century that would eventually lead to the end of unrestricted immigration. One such factor was that the American economy was becoming less dependent on European labour and capital. Another was the difficulty encountered in ensuring that the Chinese coolies returned home. A third was that America had become a safe haven for those European Jews who fled from the rising anti-Semitism prevalent in Russia and Eastern Europe. Between 1881 and 1914, nearly 2,3 million Jews emigrated to the USA.[20]

Immigration was, however, never effectively restrained, despite much new legislation, because American employers and immigrants themselves put up a fight. It was only with the outbreak of war in 1914 and, later on, the Russian revolution in 1917, that effective controls and restrictions were placed on immigration in the name of national security.

In 1914, many countries began systematically checking passports, and when the war ended four years later, virtually all the states, both old and new, had introduced strict controls on their borders. The open world had passed on into history.

4.7 Stateless refugees

In this century, migration took on a new form in that refugees moved to centre stage. Many demographers hold that from the beginning of this century until the present day, the number of people who have crossed national borders in order to escape war, persecution or internal unrest is greater than the number of those who migrated due to economic necessity or opportunity.[21]

From the very start of the twentieth century, Europe has been affected by several migrations caused by local and regional conflicts. The decline of the Ottoman Empire in the Balkans allowed the growth of an initially smouldering nationalism and the subsequent waves of refugees.

Large migrations occurred throughout the Balkan powder keg and, in the period after the First World War, the areas bordering the newly created Turkish Republic where the Armenians were the most affected. Unlike the developments in recent years in ex-Yugoslavia, the Balkan refugee flows did not affect the rest of Europe; it was a matter of redrawing the ethnic map at local level.[22]

The new national boundaries drawn up at the peace negotiations at the end of the war were the cause of massive migration involving 7.7 million people.

Elsewhere on the continent, an almost equally all-embracing refugee situation arose as millions fled persecution, famine and the collapse of social order in the wake of the Russian revolution. Most remained within the borders of the new Empire although about one million did manage to escape before the Communist authorities solved the problem in the mid-1920s by denying the right to travel.

Russians were the first of many large groups of refugees who could be called "stateless". The Soviet Union had stripped them of their citizenship and thus they did not have valid passports. Their situation was hopeless – they were not allowed to stay where they were, they could not travel on without valid documentation and return was out of the question. At the time, refugees were not welcome anywhere.

The newly created League of Nations appointed its first High Commissioner for refugees in 1921, whose task was precisely to sort out the problem caused by the many Russians. Fridtjof Nansen, a Norwegian, was appointed. The future Nobel Peace laureate was famous for his earlier exploits in the polar regions and in 1888 he had become the first to cross the Greenland ice cap from east to west on skis.

Nansen's priority was helping the stateless refugees who had no travel documents. They were issued with Nansen certificates which over fifty countries had been persuaded to recognize as valid travel documents. Although his set task had been to help the Russian refugees only, others ended up in the same predicament. Nansen certificates were also issued to Armenians, Syrians, Kurds and Turks.[23]

The High Commissioner's task was well-nigh impossible. On the one hand the extent of the problem had assumed colossal dimensions in that there were 9.5 million refugees in Europe by 1926[24] while on the other, the immigrant nations had closed their borders throughout the 1920s. Only temporary labour, relatives of earlier immigrants or a few hailing from the "original" nations of Northern and Western Europe were allowed into the USA. The immigration controls that exist today were built up in those years.

In 1921, the USA adopted very restrictive immigration legislation on a provisional basis, which set up quotas for immigration. In 1924, this legislation was made permanent. The nations of Western Europe followed suit in the 1930s by drawing up laws which effectively kept refugees out.

Migration inside Europe was also reduced though on the whole it was only Poles or Italians who travelled elsewhere in Europe. 630,000 Poles emigrated in the 1920s, some of them coming to Denmark, and 390,000 Italians left in the same period. Another type of immigration started up gently – immigration from the colonies. In 1921, 200,000 arrived in England and, in 1930, a little over 100,000 arrived in France.[25]

The general situation worsened as a result of the recession of the 1930s as most states sought to protect their own labour force when faced with mass unemployment. Then, all "non-Aryans" such as Gypsies were persecuted in Germany along with Social-Democrats and

Communists, and the number of refugees grew. The truncated League of Nations was powerless to intervene.

In 1938 the American President, Franklin D. Roosevelt, called an international conference on the refugee question at the French Alpine resort of Evian. The Inter-Governmental Committee on Refugees, IGRC, was set up to negotiate with the government of the Third Reich about the right of Jews to emigrate.[26] This initiative, however, was overtaken by evvents and no nation would take in more refugees. There was a widespread fear of Jewish mass emigration from Poland, Hungary and Romania.

The scene was thus set for the continental tragedy. In the same year Austria was annexed by Germany while the following year saw the occupation of rump Czecho-Slovakia. The number of refugees in the Reich doubled from 1938 to 1939, and on 3rd September 1939, the Second World War broke out. European refugees had nowhere to go as all doors were slammed shut – they were on their own.

4.8 War refugees

The end of the war almost six years later gave rise to massive migrations throughout the countries of Europe. Millions of soldiers and workers pressed into forced labour had ended up far from home during the war, and as many again had been forced to flee in their own countries. Several authorities are of the opinion that up to thirty million Europeans had been made homeless during the war[27], and as the peace brought with it several border revisions, the result was endless waves of refugees flowing along the shattered roads of Europe.

Nearly fifteen million people had to move to another country[28], the bulk of these were Germans who returned to a geographically shrunken Fatherland. When the post-War national borders were drawn up, twelve million Germans found themselves outside the new Germany. In the years after the war, most of them went to West Germany. A census taken in 1950 showed that 9.6 million Germans had arrived in West Germany both during and after the war, and constituted one-fifth of the forty-eight million population. The emigration of Germans continued, particularly from East Germany, and by 1956 the resettled Germans constituted 25 per cent of the population of West Germany.[29]

The years up until the early 1950s were the years of resettlement and reconstruction. This period was also marked by two factors of decisive importance for the refugee flows of the future. One was the Cold War with its many refugees from East Germany and Eastern Europe. The other was the rising clamour for independence in the European ruled colonies which led to a considerable migration to Britain, France, the Netherlands and Portugal.

While the war was raging, the United Nations Relief and Rehabilitation Agency, UNRRA, was established and it played an important role in repatriating the many people who had been made homeless during the war. However, soon after the end of the war, the organization was caught up in and by the Cold War.

Opposition to sending people back to Eastern Europe and the Soviet Union soon became widespread and in 1947, due to American pressure, UNRRA was supplanted by the newly created International Refugee Organization, IRO, which was not a part of the UN system.

The new organization soon established its guiding principle that protection was to be afforded to the individual on the basis of "a well-founded fear of being persecuted for reasons of race, religion, nationality, membership of a particular social group or political opinion."

Thus the definition of a refugee now depended on whether the individual was persecuted or had a well founded fear of persecution whereas the inter-war definition had depended on whether a person belonged to a group that was being persecuted.[30]

This new individualized definition of a refugee was admirably suited for use as a tool in the Cold War and the many refugees from the East were seen by the West as proof positive of the bankruptcy of Communism.

The new refugee organization was solely concerned with European refugees and ensured that nearly a million people got to the USA, Canada, Australia or Israel. The IRO did not deal with, for instance, the colossal refugee flows generated on the Indian sub-continent in 1947 by the partition of India when up to fifteen million Hindus and Muslims were forced to flee as a consequence of Indian independence and the creation of the Muslim state of Pakistan.

The total eurocentricity of the international community was also apparent a year later when the creation of the state of Israel led to 700,000 Palestinians becoming refugees. To cope with this contingency, the UN created special organizations whose sole purpose was to provide and organize the humanitarian aid in the refugee camps.[31]

In 1951 the IRO was replaced by the United Nations High Commissioner for Refugees, UNHCR. Originally this organization was only supposed to work for three years and was only to deal with those people who had become refugees before 1951. In other words, the international community only felt obliged to solve the refugee problems that had arisen as a consequence of the Second World War and the ensuing Cold War.

The UNHCR was to become permanent as it soon became apparent that the refugee problem was not a transient phenomenon. The first major task it had to face was in 1956 when 200,000 Hungarians fled as a result of the Soviet invasion. In the early 1960s the UNHCR evolved into a worldwide refugee organization and, in 1967, the definition of a refugee was universalized through the adoption of an additional clause to the Geneva Convention of 1951.

Many refugees of the war were thus repatriated with international assistance or obtained refugee status as a result of the Cold War. At the same time, the old immigration nations eased open their doors just a little.

In the years immediately after the war and throughout the fifties there was strong migratory pressure on the USA, Canada and Australia as many Europeans wanted to leave this recently heavily traumatized part of the world. Most of the emigration to the USA did come from Europe and the USA's neighbouring countries, Canada, Mexico and the West Indies.

From the war's end until 1963, the USA received 2.3 million European immigrants of whom 600,000 came as refugees, Australia received two million during the same period of whom the majority were from Europe. The same number and tendency applied to Canada which did, however, display more openness to refugees.[32]

This emigration was not supported by national governments. With the exception of the Netherlands, every European nation feared that its labour force was too small to undertake the demanding task of reconstruction. The almost eight million dead in Western Europe had left ominous traces in the national demographies.

The fears were to prove to be well-founded.

4.9 Immigration to Europe

In the course of the 1950s, the economic repercussions of the war had spent themselves and the continent was about to enjoy one of the most powerful and prolonged economic upturns in history. From 1950 until the first oil crisis in 1973, the western OECD countries experienced an average growth rate of 5 per cent a year. This was a historic record in terms of economic progress as the rates of growth were double those experienced over the past forty years.[33]

This almost explosive rate of development required labour, and one would have thought that the labour force could have been augmented by two obvious measures. One would have been the gradual shift of women from being housewives into becoming wage earners and the other would have the modernization and rationalization of agriculture which would have freed labour for the expanding economies.

According to studies there was some degree of movement from the countryside to the big cities. However, France was the only large country where this occurred on a significant scale. As for women finding their way to the labour market, public opinion was not ready for the process which did eventually take place many years later.[34] In the case of most European nations it was only by 1973–74 that women entered the labour market to any significant extent. In Denmark the process was somewhat different as there had been movement from rural areas to the towns at a relatively early point in time and women had also entered the labour market early on.[35]

Although Western European labour was eventually augmented from these two sources, it was by no means sufficient as the demand for labour was insatiable.

Suddenly, for the first time in the history of the continent, Europe became a net importer of labour. Whereas the number of emigrants exceeded the number of immigrants by four million from 1914 to 1949, the picture was reversed by 1950 and from then until 1973 there was a net addition of almost ten million immigrants.[36]

Around 1950 the emigration from the south of Europe to the north began to accelerate, mainly to Switzerland and Sweden to start with and, to a lesser extent, Britain and France. At this early point in time, France began to import Turkish labour whereas West Germany was still able to constantly augment its work force with East Germans, many of whom were highly educated, and who were leaving East Germany at the rate of 200,000 a year. Immigration from the colonies also started up, mainly from the West Indies to Britain.[37]

4.10 The Italians are coming

From the mid-1950s to the first oil crisis of 1973, Northern and Western Europe consequently experienced a strong migration of labour as the national labour reserves were not big enough to support the explosive economic growth, and as foreigners, mainly from the Mediterranean area, came to help.

The traditional factors of "pull" and "push" came in to play as the level of unemployment in the emigrant nations was high. It was hard for many people to maintain even a reasonable standard of living and the rate of demographic growth was still high. At the same time, in the rich part of Europe, there was a shortage of labour especially in the risky, filthy and poorly paid category of the so called "3D" jobs, "Dirty, Dangerous and Demanding".

The labour shortage was greatest in West Germany which, towards the end of the 1950s, began importing foreign labour. When the Berlin Wall was erected in 1961 the East German source dried up and the labour requirement became a matter of acute urgency. Unlike France and Britain, West Germany had been able to afford to take a relaxed view of the labour shortage in the post-war years since the flow of people from the East had satisfied demand on the labour market.

In Britain, already at the end of the war there was an awareness that problems would arise before very long. "In a few years' time, we in this country will be faced with a shortage of labour and not with a shortage of jobs. Our birth rate is not increasing in sufficient proportion to enable us to replace ourselves," said Labour politician and later Prime Minister, James Callaghan in a speech to the House of Commons in June 1946.[38] In 1948, Parliament approved a Nationality Bill which affirmed the freedom of movement of labour within the Commonwealth and colonies, and during the ensuing decade, there was some immigration from India, Pakistan and the West Indies. However, the intake of labour from abroad was not on the same scale as in France and West Germany.

In France the politicians were even more worried as the nation had experienced a declining birth rate for many years. This, along with the large loss of life in two world wars, meant that the country was ready to receive a large flow of immigration. A government announcement of 1946 put it thus: "The population problem is the number one problem of French economic policy."[39] In 1947 France and Algeria reached an agreement on the freedom of entry and exit between both countries. By

1949, 256,000 Algerians had emigrated to France and, during this period, government advisers from the Institut National d'Études Démographiques were recommending a permanent immigrant presence of 5.3 million. Right up until 1962, President Charles de Gaulle talked of a France with a hundred million inhabitants.[40]

The prime migrants were the Italians. Throughout the 1950s they constituted half of the northbound emigration. The dramatic migration from Italy to the USA and Northern Europe was mainly due to late industrialization, especially of the southern part of Italy, and a high rate of demographic growth. Though when the Italian economy itself began to expand during the 1960s, emigration dropped and the Northern and Western European countries had to look around for other sources of labour.

Turkey and Yugoslavia were to be the main sources of labour for West Germany though comprehensive agreements were also reached with Portugal, Greece, Morocco and Tunisia. In France the Italians were replaced by Spaniards, Portuguese, West Africans and North Africans, the latter mostly from Algeria. Britain, as mentioned earlier, drew labour from its old colonies, India, Pakistan and the West Indies.

Table 4.1 illustrates the extent to which the then six Common Market countries, West Germany, France, Italy, the Netherlands, Belgium and Luxembourg had come to depend on foreign labour. From 1958 to 1972 over eight million work permits were issued to foreigners.

One third of the foreign workers came from other EC countries but this, however, did not indicate a rise in the migration of labour across EC borders. As Table 4.1 shows, it was mainly a question of Italian labour migrating to the other EC member states, Italy alone providing 86 per cent of those who migrated within the EC area.

The number of guest workers in West Germany soared when the borders were finally opened. In 1958 there were only 127,000 foreign workers, and in the early 1960s, they still represented under one per cent of the population.[41] By 1965 they numbered one million and by 1971 two million. The huge number of guest workers absorbed by West Germany becomes apparent when the figures are compared with those of the other major immigrant nations during the same period. France, Switzerland and the three Benelux countries received the same number, around two million all together.[42]

At the beginning of the 1970s, France and West Germany had 2.5 million guest workers which corresponded to 10–12 per cent of the labour force.[43] Migration to Britain was not so extensive where net immigration

Table 4.1. Work permits granted to foreign workers in the EC. 1958-1972.
(in thousands)

	Total	From EC countries	Thereof from Italy
1958	176	110	85
1959	152	94	73
1960	333	207	171
1961	436	229	206
1962	514	222	199
1963	516	182	158
1964	638	190	164
1965	713	261	235
1966	595	213	189
1967	286	96	75
1968	522	164	142
1969	860	166	145
1970	945	205	176
1971	767	198	166
1972	623	195	161
Total	8.077	2.732	2.345

Source: Göran Rystad: "History and the Future of International Migration", in
International Migration Review, vol. XXVI, no. 4. Winter 1992, p. 1178.

amounted to 670,000 between 1955 and 1968.[44] The foreigners were
mainly concentrated in France and West Germany as two-thirds of the
non-EC citizens lived in the two countries whose combined populations
only amounted to a third of the total EC population.[45]

4.11 The absence of an immigration policy

According to the Swedish social scientist, Gøran Rystad, the immigration policies of the European nations in the years from the end of the
war until 1973 may be categorized according to two types.[46] The first
was the so-called rotation system whereby the guest workers could only obtain temporary work and residence permits, thereby ensuring that
the business community had a labour reserve at hand should demand
rise. This situation meant that the countries tried to attract young, single, mainly male workers who could travel home if there was no longer
any work to be had which would be the reason for not renewing their
residence permits.

This scenario suited the receiver countries who could thus ensure the national workforce against unemployment when the economy was sluggish, as well as reducing the risk of great social burdens. There was the additional calculation that the importation of a large workforce would contribute to keeping down the levels of wages and prices during periods of strong economic growth.

This arrangement was also supported by the guest workers' countries of origin which in the short term could thus reduce their own levels of unemployment, and in a longer term perspective would benefit from the return of workers who would be more educated. That the guest workers often sent foreign currency to their families back at home was also an important factor as this improved the home country's balance of payments situation.

Thus guest workers formed a system from which all seemed to benefit. In terms of national economy, it was advantageous for both emigrant and immigrant nations. The European nations solved the basic problem of securing enough labour for their industries while maintaining their cultural specificity that would otherwise be threatened by the presence of large numbers of foreigners.

Switzerland was the country which most consequently and successfully applied this guest worker system. Foreigners have traditionally formed a large part of the country's population. From 1950 to 1974, the number of foreigners rose from 285,000 to a million. All the same no-one would regard Switzerland as an immigrant nation, and quite rightly, as there are no immigrants. Non-nationals are known as foreign workers, foreigners or guest workers. The sole consideration is that the foreigners form part of the Swiss economy.

Throughout the 1960s the guest worker system was the policy also practiced by the West Germans, though with far less success than the Swiss. As unemployment amongst the Germans rose in 1974, it became apparent to what extent the majority of foreigners who were supposed to go home actually remained in the country.

The other type of immigration policy of the post-war years consisted of foreigners coming to the host country with the intention of settling permanently and being slowly integrated in their new home country. Britain is an example of this policy. Although it was in terms of history primarily an emigrant nation, in the 1930s, it experienced a slight immigration surplus from the colonies.

After the Second World War, immigration resumed mainly from the West Indies at first, then from other parts of the old empire, India, Pa-

RIGHT: *There was a shortage of labour in the New World. Until 1800, this problem was solved by means of one of the most extensive transportations of people in history. Fifteen million slaves were forcefully transported from Africa to North America. (Kronborg Trade and Navigation Museum)*

BOTTOM: *The population of Europe exploded from 194 million people in 1840 to 463 million in 1930. So did emigration and the pressure was thus released from the population pressure-cooker. Sixty million Europeans emigrated in this period, the majority went to the USA. (Polfoto)*

TOP: *The Norwegian polar explorer and peace pioneer Fridtjof Nansen addressing the League of Nations in September 1921. That year, he became the first High Commissioner for Refugees, his task was to assist the millions of stateless Russian refugees who followed in the wake of the Russian revolution in 1917. The "Nansen certificates" which afforded a degree of protection were also issued to many other groups of stateless refugees. In 1922, he received the Nobel Peace Prize. In 1888, he had been the first man to cross Greenland on skis. (UNHCR)*

LEFT: *Towards the end of the 1950s, labour shortages appeared in many parts of Western Europe. The guest workers began to arrive and generally received the menial jobs that the locals did not want, the so-called "3-D-jobs" as in "Dirty, Demanding and Dangerous". (Tommy Nilsson/2maj)*

kistan and Kenya. By 1962, half a million people had arrived who were not of British origin. Until that year there had been no restriction on immigration as such because all the citizens of the colonies or of Commonwealth countries were automatically British citizens as well. Since then the legislation has been gradually tightened, especially towards coloured immigrants.

France found itself falling between two stools – the pure guest worker system on the one hand and the permanent residence permit system on the other. During the latter half of the 1950s, 400,000 immigrants arrived. Since the majority of them came from Algeria it was a case of permanent residence as they were French citizens. The same could be said about the half million who came to France in 1962, the year of Algerian independence.

Throughout the 1960s until 1974, when immigration was officially halted, there were approximately 130,000 new arrivals a year, primarily unskilled labour from Portugal and North Africa. It was also during this time that France lost control of how many and whom entered the country. In 1968, 80 per cent of the foreigners in the labour market were illegal immigrants. The pressure on the labour market was so strong that they just slipped in to the system and were granted legal status later on.

On the one hand, France tried to maintain the rotation system through the use of harsh measures such as sending back those people who could not adapt to French society or who were no longer contributing to the economy. It should be pointed out, though, that the French did not implement this policy any more effectively or toughly than any of the other European countries. On the other hand France, in many areas, maintained a relatively positive policy towards the new arrivals, for instance in such areas as reuniting families and with the acquisition of French citizenship after five years residence.

Perhaps this lack of consequence in their immigration policy is one of the reasons why France, to a greater extent than the other countries, has to face up to racism, xenophobia and extreme nationalist parties.

4.12 The failed policy

At the outset of the 1970s, all the countries of north-west Europe were in the same situation although they had implemented very different recruiting and immigration policies over the previous twenty years. They

had all experienced strong waves of immigration, often without any real control over who or how many came in, and every nation had to face
the fact that the majority of the non-Europeans were not going to go
home when the economy of Western Europe went from boom to slump.

During the time of the large migrations in the 1960s, few would have
foreseen the large number of foreigners living in Western Europe today.
The rotation or guest worker system simply did not work or, more to the
point, it only worked in times of plenty. The dramatic recession that followed in the wake of the 1973 oil crisis meant a almost complete halt to
the immigration of new labour. However, two factors were to have the
effect of neutralizing the rotation principle.

The first, which took many economists and politicians by surprise,
was that the unemployment rate among foreigners was not significantly higher than that of locals.[47] The principal reason for this, of course,
was that the foreigners did the work that the locals did not want either
because it was poorly paid and/or it was dirty and dangerous. This factor was all the more relevant as the many years of economic prosperity
and improved levels of education meant that the locals were even less
interested in menial work than they would have been earlier. In other
words, the jobs that disappeared when the recession began to bite were
not necessarily those of the foreigners.

The second factor was that most countries did not possess the political and legal tools necessary for democratic societies to send people
home against their will. Also, most guest workers did have the legal right
to have their families join them in the host country.

At the time, the flow of refugees into Europe did not pose economic
or political problems. As mentioned in Chapter 3, relatively few got
through the Iron Curtain and those who did were all very well received.
Otherwise, refugees were mainly to be found in the Third World and
very few victims of those conflicts found their way to Europe. In 1961,
the UNHCR had to assist 120,000 Chinese who had fled to Macao.
Later on, refugee flows resulted from wars of independence against
colonial powers and civil wars throughout Africa, and at the start of the
1970s, the Indian sub-continent again experienced extensive refugee
movements as East Pakistan gained independence as Bangladesh.[48]

Immigration in Europe was largely a question of importing enough
labour in the interim to satisfy the rising demand of the rich European
countries. This policy was both a success and a failure, a success initially when all the criteria applied, a failure in the eyes of those who thought

that the role of foreign labour in the reconstruction of Europe was a closed chapter. In her book "Europe and International Migration," Sarah Collinson writes: "... post-war immigration had not been a temporary economic phenomenon, but was permanent, structural, and socially and politically significant."[49]

From 1960 to 1973, between twenty and thirty million people were involved in this migration of labour. During those years the number of foreign workers in Western Europe rose from two to seven million and the number of foreigners rose from four to twelve million.[50]

4.13 The first oil crisis

The shock came in September 1973. In the next four months the price of crude oil quadrupled and the entire western world was drawn into a recession that no-one had thought possible. During 1972 and 1973 the economies of the OECD nations grew at an average rate of six per cent a year. In many places the shortage of labour was catastrophic and wages soared. So, in the midst of the overheating economies, the quadrupled oil prices were to plunge the entire western economic system into the nightmare scenario dreaded by politicians and economists alike – uncontrollable price rises alongside declining production – known as stagflation.

By 1974 all the western economies were close to stagnation and, in 1975, Western Europe, for the first time since the war, experienced a fall in production while inflation had risen over an average of 12 per cent in the previous year and remained at a level of 10 per cent the next year. The price of industrial products rose much more sharply – 22 per cent in 1974 alone.[51]

Everywhere politicians brought things to a screeching halt, partly in order to get the soaring rate of inflation under control, but also in order to correct the balance of payments towards the oil exporting countries. The outcome was inevitable.

The nations of Europe had to make a swift adjustment from many years of labour shortage to a situation where unemployment started to grow for the first time since the 1930s. Under those circumstances the politicians did not find it hard to reach a decision.

The arrival of new labour from abroad was immediately stopped. The Germans closed off access in November 1973 and the French followed suit in July 1974. Although throughout Western Europe and the EC, enlarged on 1st January 1973 with Britain, Ireland and Denmark as new members, there was no coordination of national policy in this area, each country came to the same decision. No more guest workers were allowed in from then on. However, this did not stop immigration, it just made it assume a new form.

That the immigration of labour fell during those years is apparent from Table 4.2 which shows how the number of work permits issued in the nine EC countries fell dramatically between 1973 and 1975. This fall is especially steep in the case of non-Europeans.

Table 4.2. Immigration of workers to European countries from a number of emigration countries. 1973 and 1975. (in thousands)

Country	1973	1975
Finland	6.7	8.5
Greece	12.4	4.3
Italy	82.6	50.9
Portugal	73.0	6.3
Spain	96.1	10.0
Turkey	135.8	15.6
Yugoslavia	100.0	17.6

Source: Göran Rystad: "History and the Future of International Migration", in *International Migration Review*, vol. XXVI, no. 4. Winter 1992, p. 1178.

4.14 The opposition grows

At first glance, it is understandable that all countries should impose a complete stop on the recruitment of foreign labour in view of the drastic circumstances. In most countries, immigration was, to a greater or lesser extent, a system which was meant to be closed down when the demand for labour was no longer there.

The question remains, however, whether there were some underlying factors which would have made the importation of foreign labour to Europe less profitable anyway, and whether the oil crisis with the consequent recession was just a signal event which forced the politicians to stop all immigration. In other words, would there have been a clampdown on immigration anyway for economic and political reasons? If that is indeed the case, it might go some way to explaining why continued immigration has given rise to so many problems in most countries as it has done ever since the initial halt.

The powerful flow of immigration was already coming under political pressure before the oil crisis broke out. In 1974, the OECD, in a report on the moratorium on immigration, said that it was the "result of essentially political considerations" since "the social and political drawbacks of immigration now seem to have become greater than the economic advantages."[52]

Britain differs in this respect from the countries on the continent as the debate on immigration had raged since the beginning of the 1960s. Already then, the Conservative politician Enoch Powell, who was to enjoy considerable popular support, was using arguments and expressing views that were to be deployed by the Western European extreme right in the 1980s. Immigration legislation was constantly tightened up until 1971, the year when the Immigration Act was passed by Parliament. This Act contained pretty much the same restrictions as those laws adopted in other countries after the oil crisis.

In France, public opinion had begun to make itself felt and, at the start of the 1970s, a violent debate was raging about the presence of foreigners. The government thought out loud about the possibility of reducing immigration and making it harder for immigrants to be naturalized. The opposition culminated in violent unrest in Marseilles in the summer of 1973 which was aimed principally at Algerian immigrants. Right up to the presidential election of 1974, immigration was one of the central issues and, in the summer of that year, a stop to immigration was instituted at the recommendation of a committee of ministers chaired by the newly appointed Prime Minister, Jacques Chirac.

The same pattern emerged in West Germany where the government by means of various measures sought to make it less advantageous for employers to recruit labour from abroad. Fines for employing illegal immigrants were introduced in the summer of 1973, and the government imposed a halt on non-EC immigration only a few months later.

Thus, all over Western Europe, there was a political build-up towards settling once and for all the issue of unrestricted immigration. Social costs became an important theme in public debate and nationalist tones were heard with increasing force in political debate. The winds of change not only gained strength in the political sphere, but questions were also being asked about the economic wisdom of the policy pursued hitherto.

In his book "The New Helots", Robin Cohen lists four reasons why the advantages of importing cheap foreign labour were already on the wane at the time of the oil crisis.[53]

The first reason was that internationalization based on the large multinational corporations was beginning to get under way. This meant that, in many fields, production which had hitherto been placed in Europe could be advantageously moved to Third World countries where labour costs were much lower. In other words, the import of foreign labour was to be replaced by the export of capital, plant and technical know-how to the developing nations.

This process was reasonably common. For instance, in thirty-six developing nations – fifteen in Asia, fifteen in Latin America and six in Africa – free zones were set up where foreign companies could locate their production on favourable terms. Another example of the departure of parts of industry to where labour was cheap is provided by job creation figures for West Germany at the time. From 1973 to 1976 West German industry shed a million jobs at home whereas 1.5 million jobs abroad were created through overseas investments. Research showed that the same pattern applied to Britain.

The second reason was the growing social cost of the immigrants. The really big economic advantages could only be obtained if immigrant workers were constantly being replaced by new intakes. However, in Western Europe at the time, human rights were becoming an increasingly important factor partly due to the ideological struggle against the Communists of the Eastern Bloc. This meant that there were limits to the treatment which could be meted out to the immigrants. In this light, the newly arrived immigrants could hardly be denied the rights to bring over their families, place their children in the education system, be well-housed and claim social benefits as well as the vote in local elections. All of this led to increased public expenditure.

The third reason was that it soon became apparent that the guest workers increasingly began to behave like the locals in the labour market. They started making demands and were often able to take strike action in order to improve their conditions. This became a feature of the second generation of immigrants who wanted to struggle against and change the terms that their parents had been obliged to accept.

The fourth reason was that the trade unions of most countries soon realized the dangers inherent in new immigrant labour being paid less than the locals. Thus, more and more foreigners joined trade unions thereby nullifying one of the advantages of hiring foreign labour.

There were other changes in society which affected the balance of the labour market. The oil crisis with the subsequent fall in production naturally meant a decrease in the demand for labour. There were, however, changes under way on the supply side too.[54]

The baby-boomers of the post-War period began to enter the labour market in the mid-1970s. At the same time, women began to work outside the home to a significant degree. A third change was that of women's behaviour in that whereas previously they would leave the labour market for some years in order to raise their children, it became more common for them to stay on at work after having given birth.

Furthermore, there was a debate on competitiveness, particularly in West Germany and Switzerland, the main point being that national industries should no longer rely on cheap foreign labour as this discouraged industry from investing in capital intensive production methods, an area where countries like West Germany and Switzerland should enjoy a comparative advantage.

The situation was such that as the demand for labour declined, the amount of labour on offer rose. The prognoses showed that the latter phenomenon had come to stay.

4.15 A halt to immigration – yet still more immigrants

The immigrants too had come to stay. Many had settled in Europe and were not in a position to just drop everything and go home although, because of the crisis, two to three million of them did return home in the ensuing years. In 1978 the number of guest workers was the same as it was in 1974, around five million. However, if their families are included in the count, the total number of immigrants rose from ten million in 1974 to eleven million by 1978. In other words, although there was a moratorium on immigration and many immigrants did go home, the number of foreigners increased because the remaining immigrants got their families to join them in Western Europe.

The paradox was that although Western Europe shut off immigra-

tion, the total number of immigrants grew through the reuniting of families. The number of foreigners was to rise even further as reunited
families meant many more foreign births. This rise was augmented by
the fact that most of the immigrants are young in comparison with the
rest of the population. After the 1973 oil crisis many Western European
countries found that although there was no immigration per se, there
was de facto immigration and a rising number of foreigners instead.

The closed door policy led to another paradox which the authorities
had not foreseen, namely that only very few would now go home as they
knew that they would not be allowed back in a second time. Because of
family ties, the immigrants who stayed were the only way into Europe
for their compatriots still at home. To this could be added that the crisis experienced by the industrialized countries was often far worse in the
immigrants' own countries. So the prospects connected with going
home were not too rosy either.

From 1974 onwards, European immigration policy was implemented according to the presupposition that it was possible to control immigration. The policy whereby new guest workers were shut out and
those already resident were sent home was, to a certain extent, successful because there was a large overall drop in the legal immigration of
labour.

However, immigration continued through new channels, as mentioned earlier in the form of reuniting families but, from then on increasingly also in the form of refugees seeking political asylum in Europe
and, finally, through illegal routes as well. The disinction between asylum
seekers and illegal immigrants was very often fluid as 80 per cent of those
whose asylum applications were turned down remained in Europe.

In many countries the fact that this group constitutes the bulk of illegal immigrants[55] clouded the distinction between "economic" and
"political" refugees. Thus the seeds were sown of the often hate-laden
debate which was to characterize the ensuing two decades.

4.16 Self-created problems

The moratorium on immigration of 1973–74 was imposed ostensibly
because of the slump. It is far from certain that the economic reasoning
behind it is sound. The arguments put forward, however, gained

widespread currency in the population at large which, in turn, increased their political appeal. The halt to immigration was justified in some circles by the somewhat dubious argument, with its ill-concealed racist undertones, that when the foreigners were not stealing jobs from the locals, unemployment in their ranks led to a rise in public expenditure which, in turn, meant that they were a burden on European welfare systems.

This was exactly the same kind of argument as that used everywhere against immigration in the inter-war period. In the 1930s, even the USA experienced some years when more people left the country than entered it. Australia also experienced a net emigration from 1930 to 1935.[56]

It is extremely difficult to substantiate the claim categorically that immigrants take jobs away from the locals. Much research shows that, during and after the mid-1970s recession, many employers continued to employ foreign workers. This was particularly true in certain sectors of the economy such as hotels and restaurants, parts of the textile and clothing industry, agriculture at harvest time and low-wage labour in industry and the building trade. These sectors had continued to depend on this supplementary labour. As mentioned earlier, unemployment amongst immigrants did rise after 1974 but no more so than among any other group on the labour market.

The argument that immigrants take work away from locals presupposes a fixed number of jobs. In this particular context, nothing could be further from the truth as immigrants are also consumers who through their activity provide work for others.

Thus it is hard to establish whether the argument is true or false. There is, however, much circumstancial evidence which indicates that it is false. For instance, development in the main immigrant nations such as the U.S.A., Canada, Australia, Israel and Germany, during the great immigration booms of the late 1960s and 1990, was definitely not marked by a low rate of economic growth.

Studies which have analysed sudden waves of immigration do not substantiate the claim that immigrants steal work from locals either. In 1980, the Cuban President, Fidel Castro, allowed anybody who wished to leave Cuba to do so. Four months later, 125,000 Cubans, mainly unskilled workers, had arrived in Miami, Florida. Although the Miami workforce had been increased by seven per cent, employment and wage levels for the locals, including the poorly paid blacks, were not affected.

The migration from Algeria to France of 900,000 people of European origin, the Pieds Noirs, in the years after 1962 had only a minimal effect. Where immigrants increased the labour force by one per cent, the rate of unemployment rose by about 0.2 per cent.[57]

The question as to whether immigrants were a burden on welfare societies can be answered with a little more certainty. Studies from the USA, Canada, Switzerland and Germany show that, in net terms, the foreigners, after tax and not counting social benefits, contributed more to the economy on average than the locals.[58] This conclusion was not surprising as most of the foreigners were young, single and employed, so their use of child and pension benefits was limited.

Although – as mentioned earlier – there may have been some economic mechanisms at work that reduced the economic advantage of immigrant labour, the implementation of the moratorium should also be seen as a largely political decision. When the crisis bites, scapegoats must be found. It is ironic that the arguments initially advanced in favour of a complete moratorium became more and more correct as a result of the subsequent reuniting of families.

4.17 We asked for workers…

After the first oil crisis, the Western European countries tried to help the foreigners go home. In France, from 1977 until 1981 when the law was rescinded, 55,000 people received financial help in resettling in their countries of origin. However, the "wrong" people took advantage of the offer as the vast majority of them went back to Portugal and Spain. It was only in 1983 that the West Germans offered economic assistance to those who wanted to go home. They set up financing offices and funds in Greece and Turkey to help those who returned voluntarily.

All these schemes, however, amounted to nothing. More and more foreigners decided to stay and have their families join them in Europe. Until 1980, only two countries, Switzerland and Sweden, managed to bring the number of foreigners down by 180,000 and 5,000 respectively. Everywhere else in Western Europe, the number rose.[59]

A French official put it thus: "On ferme la porte et on ouvre la fenêtre." This was an elegant way of saying that the moratorium throughout Europe led to a strong rise in family reunifications.[60]

4.18 …and we got people instead

Many attempts were made at slowing this process down. After all, the idea of the moratorium was not that foreigners should continue to arrive. To make matters worse, this process meant that the immigrants were transformed from being solely a labour resource into families where the woman did not necessarily work and the children went to school. In this case it was a Swiss official who put it succinctly when he said: "We asked for workers and we got people instead."[61]

In many countries legislation was tinkered with in order to stop families being reunited. France and Germany introduced rules requiring residence over a certain length of time before the family was entitled to come as well. In some cases, Germany would not issue work permits to members of the newly arrived families or would only do so after a certain period of time. Attempts were also made to deny entry to family members unless those already there could guarantee their accommodation.

These attempts to tighten the rules encountered strong resistance from several humanitarian and religious organizations while those amendments which were not removed were later reversed either by administrative decisions or by the courts.[62]

The rapidly increasing immigration through the uniting of families could not be stopped in those years. The Western European countries were caught up in the conflict between, on the one hand, economic and political arguments against immigration and, on the other, humanitarian considerations. It was almost impossible for democratic and humanistically inclined Western Europe to effectively oppose the reuniting of families and, later on, to reject refugees fleeing persecution.

It was during those years that the presence of the foreigners suddenly became a direct challenge to the democratic nations of Western Europe. This challenge was new since immigration until the early 1970s had largely been a question of providing labour for private sector industry. It was not made any easier to face by the fact that Western Europe had to present a credible profile in the area of individual human rights towards the countries behind the Iron Curtain.

There was the additional fact that the right to unite families was enshrined in several international conventions on human rights. This right had been further established as late as 1985 in the United Nations Declaration on Human Rights for Non-Indigenous Peoples.[63]

What with internal opposition, the Cold War as well as international obligations, the governments of Western Europe were left with precious little room for manoeuvre on the question of limiting the new type of immigration.

4.19 The families arrive

On the eve of the 1980s, the industrialized nations were again thrown into recession. Unrest in Iran, a major oil producer, gave the OPEC nations another opportunity to strike. Economic growth had fallen to 1.5 per cent by 1981, and in the next year there was zero-growth in the OECD area. The currency markets were in a state of chaos, inflation had risen to well over ten per cent in most countries and unemployment had again begun to rise sharply. This time, the immigrants in Europe were to be hard hit by the crisis.

Until 1980 the unemployment rates for immigrants and locals had, by and large, been the same. However, from 1979 onwards unemployment rose and immigrants were the hardest hit. In West Germany the rate of unemployment had varied between four and five per cent for both groups until 1980. By 1982 unemployment stood at a little over nine per cent, whereas for immigrants it had reached twelve per cent. In France approximately ten per cent of immigrants were unemployed, which was a little above the national average.[64]

The Swedish Ministry of Finance carried a similar survey in 1995 where the conclusions were the same. Throughout the 1970s the rate of employment among immigrants was often higher than that of the locals. However, during the 1980s, the problems really set in, partly due to the new arrivals coming from cultures that differed greatly from Swedish culture, and also because industry began to require relatively high levels of education of its new intake of labour.[65]

That unemployment amongst immigrants should rise was not remarkable. Reuniting families meant that a relatively large part of the foreign community now consisted, in contrast to previous times, of people who could not just go and present themselves on the labour market. The large component of women and children obviously did not have the same relationship to working life.

The strength of this development from 1974 onwards is apparent from Table 4.3 which covers the largest immigrant groups in Switzerland, West Germany and France. The pattern is the same for all the groups in that the share of foreigners not on the labour market has risen sharply.

In France the average share of foreigners on the labour market fell from 53.8 per cent in 1974 to 40.0 per cent by 1989. In West Germany, the drop was from 71.8 per cent to 47.2 per cent. In Switzerland the level of foreigners outside the labour market is much lower. However, even here, there has been a tendency for the share of foreigners on the labour market to fall from 75.8 per cent in 1974 to 62.4 per cent by 1989.[66] The figures for these averages are untreated and they do not reflect variations in the size of the various immigrant groups. Thus these averages solely reflect the tendency which, according to the table, can be discerned in all immigrant groups.

Table 4.3. Foreign workers as proportion of total foreign population in France, West Germany and Switzerland in 1974 og 1989. (per cent)

Receiving country / Sending country	France		West Germany		Switzerland	
	1974	1989	1974	1989	1974	1989
Greece	-	-	73,5	39,6		
Italy	45,1	37,5	64,7	39,8	75,6	61,3
Portugal	52,2	55,0	77,3	56,7	-	-
Spain	49,3	37,9	87,3	53,0	83,3	64,6
Turkey	60,3	44,5	50,6	40,4	-	-
Yugoslavia	-	-	77,0	53,9	68,4	61,6
Algeria	53,2	31,5	-	-	-	-
Morocco	55,0	36,2	-	-	-	-
Tunisia	61,2	37,6	-	-	-	-

Source: Russel King: "European International Migration 1945-90: A Statistical and Geographical Overview", in Russel King, ed.: *Mass Migration in Europe*, Belhaven Press, London 1993, p. 34.

The reuniting of families has continued right up to this day. In the years after the moratorium, this was primarily of the so-called "first generation" variety. In this instance, the original immigrants were joined by their wives and children in Western Europe. Then, throughout the 1980s, many of the children found a spouse in the home country.

The reuniting of families meant that the immigrants to a far greater extent became part of society. Many second generation immigrants went to school and the families began to use the healthcare systems. The families formed large enclaves in the cities and the process of integration was entrusted to the local authorities. It was then that the general public became aware of the social cost which was an inevitable consequence. The "immigration problem" was becoming a hot political issue.

It was, however, only by the mid-1980s that the mounting political resistance gained any serious purchase and assumed a violent and racist stance towards the foreigners. This political development was due to another phenomenon – that a rising proportion of the foreigners were of non-European origin. This was primarily due to the fact that another group of people was now arriving in Europe in increasing numbers, a group whose numbers are connected with the complete moratorium of 1974 – political refugees.

4.20 The refugees are coming

Before the first oil crisis there were, by comparison with subsequent developments, few refugees. According to the UNHCR, the total number of refugees throughout the world during the 1960s up until 1974 was between 1.3 and 2.4 million per annum. Afterwards the number was to rise dramatically every year until it peaked at 18 million refugees in 1992.[67]

Right up until the mid-1970s, the refugees came from Europe. During the first half of the seventies 13,000 people each year sought political asylum in Western Europe.[68] This was slightly less than the number seeking asylum in Denmark in 1992.[69]

When the UNHCR was created in 1951, it was based on earlier experience where refugees had come primarily from neighbouring countries where culture and religion were relatively similar. When persecution again forced Europeans to flee, first in Hungary in 1956, then East Germany in 1961, Greece in 1967 and Czechoslovakia in 1968, the refugee flows did not give rise to any political problems. The neighbouring nations had a historic responsibility for the refugees of the region.

As colonies began to gain independence in Africa and Asia, the pattern changed. Refugees were no longer a European phenomenon. Conflicts in North Africa, the Congo, Ghana, Togo, Uganda, Burundi and Senegal gave rise to massive population movements. The same applied in 1970–71 when the creation of the state of Bangladesh forced millions to take to the roads. These conflicts were also resolved in the region, and the Western European effort consisted of financial assistance.[70]

Another era dawned in the mid-1970s when the fighting in Vietnam, Laos and Cambodia triggered mass migrations and, for the first time ever, a regional solution was not possible. The bordering countries would only accept refugees inside their borders if they could travel on to a third country. Subsequently, more than a million people from Indo-China were to arrive in the West.[71]

There were also various other reasons for these refugee flows not causing any political problems in the West either. Because of the Vietnam war, the humanitarian aspect of the assistance was both obvious and heavily covered by the media. Also, the majority of the OECD countries participated in a burden-sharing scheme in order to solve the Indo-Chinese refugee problem. The Vietnam solution did not create a precedent as the ensuing crises in Afghanistan, Central America and the Horn of Africa remained localized.[72]

A third era started in the 1980s, characterized by large, often intercontinental, refugee movements where European refugees are no longer predominant. This development is parallel to ordinary immigration which becomes less and less European in complexion.[73]

From 1983 until 1988 almost 800,000 asylum seekers came to Western Europe, a third of them from the Middle East, 15 per cent from the Indian Subcontinent and 10 per cent from Africa. Almost half of these asylum seekers went to West Germany. However in relationship to size of population, it was Sweden which received most refugees in this new period of globalized asylum seeking.[74]

Towards the end of the 1980s, a new feature arose in the stream of refugees as the migratory movements from Eastern and Central Europe begin to gain momentum. From 1988 to 1990, for instance, there were 90,000 asylum seekers from Poland, 320,000 Romanians sought asylum from 1990 to 1993. The flow of refugees from Turkey also rose to almost 200,000 from 1988 to 1992.[75]

It is quite clear that many from these groups arrive primarily with the hope of obtaining a work permit. Their countries of origin were undergoing an improvement in political conditions whereas the economic conditions were undergoing serious deterioration. The rise in the number of asylum seekers led to a sharp decline in the number who were granted refugee status – from approximately 65 per cent in 1980 to under ten per cent in 1993.[76]

By then the Balkan tragedy was unfolding as ex-Yugoslavia fell apart from 1991 onwards in a bloody civil war. This caused almost 3.7 million people to flee from their homes. All of a sudden, Western Europe was faced by seemingly endless columns of refugees right on its own doorstep. The majority of the victims of the civil war remained in what used to be Yugoslavia, though 700,000 did reach Western Europe.[77]

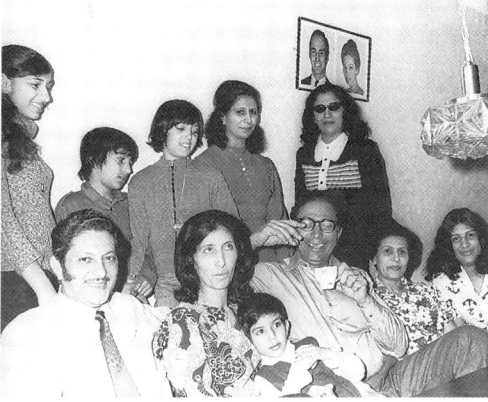

LEFT: *After the 1973 oil crisis and the onset of economic recession, a halt on immigration was implemented throughout Western Europe. However, immigration continued in the form of family reunification. "We asked for workers - and we got people instead" as a Swiss official put it. Family reunification has been a political bone of contention ever since. (UNHCR)*

BOTTOM: *A bloody civil war erupted in the former-Yugoslavia in 1991, in the ensuing four years, it was to force almost four million people to flee for their lives. In the period of April 1992 and three months onwards, 2.6 million people were made homeless in Bosnia-Herzegovina. During these years, 700.000 people came to Western Europe. (UNHCR)*

LEFT: *Communism collapsed while Mikhail Gorbatchev was Secretary General and the Soviet Union dissolved. Nowadays, about 60 million erstwhile Soviet citizens live outside their country of origin. Perhaps it is this group of people who form the most insuperable potential refugee threat against Western Europe. (Polfoto)*

BOTTOM: *The number of refugees has risen dramatically worldwide. In 1980, the UNHCR figure for refugees outside their home country was eight million people. By 1995, the total number of refugees throughout the world was 27 million. (UNHCR)*

5. The pressure on Europe

5.1 The global landscape

Ever since the 1950s the international economy has been marked by two fundamental factors – gradual economic liberalization and growing internationalization. These two tendencies were to emerge fully during the 1980s. These developments are often explained as being attributes of the neo-liberal political wave that swept through the Western World, personified by Ronald Reagan in the USA and by Margaret Thatcher in Britain.

However, the sheer force and thoroughness of these developments were only made possible due to technological evolution in the areas of information technology and transport. Without decisive developments in technology it would have been virtually impossible to carry out the extensive deregulations which have taken place at all levels of society whether national, regional or global.

Thanks to these great leaps forward in technology, market forces were let loose to a hitherto unseen degree and, over the past fifteen years, huge steps have been taken towards a global single market.

This process of integration has progressed in historic terms at break-neck speed in all domains. The growth in the volume of international trade has outstripped that of production. Over the past forty-five years, the volume of international trade has grown fourteenfold whereas the volume of production has only grown 5.5 times in the same period. The gap between these figures has widened further during the 1990s.[1]

This development was not just an internal matter which solely concerned the rich countries of the Northern Hemisphere, but also impinged on the relationship between industrialized and developing nations. In 1980, industrial products only formed 15 per cent of exports from Third World nations to OECD members; by the end of the decade they made up 53 per cent of their exports.[2]

Foreign investment has grown even more than trade has. The overseas investment of the OECD nations more than quadrupled during the

1980s, and this development reflected the strong build-up of global production which was primarily generated by the numerous and large transnational companies.[3] The evolution of the international electronic money markets marks an even more advanced stage in the process of internationalization. The daily foreign currency transactions are now in the 1.000 billion US Dollar category of which only a fraction is used as payment for actual physical transactions.

However, it is not just the transaction of money and goods which includes the whole world as its working area. Without giving it a second thought, the media industry broadcasts advertising, talk-shows and news directly to the most remote parts of the globe. The tragedies of Somalia and Kurdistan unfolded in living rooms all over the world, just as the wealth and affluence of the Western World were put on display to rich and poor alike in every region on Earth.

The tourist industry has put even the most exotic travel destinations within the reach of the wealthy countries' middle classes. The number of tourists crossing an international border rose from sixty million in 1960 to five hundred and thirty-one million in 1994.[4]

In every area, development has been dictated by liberal ideology. This has been based on classical economic theory which itself rests heavily upon the following assumption: that the greater the degree of freedom for all, the greater the level of competition. This, in turn, should lead to more efficiency and, consequently, a general rise in living standards.

This wave of liberal internationalization has swept over the entire globe. For the former Soviet Union and its satellite states it meant a complete collapse of their then existing systems. Although the Communist People's Republic of China does not proclaim adherence to political liberalism, that nation has taken some giant strides down the road towards economic liberalism.

By and large, there seems to be agreement in most of the world's countries and political systems that it is neither possible nor desirable to modify this course of events. Ingenious international mechanisms are being erected, the purpose of which is to ensure that everybody adheres to the set rules.

The newly created World Trade Organization, WTO, has the task of ensuring that international trade takes place on a level playing field in terms of competition. In relation to its predecessor, GATT, the WTO has been granted greater powers of intervention and mediation in trade disputes between nations or regions. In the area of capital, the freedom of movement for capital is supposed to ensure that no single country fundamentally alters its rules to its own advantage. Should that happen, the country in question would be subject to punitive interest rates and a run against the national currency might be organized on the international money markets.

In every area nowadays new regional economic communities are being created in order to extend regional economic integration by means of a common policy. Examples of this growing regionalization of the world economy are provided by the EU in Europe, the North American Free Trade Area – NAFTA – in the Americas and the Preferential Trading Arrangements of the ASEAN countries.

In the midst of this vast process there is one area where international cooperation does not work or, more to the point, does not even exist. That area is migration.

There is no international regulation in the area of migration just as there seems to be no political agreement on how to view this particular question. Nor does an ideological base exist upon which the countries could build up a common policy. There are not even mechanisms which come in to play when one country tightens its regulations to the detriment of its neighbours, a principle that has otherwise been applied in all other areas of international cooperation since the Second World War. In most areas complicated mechanisms have been created which are supposed to prevent individual countries introducing legislation and regulations that just pass the problem on to neighbouring states. The shadows cast by the inter-war period still affect us.

There seem to be only two principles that govern the entire area of migration. The first is set down in the Geneva Convention of 1951 with its subsequent protocols whereby the signatories undertook to afford protection to a person or persons if they were subject to persecution for various reasons. This policy is in perfect accordance with the political aspect of liberalism which stresses the protection of individual human rights.

The second principle seems to be that of the closed door in all the Western European countries since the 1970s. The only forms of legal immigration to Western Europe since have been either on compassionate grounds, i.e. family reunification or the granting of political asylum. This principle, however, is at odds with both the political and economic aspects of liberalism. The latter aspect, in its purest form, requires freedom of movement for all factors of production, including labour.

How can it be that the international community does not cooperate in this vital area? There are not even uniform rules governing the compilation of statistics so that they can be compared across national boundaries. Even within individual states, the immigration figures fluctuate according to which ministry one is dealing with. In France, for instance, at the beginning of the 1980s there was a discrepancy of up to half a million in the figures when the various ministries had to determine the number of foreigners.[5]

As mentioned earlier, there are not even rules determining what makes someone a foreigner in a country. A surprising degree of modesty is displayed in this area by the 15 EU member states which, elsewhere, take upon themselves the heroic task of harmonizing all statistics and regulations.

Could this glaring lack of international cooperation be explained by immigration to Western Europe not in reality posing a problem? Or could it be, perhaps, that immigration is indeed desirable and that all the attention lavished upon it by the various populations, the media and politicians is more an expression of general insecurity in the face of the unknown than anything else. Part of the answer to this is given in Chapter 3 which relates why, during the 1980s, this issue suddenly became as urgent as it still is today. And Chapter 2 contained a discussion of how one of the prime duties of a nation-state is precisely to protect its own citizens against people who come from outside its borders.

There is a further important reason for the international community's hesitancy in committing itself to a binding cooperative scheme in this field. This is that migration itself has evolved to become a far more complex and confusing problem than it was earlier. The question is no longer whether industry may or may not need labour irrespective of its level of qualification. Nor can Western European nations determine which people satisfy the Geneva Convention's criteria for political asylum with the certainty that they had in the past. All the while, the continent is witnessing a sharp rise in illegal immigration.

One solution to all these problems would be to seal all the borders in an attempt to stop all migration from outside This solution is already being applied, although it does encounter, when not actually running counter to, aspects of the process of internationalization mentioned earlier.

Growing globalization, on the one hand, automatically gives rise to a certain degree of necessary and desirable emigration and immigration. On the other, the fifteen EU countries' aim of establishing an economic and monetary union requires increased migration levels between member states because if the area of the common currrency is to work, there has to be a certain level of mobility among its citizens. Again this means that the EU countries will be forced to implement a common immigration policy in the years to come.

This chapter seeks to answer two further questions. First, does the intensifying process of internationalization by itself imply increased immigration and, second, do developments in the countries bordering Europe justify fears about future immigration.

5.2 No need for immigration

The process of internationalization presently under way will of itself lead to extensive migration, though not in the form of the traditional immigration of unskilled labour experienced by Western Europe up till the early 1970s but in the shape of a far more varied group of people.[6]

They could be contract workers hired to do a specific job within a set time span as were the Irish tunnel diggers who worked on the Danish Great Belt tunnel. They might be highly qualified technicians or executive managers hired for a certain period of time or, again, employees of multinational corporations posted abroad. Seasonal workers, au-pairs, bartenders, artists, students and sundry others belong to the growing group of people who change their country of residence for shorter or longer periods of time.

To these can be added all those people who travel abroad not in order to find work but end up doing so anyway. They are people such as foreign students wanting to supplement their grants, relatives visiting former immigrants, asylum seekers who enter the labour market before their case is decided and tourists who remain illegally in the country.

The result of this migration of labour in the wake of generalized internationalization is that the receiver countries are increasingly selective in their choice of whom they allow to work in the country. This means, in practice, that all the countries grant admission to immigrants with either high qualifications or specific skills.

So immigrants are now, as a result of increased globalization, distinguished by their following the globalization of production, apart from their high levels of training or a particular skill, This often means that they will only perform their given function over a limited period in time.

According to the OECD's annual report on migration for 1994, this is the fastest growing category of migration. However, no-one knows its true extent as it "does not present any particular problems" as the OECD puts it.[7]

There is, however, a lot of evidence which indicates that "mass migration" of labour to take over those jobs the locals do not want is becoming a thing of the past in Western Europe. There are many reasons for this.

To start with there is a restructuring under way in Western Europe away from low wage work in industry and the basic professions. One of the causes of this development is that parts of European industry have been made redundant by imports from the newly industrialized countries. The evolution of technology has enabled multinational companies to diversify and split up their production processes, and to place the labour intensive elements in Third World countries where wage costs are much lower. This means that the Western European countries have to concentrate on the high-technology sectors which require highly qualified labour.[8]

There is no doubt that until now we have only seen the tip of the iceberg as far as this process is concerned. In part, this is due to the exports of the newly industrialized developing nations still only amounting to two per cent of the GNP's of the OECD countries[9]. It is also due to the probability that the ex-Communist countries of Eastern Europe will play a similar role to that of the newly industrialized nations as Western European nations move the more labour-intensive elements of their production eastwards.

As a consequence of Western European imports of cheap, labour-intensive products, it has been possible to maintain relatively high wages for unskilled labour in the service sector, for instance, where there is no competition from outside. The imports have thus contributed to maintaining a relatively high minimum wage for those without training or skills as those elements of production requiring only low rates of remuneration have been largely farmed out. However, the question remains whether the Western European countries can continue this policy if they start to recruit cheap labour from abroad.[10]

In other words, internationalization and technological development mean that the need for "mass immigration" in the traditional manner is waning. Immigration can be replaced by the relocation of labour intensive production. Developments in Germany indicate that this is a process which, in all probability, will grow in strength over the years to come.

The first ten months of 1995 saw a 212 per cent rise in German investments abroad compared with 1994.[11] One of the consequences of continued immigration, should it occur, could be the impossibility of maintaining the relatively high wages of the most poorly qualified section of the work force.

Another factor to consider is the relatively high number of people out of work throughout the whole of Western Europe where the level of unemployment is highest among those with little or no training. At the same time, developments throughout the 1980s have shown that this particular element of unemployment has settled at ten per cent, no matter how healthy economic growth might be.

There is also the fact that unemployment is, in reality, much higher than the figures show because several countries have implemented a plethora of schemes whose purpose was to keep people out of the labour market. Thus it is only a ten per cent minority of people between the ages of 65 and 69 who still work in the original 12 EC member states. Between 30 and 45 per cent of people aged from 55 to 64 years have left the labour market in most of these countries.[12] Thus it is a reasonable assumption to make that demand for largely unskilled labour will decline in the future.[13]

Furthermore, in several Western European countries, there is a considerable labour reserve in the form of women who could enter the labour market. To this can be added the considerably higher levels of flexibility in the labour market engendered by the restructuring of the economies. Part-time jobs, leaves-of-absence whether paid or otherwise and working at home are all features that not only increase flexibility, but also increase a nation's labour reserve.

In other words, on the one hand, it looks as though increasing globalization leads to large migrations dependent on this trend and which therefore focus on certain categories of people. On the other hand, internationalization leads to a reduction in the demand for the hitherto most common type of immigrant labour made up of people who could not speak the language and had not been educated in the receiver country. Production, as opposed to people, is now on the move.

In the near future, it is unlikely that Western European employers will press for more immigration as they did in the 1960s when there was a definite labour shortage. There are, however, a couple of factors in the equation which could render the above statement invalid.

To start with, there is the question of whether European labour markets will be afflicted by bottlenecks of a geographic and professional nature. Should such delimited labour shortages arise in certain areas, it is not hard to imagine a resurgence of immigration. This should be seen in the light of what many surveys have shown which is that large parts of the European economies are marked by inflexibility and low levels of mobility.

Then it is quite likely that parts of Western European industry will still have to rely on cheap foreign labour as they do at present, though this potential demand might be satisfied by illegal immigration. This particular question will be dealt with at the end of this chapter.

A more important issue, however, is the uncertainty surrounding European demographic development. If present tendencies persist, the nations of Europe will experience a decline in their populations in the decades to come. Among those left will be an ever increasing proportion of old age pensioners who will have to be supported by the active part of the population. The question as to whether this will increase demand for foreign labour will be discussed in the next chapter.

When the topic of "immigrant pressure" arises, what is meant is "potential pressure" or the "feared pressure". The wish for increased immigration does not come from the inside, from within the Western European business community. It is the pressure from without, the desire of outsiders to emigrate to Western Europe, which could turn into a problem. It could also turn out to be challenge on an hitherto unheard of scale.

5.3 The population explosion

In 1990, the award-winning BBC drama-documentary, "The March", sparked off a heated debate. In it, tens of thousands of Africans joined a march which started off in the Sudan, crossed the northern part of the continent and proceeded in this quest for survival towards affluent Europe.

This film clearly played on the fears of the white race towards foreigners. It drew unmistakeable parallels with Mahatma Gandhi's peace march against British colonial rule on the eve of independence in 1947 and Martin Luther King's march for civil rights in 1963. The film stops at Gibraltar which is where the march ends as well. Well-armed soldiers with the twelve yellow European stars on their helmets were there to ensure that the starving Africans came no further. What then happens is left to the viewer's imagination.

The film caused a violent reaction in Western Europe. Most agreed that it had broached a worst-case scenario that lay within the bounds of possibility. However, many also agreed that the consequences of over-population in Africa shown by the film were not the most probable. Objections to the film were legion. Such an army of the destitute could not cross the barren wastes of the North African desert. The various nations along the route of the march would be incapable of such cooperation in practice. The starving legions would have broken up and dispersed long before arriving in sight of the sunny coasts of Spain. All these contentions are probably correct, though they do not provide an answer to the question of whether such a scenario could unfold in the future.

Not, of course, in the way shown in the film, but the major elements of the story are already in existence. Demographic growth in the world has been very uneven during the last few decades and, in historic terms, explosive. Most of the world outside Western Europe and other affluent areas of the globe is experiencing a violent rise in population. Never before has the number of people in the Third World risen at the rate of the past few years. It is certain that this development is going to continue far into the foreseeable future.

One and a half billion people will be born over the next ten years – roughly the same number of people as the total population of Earth at the turn of the century.[14] About half of these are women and, in approximately twenty years time, they will give birth to their own children. So even if the women of the Third World have fewer children in the future, there would still be many births simply because there will be so many mothers. Reducing population is often compared to turning a supertanker in that, even if action is taken today, a long time will pass before the results become apparent.

In 1992, world population was estimated to be 5.48 billion people. At some point in 1998 it will have risen to 6 billion. The present annual rate of demographic growth is around 100 million. One and a half billion people will be born in the coming decade and half a billion will die. In other words, global population will increase by a billion in ten years or there will be 3 billion births in the time it takes for the Danes to pay the instalments of their recently drawn up thirty-year mortgage agreements.

A clearer picture of demographic growth is obtained by looking at how many years it took to reach a total of 1 billion. It also shows that such rapid growth is, relatively speaking, a recent phenomenon in historical terms.

It took a century – from 1830 to 1930 – for the global population to grow from one to two billion people. The third billion had already become reality thirty years later in 1960. The fourth only took fifteen years, while the fifth in 1987 had taken twelve years. The next billion will only take about ten years.[15]

This development becomes really confusing when one looks at how many children the women of the Third World are having these days. While the rate of demographic growth has soared, this particular figure has dropped drastically in recent years. The average family size throughout the Third World at the beginning of the 1960s was 6.1 children per woman. At the outset of the 1990s, women were giving birth to only 3.9 children on average.[16]

The United Nations Population Fund, UNFPA, has produced many prognoses for the entire population of the planet. According to the organization's median evaluation it will have reached a total of 8.5 billion people by the year 2025. By 2050 the total will be 10 billion, after which it will rise gently before stabilizing at 11.6 billion by the year 2150.

Prognoses such as these are tentative at best when they go forward beyond a few decades in time. It is more reasonable to view these calculations as examples which demonstrate an outcome under given criteria. The UNFPA's median estimates are widely used in the population debate, mainly because the idea of a median estimate is reassuring. Realism and credibility are associated with the use of figures which lie in between the optimal and the catastrophic as opposed to either painting too pretty or too gloomy a picture.

However, behind even this median estimate, there is the problem of definite presuppositions about the extent to which women in the Third World will reduce their fertility. These presuppositions are, to say the least, wildly optimistic. If the median estimate is to be borne out in fact it would require women to bring down the birth rate to reproduction level over the next 35 to 55 years. This would mean 2.1 children per woman, which would ensure a stable population level over a long period of time.

Should the women of the world just have 2.2 children each on average, by the year 2050, world population would be up to 12.5 billion people and a hundred years on the total would be 20.8 billion. If they were to have an average of 2.5 children each, then the world population would be 28 billion by the year 2150. One can go to extremes and imagine that the women of the world maintain the fertility rates of 1980, which would mean that the population would explode like an anthill to 694 billion by the year 2150.[17]

The likelihood of the latter scenario is minimal as, among other things, the birth rate of women throughout the world is falling and, in many countries, this decline in fertility is rapid indeed. However, calculations show that the number of people in the poorer developing countries will rise at an uncontrollable rate if birth rates do not fall even further. This rise will be so dramatic that it would justify the very real fears that many people have that, within the foreseeable future, world population figures will be such that the result could be a march of the starving like the one shown in the BBC drama-documentary.

5.4 The decline of the white race

The Russian nationalist Vladimir Zhirinovski who obtained 11 per cent of the votes cast in the elections for the Duma in December 1995, used to tell his audiences during his election campaign that the white race was almost on the verge of extinction. Before long it would represent less than ten per cent of the world's population. This message was to serve as a justification for pre-emptive military strikes against the Muslim areas on Russia's southern flank.

The BBC production, Vladimir Zhirinovski's outbursts and much of the rhetoric of the European right wing are underpinned by the same message complete with racist overtones. That message is that the white race is rapidly becoming an ever smaller minority in the world, irrespective of whether the majority is defined either by creed or colour or both.

That the inhabitants of Europe, the part of the world which created the rest in its image so to speak in the eighteenth and nineteenth centuries, should now represent a rapidly dwindling portion of the global population is the outcome of a process under way since the end of the 1930s. Furthermore, this is a development which, in decades to come, will intensify with unpredictable consequences for the future global position of the continent.

Figures illustrating this trend are shown in Tables 5.1 and 5.2. They were published in *Population*, the journal of the French Institut Na-

Table 5.1. Population growth in broad regions of the world, observed (1800-1985) and projected (1985-2100). (Millions of inhabitants)

Continents Regions Countries	Years					
	1800	1939	1985	2000	2025	2100
World	954	2.195	4.842	6.127	8.177	11.011
China	330	455	1.063	1.256	1.460	1.481
Japan	25	72	120	128	128	128
India, Pakistan and Bangladesh	180	381	964	1.250	1.621	2.538
Rest of Asia	96	254	677	910	1.258	1.793
Asia	631	1.162	2.824	3.544	4.467	5.940
Europe	146	403	492	513	527	553
Former USSR	49	170	278	315	367	377
North America	5	143	264	298	347	325
Oceania	2	11	25	30	40	40
Population of European origin	202	727	1.059	1.156	1.281	1.295
North America	10	49	125	185	295	460
Rest of Africa	92	126	428	692	1.348	2.376
Africa	102	175	553	877	1.643	2.836
Latin America	19	131	406	550	786	940

Source: Jean Bourgeois-Pichat: "From the 20th to the 21st Century: Europe and its Population after the Year 2000", in *Population*, vol. 44, no. 1. Institute National d'Études Démographiques, Paris, September 1989, p. 65.

tional d'Études Démographiques, and are based on estimates from the UN and the World Bank. The two tables make use of the UN median projections from 1989 which were subsequently revised upwards in 1992. Thus the global population is expected to number 8.2 billion by 2025, the "only" presupposition being that the birth rate would stabilize at an average of 2.1 children in all parts of the world. This would mean a stable world population of 11 billion by the year 2100.[18] Those parts of the tables which project into the future should therefore be treated as realistic calculations.

The European part of the world population peaked in 1939 when Europeans constituted 18.4 per cent of humanity. At that time Europeans had spread all over the globe either as colonizers or emigrants to the New World. If all of these are included, along with the population of

Table 5.2. Distribution of world population among broad regions, observed (1800–1985) and projected (1985-2100). (Millions of inhabitants)

Continents Regions Countries	Year					
	1800	1939	1985	2000	2025	2100
World	100.0	100.0	100.0	100.0	100.0	100.0
China	34.6	20.7	22.0	20.5	17.8	13.4
Japan	2.6	3.3	2.5	2.1	1.6	1.2
India, Pakistan and Bangladesh	18.9	17.3	19.9	20.4	19.8	23.0
Rest of Asia	10.0	11.6	14.0	14.8	15.4	16.3
Asia	66.1	52.9	58.3	57.8	54.6	53.9
Europe	15.3	18.4	10.2	8.4	6.5	5.0
Former USSR	5.2	7.7	5.7	5.1	4.5	3.4
North America	0.5	6.5	5.5	4.9	4.2	3.0
Oceania	0.2	0.5	0.5	0.5	0.5	0.4
Population of European origin	21.2	33.1	21.9	18.9	15.7	11.8
North Africa	1.1	2.2	2.6	3.0	3.6	4.2
Rest of Africa	9.6	5.8	8.8	11.3	16.5	21.6
Africa	10.7	8.0	11.4	14.3	20.1	25.8
Latin America	2.0	6.0	8.4	9.0	9.6	8.5

Source: Jean Bourgeois-Pichat: "From the 20th to the 21st Century: Europe and its Population after the Year 2000", in *Population*, vol. 44, no. 1. Institute National d'Études Démographiques, Paris, September 1989, p. 66.

the Soviet Union, then the group which could be loosely labelled "population of European origin" represented about one third of humanity at the time when the Europeans unleashed their Second World War.

After this point the European portion falls drastically as can be seen in Table 5.2. Today, it only stands for a little over 8 per cent and, by the year 2025, the Europeans will represent 6.5 per cent and the group of "European origin" 15.7 per cent.

So, in less than a hundred years, the European element of the world population has fallen from over 18 per cent to 6.5 per cent. This trend is set to continue.

As for the "European origin" group, the trend will be that from approximately every third person belonging to it in 1939, the ratio will drop to every sixth person by 2025. Table 5.2 shows that, further on in

Table 5.3. Evolution of the World population according to civilization, observed (1980 and 1985) and projected (1985–2100). (Millions of inhabitants)

Civilization	Years				
	1980	1985	2000	2025	2100
World	4.453	4.842	6.127	8.177	11.011
Christendom	1.385	1.463	1.703	2.061	2.228
Islam	800*	857	1.429	2.503	4.412
China	1.003	1.063	1.256	1.460	1.481
Rest of world	1.265	1.459	1.739	2.153	2.890

* The estimate of 800 millions followers of Islam is given by Nafis Sadik in "Moslem Women Today". Populi, XII, I, 1985, p. 38.

Source: Jean Bourgeois-Pichat: "From the 20th to the 21st Century: Europe and its Population after the Year 2000", in *Population*, vol. 44, no. 1. Institute National d'Études Démographiques, Paris, September 1989, p. 68.

the future, the "white man" will only be one out of every eight humans. Therefore, it is quite correct, seen from this perspective, that the "white race" has declined in terms of numbers over the past fifty years. This development will continue in the same direction throughout the whole of the next century.

Some might raise the objection that this kind of projection depends on the presuppositions made about people's average life expectancy. In the case of the figures in Tables 5.1 and 5.2 the presupposition was that the average lifespan throughout the forecast period would be 75 years, a clearly unrealistic premise even today.

The "Population" article also relies on the over-optimistic premise that longevity will increase to reach a level of a hundred years. This will not happen. However, the example does illustrate the fact that, as life expectancy goes up, then the indicated trends will become even more pronounced.

If this premise were somehow to hold, then the world population would become stable at a higher level of 13.6 billion people. The above-mentioned trends would manifest themselves with even greater disparities meaning that, in the year 2100, the Europeans would constitute less than five per cent of the Earth's population. As shown in Table 5.2. they would only constitute three per cent. So the highly probable rise in life expectancy in the future means that the European element of the global population will decline even more rapidly than it otherwise would have done.

Table 5.4. Distribution of the World population according to civilization, observed (1980 and 1985) and projected (1985–2100)

Civilization	Years				
	1980	1985	2000	2025	2100
World	100.0	100.0	100.0	100.0	100.0
Christendom	31.1	30.2	27.8	25.2	20.2
Islam	18.0	17.7	23.3	30.6	40.1
China	22.5	22.0	20.5	17.9	13.5
Rest of world	28.4	30.1	28.4	26.3	26.2

Source: Jean Bourgeois-Pichat: "From the 20th to the 21th Century: Europe and its Population after the Year 2000", in *Population*, vol. 44, no. 1. Institute National d'Études Démographiques, Paris, September 1989, p. 68.

The French article also takes a look at future developments among the world's great religions. Christians, Muslims, the Chinese and the rest of the world. The share-out between these four categories can be seen in Tables 5.3 and 5.4.

The relative number of Chinese will drop in the future due to the population policy in force at present and the expected positive economic development in the People's Republic of China. The "Rest of the World" category is reasonably stable and comprises those people left when the other three categories are subtracted. The interesting aspect of this table is the distribution between and development of the populations in the Muslim countries and the number of Christians of all denominations. It is in these areas that the greatest divergences will appear.

In 1980, almost every third person on Earth belonged to one Christian denomination or another while 18 per cent of the global population was Muslim. There will be more Muslims than Christians by the year 2025: 30.6 per cent as against 25.2 per cent. The cause of this divergence is the rapid demographic growth in North Africa and the Middle East.

In the more distant future, Table 5.4 indicates that many of the Muslim countries fit into the category of those with the highest birthrates. According to this table, 40 per cent of the 11 billion people who will constitute the world population when it stabilizes in 2100 will be Muslim. Christians of all types will only amount to about half of this figure at around 20.2 per cent of the world's population.

These tables were also drawn up according to the premise that life expectancy would reach a hundred years. Were that to be the case, the percentage of Muslims in the year 2100 would be 43.3 of the global population while that of the Christians would be 14.6.

5.5 The myth of the Muslim menace

It is important to point out at this stage that this is not a struggle between two religions as in the days of the crusades. What is happening is that two geographical areas with their particular political systems are going along different paths of economic and demographic development. There are the rich western secular Christian nations, with their declining populations and relatively high levels of economic growth, on the one hand while, on the other, the often very poor countries who organize their society on Islamic lines where birth rates are soaring and the populations, partly due to this, are experiencing a constant fall in living standards.

The distinction drawn in the table between Muslims and Christians is, therefore, less of a religious nature than social and economic. By and large, the high rates of demographic growth will occur in those countries which are at present Muslim, and this process will continue for many decades. Thus the figures in Tables 5.3 and 5.4 are really an expression of how the impoverished part of the world population will grow to be an ever larger component of humanity, whereas the exact opposite is true in the case of the western countries which still hold the lion's share of global economic, military and political power.

So the truly threatening scenario is not that of the many Muslims close to the borders of Europe. It is that of a rich Western Europe surrounded by countries where the majority of the populations are living in extreme poverty. Had these countries not built up their political systems on an Islamic basis, the worst case future scenario would still have arisen although the characterization of the enemy would have been different.

The future danger for Western Europe lies in those countries undergoing such negative social and economic developments that it might bring fundamentalist forces to power along with all the consequent internal and external tensions. Therefore, it is of key importance that those countries which are moderately Muslim nowadays are able to pro-

mote their particular answers in the religious sphere for the faithful in a
materially much-improved setting. If this is not the case, then extremist
forces will probably gain greater influence.

Thus, in the long run, it would be these forces which would bring
about the necessary economic improvements in order to maintain their
grip on power and popular imagination. Whatever the nature of the
Muslim forces which hold sway in those countries, the main condition
for their survival will be whether they are able to lead their populations
out of the poverty trap in which they are caught at present.

Furthermore, there is the fallacious view, often bandied about in
public and political debate in Western Europe, that the Islamic countries can be viewed as a single bloc. Dr Jørgen Bæk Simonsen, lecturer
at the Carsten Niebuhr Institute of Near-Eastern Studies in Copenhagen has the following to say about this:[19]

> "When evaluating political Islam it is of key importance to point
> out that, since the early 1970s, all Arab states have witnessed the
> appearance of a religiously based opposition, often in the form
> of groups with Islamic tradition as their point of departure who
> would then argue for an alternative route of political develop-
> ment. This applies equally to Egypt, Iraq, Saudi Arabia and
> Kuwait as well as non-Arab countries. This international ten-
> dency has, however, not given rise to an all-encompassing Is-
> lamic opposition with common goals at the level of practical
> politics, or one which is capable of coordinating the efforts and
> aims expressed by the various individual movements. Wherever
> there are political groupings based on and guided by Islamic tra-
> dition, there are also constant references to the inherent superi-
> ority of the Islamic solution. However, in the real world of poli-
> tics, it has become apparent that there are often enormous dif-
> ferences between the myriad and mutually-divergent political
> groupings who seek inspiration from the shared Islamic tradi-
> tion. The concrete solutions proffered by the various groups are,
> in all instances, clearly influenced by the development under-
> gone by the individual states over the past few decades. That the
> Islamic groups mean business is obvious. However, the political
> plurality that they also undoubtedly represent is proof that they
> do not constitute an efficiently cohesive homogeneous entity,
> able to operate across national borders at will. Thus, in this re-

spect, there is no Islamic threat against the West in general or Europe in particular."

The anxiety about future refugee and immigration pressure is therefore rooted in reality as well as in a less well defined fear of strangers who differ from us both culturally and religiously, and are therefore perceived as a threat.

The real source of anxiety is in the drastic demographic divergence which will emerge between the industrialized nations, principally those of Europe, and the impoverished developing nations. However, no-one can say with any degree of scientific certainty to what extent this rapid demographic growth in the developing nations will translate itself into increased migration to Europe.

But to believe that a global rise in population of about three billion people in the next three decades would not lead to increased migratory pressure on Europe would be, to say the least, naive. That proposition does not need scientific models. During the nineteenth century, Europe was at the stage of demographic development at which many Third World nations find themselves nowadays. As described in the previous chapter, a massive wave or waves of emigration was the outcome.

In addition to this, it can be reasonably assumed that this growth in population in certain areas of the world will have the effect of increasing tensions in many places and because of ensuing local conflicts, it will lead to an increase in refugee pressure. According to a survey carried out in 1995 by the Worldwatch Institute, an American think-tank, internal conflicts and civil wars are the chief cause of the refugee flows of today. Out of 20 countries which have given rise to the largest refugee problems, 19 were in the throes of armed internal conflict.[20]

It is, however, important to note that the refugee flows for many years past have, in the main, been dealt with locally by the neighbouring states. In 1992, the official number of registered refugees throughout the world was around 18 million people of whom 80 per cent were in Third World countries.

To this should be added about four million people in the Third World who found themselves to be in a "quasi-refugee situation", while a further 23 million were refugees inside their own country. So when Western European politicians talk, as many of them do, about the importance of dealing with the refugee problem close to its source, it is more a question of rhetoric than reality since this is already the way in which most refugee situations are handled.[21]

Therefore, it is difficult to guess to what extent the present global population rise will lead to greater emigration towards Western Europe. That there is a lurking anxiety is hardly surprising in view of the fact that Western Europe is far closer to the demographic hot spots of the near future than are, for instance, the USA, Canada or Australia.

Figure 5.1 shows how the greatest population increases will occur in countries that are geographically relatively close to Europe. Apart from Central America and Mongolia, all these countries are within a few hours' flight time from Europe.

Figure 5.1 Population growth in different parts of the world.

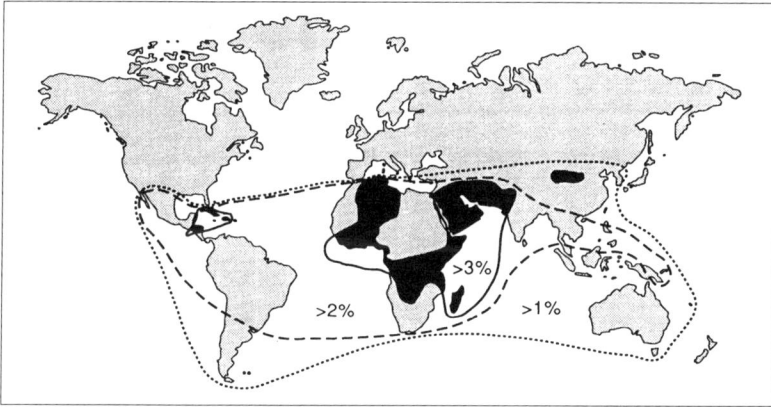

Source: Sture Öberg: "Europe in the context of world population trends", in *Mass Migration in Europe*, Belhaven Press, London 1993. p. 196.

5.6 The Rio Grande of Europe

In recent years, under Southern European leadership, the EU countries have placed the countries bordering the Mediterranean higher on their list of priorities. In political terms it has been argued that there are two threats, demographic growth and the Muslim menace and, at first sight, it is hard not to take the demographic divergence seriously.

Table 5.5 shows future demographic development in the countries bordering the Mediterranean where the population will have almost

Table 5.5. Population in the Muslim countries at the Mediterranean. (millions)

	1990	2025	Increase
Algeria	25,0	52,0	27,0
Egypt	52,4	90,4	38,0
Libya	4,5	12,8	8,3
Morocco	25,1	45,6	20,5
Tunisia	8,2	13,6	5,4
Lebanon	2,7	4,7	2,0
Syria	12,5	34,1	21,6
Turkey	55,9	87,7	31,8
Total	186,3	340,9	154,6

Source: Poul Christian Matthiessen. "Verden på vandring mod Europa", *TEMA-SPOT*, no. 1, 1992, p. 2.

Table 5.6. Population in world regions. 1980–2030. (millions)

	1980	1991	2000	2030
Sub-Saharan Africa	351	489	635	1.313
East Asia and the Pacific	1.399	1.667	1.891	2.442
South Asia	903	1.152	1.368	2.004
Europe and Central Asia	448	492	517	566
Latin America and the Caribbean	358	455	516	721
Middle East and North Africa	173	244	315	600
OECD-members	733	783	820	871

Source: World Development Report 1993, The World Bank *1993, p. 199.*

doubled by the year 2025,[22] whereas, during the same period, the total population of Western Europe will be much the same, unless there is considerable immigration.

Table 5.6 shows the development of the World Bank's median estimates of population figures in the major regions of the world.[23] A similar picture emerges here in that, from 1980 to 2030, the population of the OECD countries will rise from 733 million to 871 million. Most of the growth, however, will take place in the old immigrant nations, Canada, Australia and the USA.

Over the same period, the population of Africa south of the Sahara is expected to grow from 351 million to 1,313 million, an almost fourfold increase. In the area comprising North Africa and the Middle East, demographic growth will be just as spectacular increasing from 173 million in 1980 to 600 million fifty years later.

When population growth is as rapid as it has been in recent years, there are two consequences, both of which make the task of lowering birth rates more difficult.

To begin with it means that there will be many more people coming into the labour market. According to the World Bank's projections, the number of people in North Africa and the Middle East of working age between 15 and 64 years will rise at a rate 15 per cent higher than the general rise in population in the period from 1990 to 2025. This is a development which places colossal demands on investment in new workplaces. If this addition to the labour market is to be absorbed, it requires exceptionally high rates of economic growth in order to avoid a decline in living standards for the individuals concerned.[24]

Furthermore, only 14 per cent of women are on the formal labour market.[25] If this percentage is to rise, even more demands will be placed on economic growth. Economic progress and increased female participation in economic and social life are both crucial factors in reducing fertility rates.

The other consequence of rapid demographic growth is a relatively high number of young people. About 40 to 45 per cent of the populations of the Muslim countries bordering the Mediterranean are under the age of 15.[26] With such a composition, it is inevitable that the population will rise, even if women have fewer children.

In fact, women are having fewer children, which brings us to a bright aspect of an otherwise gloomy picture. If viewed from an historical perspective, birth rates are falling very rapidly indeed. In Morocco, Tunisia and Algeria, the average number of children per woman was 6.8 in the early 1970s. Twenty years later, this average had fallen to 4.7, an impressive drop of almost a third. However, in view of the rapid population growth in the years to come, this is still too little.[27]

The big question remains as to whether this dramatic population growth will, especially among the young, lead to increased migration towards Europe.

5.7 Why do people migrate?

There is no scientific basis upon which to answer this question. The best that can be done is to provide some explanations, each of which cast light on aspects of the factors which trigger the processes of migration. The main focus of migratory research has, for many years, been placed on examining the factors behind the early mass migration from Europe to the USA, Canada and Australia. As a result of this work, some parallels can be drawn with contemporary migrations. Among the most important explanations for European migration are the following:

Demographic transition

As explained in Chapter 4, there was a population explosion in Europe during the Industrial Revolution from 194 million in 1840 to 463 million by 1930. It was precisely at this time that emigration grew when the continent was experiencing a sharp decline in mortality while fertility remained at its earlier high level. Research has revealed a link between demographic growth and emigration. Countries with rapidly rising populations also experienced extensive emigration.[28]

Differences in real wages

A characteristic of the process of demographic transition is that the birth rate declines at a later point in time than the death rate and the period in between is when the population surges upwards. However, the speed with which the decline in fertility makes itself felt is very much dependent upon the living conditions of the population. All other things being equal, a high standard of living leads to a fall in fertility. The standard of living is not just set by the level of income but is just as dependent on factors such as levels of education, the position of women, social security and levels of health in the population at large.

Examination of earlier migrations has revealed that differences in real wages, as a measure of living standards, between the countries migrated from and migrated to went a long way towards explaining the scale of migration. This was a significant factor in European migration where countries, except Britain, with low levels of income were generally those from where migration started.[29] In other words, high population growth and poor standards of living mean that emigration gathers momentum.

The gravitation model

The premise of this model is that waves of migration can be explained by factors in the countries of origin which push people to migrate; also known as push-factors. At the time, Europe was marked among other things by social and political unrest as well as low levels of income. Factors in the receiver countries, pull-factors, also played a part. The more important of these included political freedom, higher wages, plentiful arable land and better economic prospects for the individual. The extent of emigration finally depended on the distances involved, along with the cost of travel. Research has shown that the much increased emigration from around 1870 to 1914 coincided with a considerable fall in transportation costs.[30]

Internal and external migration

Increased levels of industrialization meant increased internal mobility, principally from the countryside to the cities. This break-up in European population patterns also contributed to external migration.

The question remains whether this historical experience can be transferred to the contemporary European scenario. The answer must be "only in part" as it is clearly inadequate, which means that a series of other factors must taken into consideration in order to fully understand modern-day migration.

The fundamental answer to the question of why people move to another country is that they do so in the hope of improving their lives. This hope has many facets; better prospects for their children, political or religious freedom, better economic opportunities or something completely different. Many people all over the world would like to move for one or more of these reasons but remain where they are anyway. So the question remains, what is it that impels some people to make their migratory move while others stay put?

According to Peter Stalker, author of the book "The Work of Strangers" written for the International Labour Office, ILO, there are two aspects to this question – the individual and the structural.[31]

Seen from the point of view of the individual, each migrant makes a rational choice and travels to wherever their hopes will be best fulfilled in general terms. This rational economic being is not only capable of deciding whether to sally forth or not, but also to where. Peter Stalker points out the example of the Philippino worker preferring to travel to

Japan instead of Saudi Arabia if wages in Tokyo are higher than those in Riyadh. A parallel may thus be drawn between this economic being and capital in that both seek out wherever the returns are highest.

However, the structural point of view holds that the destiny of a human being is more likely to be influenced by the circumstances in which he or she develops. All human beings live in a political, economic and cultural environment which shapes their existence. In view of this, demographic growth and the consequent unemployment are considered to be important structural factors which explain migration. If these factors are linked to a third, namely, the power of the media to tell people that a better existence is possible elsewhere then, according to Peter Stalker, you have part of the explanation why people want to leave Mexico City, for instance, in order to move to San Diego or Los Angeles.

Clearly both individual and structural aspects have to be taken into account. No individual person acts independently of the political and economic structures around them. It is equally true that all political, economic, cultural and religious structures are the sum of the individuals of which they consist. Therefore the analyses of migratory patterns must be based on both premises as well as their interaction.

The "network explanation" is a good example of the interaction of both perspectives. This explanation holds that a few individuals or small groups initiate a migration and build up the structures through which others from their family, village or country, will be assisted when they follow at a later stage. The whole history of humanity is laden with examples of how these networks led to people from a specific area settling in an equally definite area in the host country.

Analyses of these networks may now be broadened in the light of the wider perspective afforded by the contemporary process of internationalization. Thus light is shed on another common connection between the countries of origin and the host countries; if there are close ties in terms of trade and/or investment then it is likely to be the case in terms of migration. A network is thus built up in the host country which acts as a catalyst for immigration as well as other economic ties between the home and host countries.

By combining the three aspects – the individual, the structural and the international – it should be possible to furnish a reasonably qualified answer to the next question: are they coming to Europe?

5.8 Europe as a continent of immigration

Fundamentally this question is false. In view of the Europe-wide immigration policy already in place, the question cannot be whether or not the immigrants come from the Third World. A solid wall has already been built up which stops unwanted people getting in. The only ways in are either illegally, as political refugees or through family reunification.

Therefore it is more to the point to ask whether there would be migration to Europe if it were possible to freely enter the countries involved? In order to answer that question, the above-mentioned theories derived from earlier migrations may be used. Furthermore, irrespective of the methods used, all the indicators point towards the same conclusion.

There would be massive migratory pressure on Europe if the present highly restrictive policies were relaxed or wholly given up. Generally speaking, all the causes of earlier mass migrations exist nowadays between the industrialized countries and the Third World.

Demographic transition

As described in Chapter 4, this process can take several years. In England it took almost 200 years for the rate of population growth to stabilize. If this process were to be as protracted in most underdeveloped countries, it would spell disaster. These countries underwent the first phase of demographic transition when they were colonized during the eighteenth and nineteenth centuries. It was, however, only with the medical developments after the Second World War that serious inroads were made in the mortality rates of the colonized nations. Death rates fell from the levels of 35 per thousand inhabitants of the pre-war years to 16 per thousand by the end of the 1960s.[32]

Most developing nations have reached the so-called third phase where mortality has declined considerably and birth rates have begun to go down. As mentioned above, birth rates have fallen dramatically in some Third World nations – on average from 6.1 children at the outset of the 1960s to 3.9 in the early 1990s. By comparison with developments in Europe during the Industrial Revolution, this represents a significantly sharper decline in fertility.

One might, therefore, believe that it is only a matter of time before Third World fertility reaches a level where the populations no longer grow, just like the pattern of European fertility. There are, however, several reasons for such optimism being dangerous.

To start with, the very concept of demographic transition is based upon development which has already taken place in the highly industrialized world. Later on, this pattern has emerged in some developing countries such as Taiwan, South Korea, Hong Kong, Singapore as well as Cuba and Barbados.

It cannot be taken for granted that other cultures should follow this pattern. For instance, it is obvious that the Chinese Communists do not believe that this pattern automatically applies to their society and they have, therefore, resorted to exceptionally harsh measures in order to bring down birth rates. There are many other cultures where demographers are not at all sure that the fall in fertility they have already registered will actually continue.

Although the average number of children borne by each woman has fallen from six to four, there is no guarantee that this development will continue as was the case in the developed nations. It could be that other cultures are not affected in the same way by the factors that affected Europe, and which still do. Perhaps the fertility rate will never get down to the level of 2.1 children per woman presumed by all the otherwise gloomy forecasts. A lack of definite knowledge and uncertainty on this point are widespread among demographers.[33]

A further essential point is that the women of the European countries which experienced the demographic transition never had as many children as their counterparts in the Third World. Two centuries ago, the fertility rate in Europe was about 4.5 children per woman whereas, in many developing countries, the fertility rate was over six children per woman. The main reason for this birth rate gap was that European women married at a relatively late stage.[34]

This is the factor which causes many demographers to doubt that the birthrate in many developing countries will ever sink to the level of 2.1 children per woman, the level necessary for a stable population. This doubt is further fed by the observation that the European countries experienced a lengthy and continuous process of economic development as birth rates slowly declined all the while. This contrasts sharply with the situation of many underdeveloped nations which have to undergo accelerated economic development if the birth rate is to be decisively affected.

It is also a race against time in that the migrant pressure on Europe, for the reasons outlined earlier, will be fed by massive demographic growth which itself will continue well into the next century. This is primarily because the relatively large number of young people means that, in the decades to come, a very large number of women will reach childbearing age.

So it is apparent from the purely demographic point of view that future developments will invariably bring increased migratory pressure on Europe. Those countries which are relatively close to Europe belong to the category of those lagging furthest behind in terms of the process of demographic transition; that is to say those with the highest birth rates and, consequently, high rates of population growth. Positive economic development is the only way that these countries have of speeding up the process. This, however, can only be done over a long period of time and the short-term prospects afford no cause for hope.

Differences in living standards

The fundamental reason for migration is the enormous divergence in incomes and opportunities around the world, mainly between the industrialized nations and the countries of the Third World.

At the beginning of the 1990s, 82.7 per cent of the entire world's income went to the wealthiest 20 per cent of nations. At the other end of the scale, the poorest 20 per cent only received 1.4 per cent of the cake. What is even more worrying is that this imbalance has kept on growing larger year by year. Thus in 1960 the wealthy 20 per cent "only" received 70.2 per cent of world income while the poorest fifth received 2.3 per cent. In absolute terms, this means that the difference in per capita income between the two categories has grown from $1,864 to $15,149.[35]

Despite the great economic progress made in many Third World countries, the truth is that they are facing an almost hopeless uphill struggle. Although the share of those inhabitants of Third World countries deemed to be living in poverty by the World Bank fell from 52 per cent in 1970 to 44 per cent by 1985, the actual number of people living below the poverty line rose from 944 million to 1,156 million. Rapid demographic growth nullifies what progress has been made in many parts of the world.[36]

Clear examples of this hopeless development are provided by the underdeveloped nations around Europe where migratory pressure will arise due to the great imbalances which exist between the northern and southern shores of the Mediterranean. The average income of an EU citizen is twelve times the average wage in those countries on the eastern and southern Mediterranean shores.[37] In this instance as well, the gap between levels of income, already skewed and divergent, has widened on the whole as each year went by.

The EU Commission, in this connection, set up a survey of the development of the Maghreb countries, Morocco, Tunisia, Algeria and Libya. From 1970 onwards until the present day, except for the period between 1975 and 1980 and again in 1991, the general trend has been a decline in per capita income. In other words, while the inhabitants of the countries north of the Mediterranean have grown richer with every passing year, those to the south have sunk ever more deeply into poverty.[38]

Generally speaking, the Muslim countries around the Mediterranean find themselves in a situation where economic and social conditions are worsening in all areas year by year. In connection with the 1994 Population Conference in Cairo, the World Bank produced a series of key figures for the area which, among other things, pointed out the fundamental problem for these countries posed by a catastrophic shortage of water, which was detrimental to their prospects for economic development. The amount of water available for each inhabitant throughout the Middle Eastern and North African regions has declined from 3.5 cubic metres per annum in 1960 to 1.6 cubic metres by 1990; and by the year 2025, this amount is expected to have fallen further to 0.7 cubic metres.[39] For purposes of comparison, the equivalent Danish water consumption per inhabitant, per year, is 62 cubic metres.

That something as basic as clean water should be a commodity in ever shorter supply is a better expression than economic growth figures of how tough the struggle to survive is, and will be in the future, in the Muslim countries bordering the Mediterranean. That many would want to migrate in order to find better opportunities is more than understandable.

Higher growth, more emigration

From the point of view of this book, the solution to this problem must be Western European countries actively seeking to relieve these gloomy future prospects in the Southern and Eastern Mediterranean. Economic development promotes demographic transition and would thus reduce the need for emigration, although there is the problem that, in the short term, it would have the opposite effect. Surveys from many regions in the world show that economic development leads to increased emigration, while an impoverished and destitute population does not move from where it is.

What often happens is that as the traditional social systems break down in the countryside, migration to the cities begins to swell and, as a result, a far larger part of the population become potential emigrants. This phenomenon manifested itself during the great European migrations of the previous century as well as more recently in the cases of Mexico and South Korea, which are both instances of strong economic growth leading to social break-up with consequent emigration.[40]

To which can be added the more obvious cause of this connection – that economic growth means that larger groups of people have the economic surplus with which to venture forth into the world.

Cheaper transport and improved communications
The explosive pace of development within the transport and communications sectors is a factor which increases the possibilities for travelling from country to country; and although it is impossible to measure this effect accurately, there are a series of factors which all display the same tendency.

To start with, the building-up of world-wide communications systems means that the "emotional distance" between the home country and country of destination is reduced. The number of international phone calls increased by 500 per cent throughout the 1980s and future growth in this area is expected to be between 15 and 20 per cent per annum. The creation and extension of the international communications network is one of the reasons for this growth and the constant drop in prices is another.[41]

If this rise in phone and fax use is seen in combination with the even steeper rise in the possibility of receiving certain countries' television broadcasts via satellite, then a degree of contact with the home countries exists which was unavailable to earlier generations of migrants. Nowadays, even the poorest of immigrant neighbourhoods in the Paris region can receive television broadcasts from Algeria or Morocco, and it is relatively cheap to make direct telephone calls home.[42]

It is probable that the strong spread and distribution of television programmes which come chiefly from the USA, Europe and Japan contribute to the migratory pressure. This is in part a direct result of the over-exposure to western wealth and affluence which is the background for many of these broadcasts. More indirectly, it also comes through the global spread of the western way of life and culture, with its elements which would perhaps appeal to the many young unemployed in the emigrant nations such as mass-consumption, individual human rights and better opportunities for women.

As stated earlier, it is not possible to measure the effects of this development on migration. In the area of communications it might simply mean that, for those who have left, they have a more intensive contact with their homeland than would have been the case previously. It is possible that it does not increase emigration at all, unlike the almost equally strong growth of the international tranport sector which is an area also marked by ever falling prices.

Confirmation that this is indeed the case can be seen from the multitude of very restrictive rules which the authorities of western countries have felt obliged to introduce in the areas of air and sea transport. For instance, according to the Danish police, from 1992 to 1995, 4,197 people arrived at Copenhagen International Airport carrying either forged passports, without passports or visas, or were involved in something which came under the general heading of "incorrect documentation"; and this in spite of the fact that the airlines have to pay DKK 8,000 in fines for every such passenger who arrives in Denmark.

Stowaways on ships also constitute a problem. Already in September 1992, the international shipping company association, BIMCO, the Baltic and International Maritime Conference warned its members of the considerable expense that shipping companies could incur because of stowaways. The American authorities, for instance, charge a fine of 5.000 US Dollars for each stowaway along with whatever costs the stowaway may otherwise have incurred.[43] A similar tendency can be observed in the severe tightening of visa regulations carried out by the industrialized nations, in recent years towards virtually all the nations of the Third World.

The upshot of all this has been that, in spite of extensive controls, an entire industry has grown up around the possibilities of travelling to Europe and North America. This industry has workers in both countries of departure and arrival and comprises both legal and illegal modes of transport, the production of all sorts of forged documents and the planning of travel routes, each of which may consist of as many as five to ten individual journeys whose purpose is to mask the extent of a massive traffic in human beings.[44]

Networks

The unequal development in both the areas of population and economics accompanied by growing communications and the very much expanded transport sector are all structural conditions which mean that, in the decades to come, Europe can expect to be subject to strong migratory pressure.

The form and the extent of this pressure will depend very much on the policies which Western Europe chooses to adopt in this area as well as the efficiency of the human traffic networks built up between the countries of emigration and immigration.

Research has shown that migrants often go to family or friends in the new country,[45] who often provide the new arrivals with accommodation and work, thus strengthening the ties which already exist between specific areas in the host and home countries. It is, however, very hard to determine accurately the true significance of these networks though, in view of the near-impossibility of entering Europe and finding work legally, the networks will probably gain more importance for those who want to enter Europe illegally.

In terms of family reunification, it is clear that the networks between host and home countries are of great significance. In part this is because the very notion implies that a relative, a friend or whoever, coming over to Europe belongs to the network and, partly, because emigration is the result of a decision taken by an extended family. Here the individual migrant plays a part in the overall family strategy in that he or she, as the one travelling abroad, is allocated the role of sending money back home for instance, or to return themselves with an education or capital. The network will have the same significance for another large group of emigrants – those who enter the host country illegally.

5.9 They are coming illegally

As described in Chapter 2, there are a variety of different groups of people migrating to Western Europe, so the explanations offered below as to why people migrate have to be matched with the groups in question.

The countries of Western Europe do not have any actual immigration policy on the lines of those of immigrant nations that feature set annual quotas for immigrants. As mentioned earlier, immigration can only take place in Western Europe in the cases of family reunification, political asylum or illegal entry.

There is growing agreement that this restrictive policy does lead to increased illegal immigration because, when the causes for emigration are present and the doors are closed, it is the only way in. In their low-key manner, the EU Commission have described the phenomenon in the following terms: "With increasing migratory pressure along with ever fewer possibilities for legal immigration, it is to be expected that people desiring to enter the Union, will continue to do so through the use of illegal channels of migration".[46]

The Inter-governmental Consultations on Asylum, Refugee and Migration Policies in Europe, North America and Australia, the IGC, is more direct. They wrote in the summer of 1995:

"While the number of asylum applicants in European participating states has decreased, a significant illegal population, living on the margins of society and without the controls exerted on legal residents, is a matter of increasing concern to many governments. In addition, there is a general feeling that the reduction in the number of asylum applications in participating States has been accompanied by an increase in the number of illegally residing aliens."[47]

Of course, although no-one knows the exact number of illegal immigrants now present in Western Europe, it is guessed that there are about two million North Africans in France and about one million in Italy.[48] Other educated guesses point to a figure of about three million people throughout Western Europe.[49]

According to the IGC, a series of episodes indicate that the number of illegal immigrants has been rising sharply in recent years. In one of its reports, the organization gives a series of examples of how and where illegal immigration has been at work. The following are four instances from four countries:[50]

- In 1992, 2,864 Algerians were registered in Spain while 6,160 Algerians were detained for criminal activities. The year after, the figures were 3,377 and 8,544 respectively.
- In July 1994, the illegal component of the German work-force was estimated to be about 500,000 people, which represented a net loss for the country of about GDM 10 billion per annum.
- A network of Albanians from Kosovo, who had been refused political asylum in Switzerland, have now taken over the drug trade in the

TOP: *In the next 30 years, world population will rise by 2.5 billion people, which is the same figure as the world population around 1950. In general, most of this growth will take place in the Third World. In Europe, population figures will fall. (C.Meffert/Stern)*

BOTTOM: *Economic and Social conditions in the countries bordering the eastern and southern Mediterranean are worsening each year. At the same time, their populations are exploding. By the year 2025, there will be over 90 million people living in Egypt, many of whom will live in the anthill that is Cairo. In 1990, Egypt's population numbered just over 50 million. (Polfoto)*

TOP: *The 1980s were characterized by considerable economic deregulation, privatization and internationalization. This development was boosted by the explosive pace of development in information technology and the transport sector. The main political architects behind this development were President Ronald Reagan in the USA and Prime Minister Magaret Thatcher in Britain. (Nordfoto)*

BOTTOM: *It is not just the figures for refugees and immigrants which are rising, everyone is travelling further and more often. In 1960, there were 60 million tourists in the world who crossed an international border; by 1994, this figure had risen to 531 million. Authorities have a hard time distinguishing between tourists, immigrants and refugees. (Polfoto)*

country. There are about 5,500 people from the Kosovo region who cannot be sent back because the Federal Republic of Yugoslavia refuses to let them back in.

• In March 1994, Belgian police unearthed a network of 140 petrol stations that employed over 300 illegal Pakistani immigrants who served as a cover for the extensive organized illegal sale of petrol. The extent of this fraud was found to be of the order of three to five billion Belgian Francs.

In 1993, the EU Commission and the International Organization for Migration, IOM, held seminars on the nature of immigration from Turkey, Morocco, Algeria and Tunisia. It was confirmed on this occasion that family reunification had, since the mid-1970s, been the main reason for legal immigration from these four countries, though there was a shift in the mid-1980s. "Since then, in purely quantitative terms, illegal immigration has been greater than legal immigration, this factor has been of prime significance for the countries of Southern Europe, Spain and Italy in particular", according to the Commission.[51]

The same research showed that, in the main, it was highly educated people with jobs who left their home countries, whereas the number of unemployed who migrated was far lower; which partly confirms the hypothesis that economic development leads to rising migration.

All the factors which usually explain migration are indeed present when it comes to illegal immigration into Western Europe. High rates of demographic growth and widely diverging standards of living are important "push factors" which engender migration. It is also the case that the existence of networks has a clear influence as, for instance, 97 per cent of the Algerian migrants settled in France. The hypothesis that internal restructuring in a given country can lead to migration is borne out by the development in Morocco where there is extensive migration from the countryside to the cities. To this can be added the role played by ethnic tensions which has had considerable influence in the case of Algerian migration as well as that from Turkey.

The fear caused by illegal immigration stems mainly from all the North Africans who travel to Southern Europe. However, in this as well as other areas, it seems that there is a process of globalization at work which means that illegal migrations are not just a phenomenon affecting the countries to the north and south of the Mediterranean.

As far as the transport of migrants goes, in recent years, extensive international networks have been built up which ensure that people are virtually transported "door to door". According to the IGC in Geneva, these networks make use of all sorts of possible routes in order to bring people from the countries of the Third World to Europe and North America. These organizations also provide the necessary documentation for, and information about, the prospective host countries.[52]

The central hub for this human traffic is Moscow where half-a-million people from all over the world, including 60,000 Chinese, are waiting to continue their journeys. Until 1994, Prague was also a major centre for this traffic until it was superseded by Warsaw. For a long time, Italy was the main point of entry to Western Europe, though recent legislation and new political measures might alter this picture.

Illegal immigrants come from ever more countries, though the main sources of illegal immigration which use these international networks are China, Pakistan and India with Iraq, Sri Lanka, Nigeria and other African countries also contributing sizeable numbers to the flow of people seeking to reach the wealthy West.[53]

However, for migration to take place at all, there has to be a further something; in this case, a "pull factor" or factors in Europe. In other words, extensive illegal immigration can only take place if there is a real demand for the labour it brings.

The general labour shortage of the 1960s is not the situation we are in nowadays; though with about half-a-million illegal immigrants arriving in Western Europe anyway,[54] this must mean that there is a considerable demand for their labour after all.

According to the IGC, it is a truism that the vast majority of illegal immigrants serve as "gap fillers" in certain sectors of the western economies, mainly in agriculture, construction, textiles and cleaning. These four sectors take advantage of the increased flexibility and low wage costs of such labour and many of the firms which use it would undoubtedly go to the wall if they did not have that option. Investigation of the Dutch textile industry showed that, in those cases where illegal immigrants were employed due to low wage costs, the firms in question would have to close down if they were forced to replace their work-force with legal labour.[55]

The general models used to explain migration seem, to a great extent, to apply to illegal immigration, mainly because there would indeed be extensive emigration to Europe if the present highly restrictive policies were not being enforced. Such a massive supply of foreign labour when faced with a relatively small Western European demand, which is prohibited into the bargain, must give rise to considerable illegal migratory pressure.

To what extent this pressure is allowed to manifest itself depends on various factors. The first is transport in the broadest sense, meaning the ability to get past the outer defences of Western Europe while providing a "door to door" service with all that it implies in terms of forged documents and contacts. The extent to which the Western European countries succeed in reducing this human traffic depends on which policies are adopted for future police collaboration.

A second factor is that the extent of illegal immigration depends on the network existing between immigrants already resident in Europe and those who arrive illegally.

A third is the question of the true extent of the "legitimate" illegal labour force. As mentioned in Section 5.2, increasing globalization means that an ever larger group of people reside and work in Western Europe without the necessary permits.

The fourth and final factor is that the extent of illegal immigration depends on how effective internal controls are in the countries themselves. The decisive area for proper supervision and control lies in those Western European businesses which employ illegal labour. Much research shows that several medium and small enterprises depend on this kind of labour which is why, in certain circles, there is a considerable vested interest in the use of illegal labour.[56]

5.10 The global refugee pattern

Up till now, the focus has been on what might be called "voluntary migration" where people seek to enter Western Europe. In the past, this was as immigrant workers, though nowadays it is either through family reunification or as illegal immigrants.

The heated debate in recent years about the presence of foreigners has generally been triggered off by the rising numbers of refugees seeking political asylum in Europe, though that there has been a real increase in their number is beyond doubt.

Before 1983, very few refugees sought political asylum in Western Europe and the bulk of those who did were from Eastern Europe. However, from 1983 onwards, the number grew, as shown in Figure 5.2,

Figure 5.2 Asylum applications in Western Europe and Australia, Canada and USA. 1983–1996.

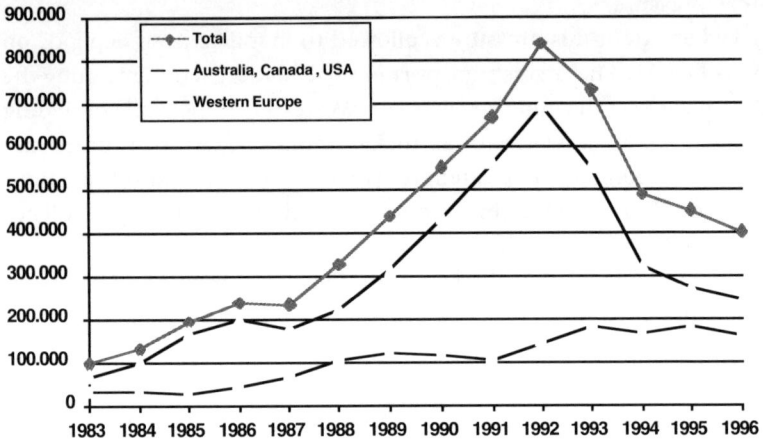

Source: Inter-Governmental Consultations on Asylum, Refugee and Migration Policies in Europe, North America and Australia, Geneva 1996 and 1997.

from 65,000 applicants to almost 700,000 by 1992 when the number peaked – an almost eleven-fold growth in nine years.

A similar development, though on a much smaller scale, was experienced by the USA, Canada and Australia. In their collective case, the number of applicants rose from 31,000 in 1983 to 143,000 by 1992, which is barely a five-fold growth in nine years. However, in contrast to developments in Western Europe, the number of people applying for political asylum in these three countries has kept on rising.

When one looks at the total number of refugees in the world during the same period, then developments have been dramatic indeed. In 1983, the UNHCR set the total figure at a little over ten million people. This was to rise to about eighteen million by 1992. If other categories are included, such as those who become refugees within the borders of their own country or those who had not yet obtained recognition of their refugee status, then the figure for 1995 rises to above twenty-seven million people.[57]

When the refugee pressure on Western Europe is put into perspective through comparison with the global refugee situation, it becomes apparent that all the talk of Western Europe acting as a magnet for groups of refugees is wildly exaggerated. Thus, in 1983, 65,000 of the world's ten million refugees sought asylum in Western Europe, which is little over half of one per cent. Although this had risen to 3.8 per cent in 1992, by 1995, the percentage of the world's refugees trying to reach Western Europe had again fallen to a little above one per cent.

Although Western Europe thus does not harbour so many refugees, it does not alter the fact that the continent did experience a historic rise in the number of people seeking political asylum within the space of a few years.

The question remains as to whether this rise represents structural factors which mean that this development could continue in the future. If that is the case, then the countries of Western Europe can expect ever more refugees.

There is, of course, no single comprehensive answer to this question, mainly because large refugee flows cannot be predicted as they, in turn, are often the result of unforeseen political, ecological or economic events.

However, it is still possible to detect some structural features behind, first, the rapid rise in refugee numbers and, second, the subsequent, almost equally rapid, decline.

To start with, it is highly likely that the globalization of transport and communications systems will have an effect on where the refugees of the future will come from. Thus, throughout the 1980s, there was a rise in the number of refugees from distant countries such as Sri Lanka, Somalia, Iran, Afghanistan and Zaire. However, since 1990, there has been a drop or levelling off in the number of refugees from many Third World nations, but the existence of networks, combined with intensively developed transport and communications systems, means that in all probability groups of refugees will be able to travel from even the most remote corners of the globe.[58]

Secondly, it is important to bear in mind that there were highly specific causes for the rapid rise in the number of refugees at the close of the 1980s, which included the initial stages of the collapse of Communism in the Soviet Union, Yugoslavia and the Eastern and Central European countries. With the peace settlement in ex-Yugoslavia and economic progress in the former Communist states, combined with an effective policy on political asylum, the number of refugees should continue its present decline.

Thirdly, the Western European countries' policy of tightening the controls on refugees has been a great success when the operative criterion is that as few as possible should be eligible to seek asylum. This was carried out in part by limiting the possibilities to seek asylum at all and partly by raising the requirements for the applicant to provide proof of genuine persecution. Further measures such as stiff fines and sanctions against airlines and shipping companies, stringent conditions for issuing visas, deportation to safe third countries from which they came, far more personnel in the asylum administration along with rapid decisions in the case of "manifestly unfounded" applications, have all played a considerable part in producing the decline which has taken place.

The single most significant step was taken by Germany when, in December 1992, it decided that asylum seekers who had travelled through a safe third country had no right in law to have their case reviewed. This regulation came into force on 1st July 1993 and the number of asylum seekers dropped from 438,000 in 1992 to just under 130,000 in 1995. The figures for 1996 show a further fall in that year to a total of 116,000.[59]

Fourthly, all these tightening measures have revealed the considerable overlap which exists between those applicants who are refugees in the sense of the Geneva Convention and those who are in fact immigrants. That this should be the case arises solely from the definition of a refugee as described earlier. There is also the fact that the number of people who fulfilled the Geneva Convention's requirements has remained constant even in the years when the number of asylum seekers rose rapidly.

On the other hand, Western Europe has sought to broaden the definition of a refugee a little by introducing other categories who could obtain temporary or permanent residence permits. This move came about as a result of the large groups of refugees from the military conflict in the former Yugoslavia and, since 1990, the number of refugees who have obtained residence permits in Western Europe on the grounds of criteria other than those of the Geneva Convention has been far higher than that of the so-called "traditional" refugees.

What the development in the number of political refugees will be is anyone's guess as it will depend largely, as mentioned earlier, on unforeseen events. It is, however, reasonable to assume that some of those factors, which are preconditions of all other kinds of migration, will also increase the risk of further flows of refugees making their way to Western Europe.

The rapid demographic rise could very well become a destabilizing factor in many areas. The same can also be said of the negative economic developments afflicting many countries, and as both factors magnify the effects of ecological disasters, the consequences may be flows of refugees.

6. Ageing Europe

6.1 The grey revolution

The countries of Europe are undergoing an upheaval nowadays which will have great consequences for coming generations. Since the mid-1960s, women on the European continent have given birth to ever fewer children so that the present birth rate is insufficient to prevent a dramatic future decline in the number of Europeans.

If the size of a national population is to be maintained at a constant level over a longer period of time, this requires that each woman should give birth to a little over two children. Table 6.1 shows which EU countries reach this level today: in fact, not a single one of them.

In 1995, the EU woman only had an average of 1.43 children. Paradoxically it is the Catholic women of Southern Europe who are the least productive with Italian and Spanish women giving birth to only 1.17 and 1.18 children respectively, the lowest level ever recorded. The gen-

Table 6.1. The fertility rate for 1995.

Belgium	1,54
Denmark	1,80
Germany	1,24
Greece	1,40
Spain	1,18
France	1,70
Ireland	1,87
Italy	1,17
Luxembourg	1,68
Holland	1,53
Austria	1,39
Portugal	1,41
Finland	1,81
Sweden	1,74
Great Britain	1,71
EU	1,43

Source: Statistics in Focus - Population and Social Conditions, Eurostat, 1997.

eral picture is, however, much the same all over Europe. Not one of the fifteen EU member states has a sufficiently high fertility rate to prevent a fall in population in the long-term.[1]

Low birth rates have occurred throughout history. During periods of recession in the 1920s and 1930s, many European states, including the Nordic countries, Britain and Germany, experienced fertility rates that were well below the level of just over two children per woman required to maintain population levels. In some areas, the birth rate was down to 1.6 children per woman.[2]

There is, however, evidence to suggest that the low contemporary fertility rate is not just a transient phenomenon where, for instance, a whole generation of women decide to delay having children. Back in 1980, the EU average birthrate stood at 1.87 children per woman.[3]

The big question is whether or not we should be pleased at the prospect of a future golden age when our descendants, fewer than we are today, will have correspondingly more to share. Progress in technology means that each individual will be able to produce more, so they need not fear a decline in living standards.

No-one knows how such a society would function, nor can anyone predict with a reasonable degree of certainty whether having many children might not come back into fashion. However, according to the theory of demographic transition discussed in Chapter 4, this is not very likely.

According to this theory, the countries of Western Europe have gone through the cycle in which people lower their fertility because they no longer have children as part of the struggle for survival when economic and social conditions are well-nigh optimal.

The creation of welfare states has removed all the earlier reasons for parents to have children. Infant mortality is extremely low and those who are born survive. The state or pension funds take care of the elderly. Children are no longer a labour source whereas, in a previous age, they would help out on farms or in the family shop. Nowadays, the age at which they may enter the labour market is strictly regulated. The emancipation of women over the past few decades is a further factor in that many women decide not to have children, while others decide to have them at a later point in life compared to previous generations.

It is thus not very likely that Western Europeans will return to having as large families as their forebears. It is also important to bear in mind that the birth rate – the number of live births per woman – has to rise from 1.43 children per woman to 2.1. This would mean an average rise of 40 per cent in the EU countries simply to reach a level at which the populations would be stable.

This development, however, is not going to lead to a golden age for our descendants in the decades to come. Low birth rates mean that a disproportionately large part of the population will consist of older people. This tendency will become more marked as the baby-boomers of the post-war period become pensioners in the next ten to twenty years.

The statistics show with alarming clarity that all the countries of Western Europe in the near future will be heavily influenced by people with their futures behind and their pensions ahead of them. This tendency is further strengthened by advances in medical science which mean that people now live longer than ever before.

At the turn of the century, the average European had a life expectancy of about 50 years. By 1950 life expectancy had risen to approximately 65 years. By 1993 the average lifespan of an EU man had risen to 72.7 years and that of an EU woman to 79.3 years.

When viewed from a larger historical perspective, we do indeed have an ageing continent. At the start of this century, every twentieth person was over 65 years of age; today, this applies to every seventh and by the year 2020 every fifth European will be over 65 years old.

Table 6.2 shows that the elderly are not the only group which is going to increase in size. The same trend will apply to the middle-aged in the decades to come. By 1990 the share of people over fifty had risen to 31.3 per cent of the population of Western Europe and by the year 2020 it will have risen to 42.2 per cent.[4]

Once rising life expectancy and the declining birth rate are linked, a picture of Western Europe undergoing a total transformation emerges. The grey revolution will completely change our view of how society is built up by different age-groups. There is already less talk of the "old" and the "elderly" and, instead, more of the "third age" comprising those aged 50 to 74, as well as the "fourth age" for those aged 75 upwards.

In one of its reports, the EU Commission did ask the question whether the member states were in the process of creating a society where most people would have a period of retirement that was as long as their working life. If this is the case, then the normal life of the average EU citizen would be divided into three phases.[5]

First of all, there would be the phase of youth and preparation, which is becoming ever more prolonged these days and which now lasts for an

Table 6.2. The older population in 1990 and 2020 as a per cent of the total population.

	B	DK	D	GR	E	F	IRL	I	L	NL	P	UK	EUR
1990													
50+	32.0	30.8	34.1	32.8	29.6	29.7	23.6	32.4	31.1	27.4	29.2	31.2	31.3
60+	20.4	20.3	20.8	19.4	18.5	19.1	15.1	20.2	19.1	17.2	18.2	20.7	19.7
65+	14.7	15.5	15.3	13.7	13.2	14.0	11.3	14.4	13.3	12.8	13.2	15.6	14.4
75+	6.6	6.9	7.4	6.0	5.4	6.8	4.4	6.3	6.0	5.3	5.3	6.8	6.5
85+	1.4	1.4	1.4	1.0	1.0	1.5	0.7	1.1	1.1	1.1	0.8	1.5	1.3
2020													
50+	43.5	40.4	47.1	40.2	41.1	39.5	36.5	46.8	42.0	40.5	41.0	38.0	42.2
60+	28.2	25.8	29.7	26.0	24.9	26.1	22.9	29.9	26.8	25.2	25.5	36.4	26.7
65+	20.8	19.5	22.2	19.9	18.3	19.7	16.6	22.8	19.3	18.6	18.8	27.6	20.0
75+	9.1	8.2	10.6	9.2	7.9	8.2	6.1	10.7	8.2	7.4	8.7	12.4	8.9
85+	2.8	2.0	2.5	5.5	2.1	2.4	1.3	2.8	2.1	1.9	2.8	3.6	2.4

B: Belgium, DK: Denmark, D: Germany, GR: Greece, E: Spain, F: France, IRL: Ireland, I: Italy, L: Luxemburg, NL: Holland, P: Portugal, UK: Great Britain, EUR: Europe.

Source: Older People in Europe: Social and Economic Policies - The 1983 Report of the European Observatory, Commission of the European Communities, 1993, p. 13.

average of twenty-five years. After that follows an active phase, a working life of about thirty years and finally, an end-phase of about twenty-five years in retirement. This scenario for the future places colossal demands on the efficiency of those who are now in the midst of their working lives, especially if the constant rise in the share of the elderly is taken into account.

This dilemma will worsen as the years go by as a result of the many who, throughout the 1970s and even more pronouncedly during the 1980s, left the labour market at an early stage. Many of these did so in order to enjoy early retirement, and the politicians were pleased since it contributed to keeping the unemployment figures down.

Most EU countries have experienced a very sharp decline in the employment rates for males over the age of 55. For instance, only one in ten males over the age of 65 is employed today. This, along with rising life expectancy, places a considerable burden on society in terms of support.[6]

The strain of this burden will become apparent not only as a problem of national finance in many countries in the near future.[7] It will also manifest itself in the steps taken by the various countries to provide real support for their senior citizens. Previously, in many EU countries, especially in Southern Europe, it was common practice for the families to support their aged members. Whether desirable or not, this pattern is breaking down everywhere since there will simply not be enough young people to care for the elderly.

If a study of the number of women between the ages of 45 and 69 is made and the figure compared with the number of people over 70, one can get an idea of whether or not women are likely to continue to take care of the elderly at home. In 1960, in the then EC countries, there was an average of 2.4 women aged from 45 to 69 for every person over the age of 70. By 1990, there was only an average of 1.6 women to take care of each aged person and, with present trends such as they are, it will not be long before both groups are of an equal size in many countries.[8]

Therefore, the good old days where the family took care of its older members will never return. Even if anyone wanted to restore the old family pattern anyway, it would take many years to bring about. The overriding premise for this would be that young people would start to have many more children than now in order to ensure that there would be more people to take care of the aged.

The question remains of how the nations of Western Europe will rise to this challenge with only 19 per cent of their total population under the age of fourteen, whereas the average portion of under-fourteens in the rest of the world represents about a third of the population. Surveys have shown that with such a relatively small number of children, several Western European countries will probably experience labour shortages in the future.

Over the next three decades, the working force of Western Europe will shrink from 145 million in 1990 to 137 million by 2020. In France, for instance, labour shortages will already be a reality by the end of the millennium. It is highly likely that there will be a general shortage of trained workers, especially those with technical qualifications, throughout the whole of Western Europe and with all the subsequent negative effects on economic activity.[9]

6.2 The immigration requirement – a model

The big question is whether the dismal future prospects may be dispelled through increased immigration. Unfortunately, there is no single clear answer to this as there are too many uncertain factors and unknowns impinging on such a calculation. However, the following discussion covers the factors which come into play when a decision has to be made as to whether the balance of probability points towards immigration being more of an asset than a threat.

The previous chapters have shown that post-war emigration to Western Europe has gone through several different phases. Furthermore, we have seen that there was no conscious or deliberate initial immigration policy like those of the traditional immigrant nations such as the USA, Canada or Australia.

Up until the beginning of the seventies, industry in many Western European nations evinced a strong desire for additional labour. This, however, was not the same as an adopted and implemented policy of immigration. What was wanted was an interim addition of labour and these workers were known as "shock absorbers".

However, once recession had set in, it was evident that this policy had failed. Like so much else, this strategy worked well enough in times of plenty but not when the going got tough. And ever since then, the countries of Western Europe have fought a losing battle against immigration which took place anyway, although no country had adopted an immigration policy and every country had instituted a moratorium on immigration.

When evaluating whether future immigration might be desirable in demographic terms, it is only natural to include the points made above. The present policy whereby immigration is simply not allowed has proved to be both ineffective and untenable, in the latter case partly because the reluctant host countries have had virtually no influence on who crossed their borders. This state of affairs might change if a more rigorously defined immigration policy were to be implemented.

The question of whether the Western European nations should adopt a proper immigration policy is discussed in the following chapter. At this point, some light will be shed on the question of whether increased immigration would provide a solution to future age group imbalance and the declining population.

Two Austrians, Wolfgang Lutz and Christopher Prinz, have developed a series of possible future scenarios which show demographic development and age distribution at different levels of immigration and integration. The following is a summary of their results.[10]

The assumptions used in making such an analysis are of key significance for the results. A model which is built to deal with immigration, integration, demographic development and the composition of populations, all in the future, has to be based on certain assumptions which themselves are subject to debate and, in the end, may prove to be wrong.

This is one of the weaknesses of all economic models because the choice of different parametres would lead to different results. So the most important aspect of the model is that it exposes some trends and connections. Should the assumptions prove to be wrong, the connections would still be valid although the actual results would be different.

The model is built up on the following six assumptions:

Assumption 1.
There are two broad categories of immigrants, one from the ex-Communist countries of Central and Eastern Europe and the former Soviet Union, hereafter called Eastern Europe. The other group comes from the Third World. Immigration from Eastern Europe is expected to drop over the next two decades while the migratory pressure from the Third World will remain constant at a high level.

This assumption is very realistic. According to Chapter 5, Western Europe will be subject to migratory pressure from the Third World for a very long time into the future. And, as described in Chapter 7, it is also reasonable to assume that, within the foreseeable future, Eastern Europe will reach such levels in economic terms that its inhabitants will no longer want to emigrate.

Assumption 2.
The point of departure here is the demographic composition of Western Europe in 1985, where it is assumed that 97.5 per cent of the population was European, 0.4 per cent consisted of immigrants from Eastern Europe and 2.1 per cent consisted of immigrants from the Third World. In this model, Western Europe consists of the present EU member states along with Switzerland and Norway. The number of second-generation immigrants in 1985 is set at zero.

The assumptions made here are also rather close to reality. Compared with the figures mentioned in Chapter 2, the number of immigrants in this model is set at a relatively low level, though with all the uncertainty which surrounds these figures, it will probably never be possible to find out what the true share of immigrants was in the general population.

Assumption 3.

The total fertility rate is constant at 1.63 children per woman in both Eastern and Western Europe throughout the entire period covered by the model. The fertility rate for immigrants from the Third World is set at three children per woman, while that of second-generation immigrants is set at two children per woman.

The European fertility rate might be set at a slightly too low level which will influence the results of this model. When this model is applied to the present day, the fertility rate used is higher, though there are many who expect that today's already low fertility rate will not be maintained in the long run. Eurostat already works with a median projection for the future total fertility rate of 1.75 children per woman and a Dutch survey reaches the same conclusion.[11]

Should it transpire that the European birth rate is actually higher than the model assumes, then it means that the population of Western Europe will rise faster than is shown in Table 6.3. It also means that the proportion of aged people will be less than shown in Tables 6.4 and 6.5, and that the non-European share of the general population will be smaller than that shown by the model.

Assumption 4.

It is assumed that life expectancy will increase in a linear fashion from 71.9 years for men and 78.6 years for women in 1985 to 83.5 years and 89 years respectively by 2050. Mortality rates are the same for all three population categories.

These are, in all probability, reasonable assumptions, although life expectancy will probably be higher in the future than is assumed in the model. If that turns out to be the case, then the share of the elderly will be larger than that shown by the tables.

Assumption 5.

The model works with three distinct immigration scenarios:

- *Low level of immigration:* from 1985 until the year 2000 there is an annual total of 500,000 immigrants from Eastern Europe and another 500,000 from the Third World. After the year 2000, all immigration is stopped and no one else gets in.
- *Medium level of immigration:* 500,000 arrive annually from Eastern Europe until the year 2000, whereas 500,000 arrive annually from the Third World from 1985 until 2050.

LEFT: *The pace of development in international communication reinforces the links between the immigrants in Europe and the areas from which they came. For instance, the number of international phone calls increased five times over throughout the 1980s, and it is still rising each year at a rate of 15 to 20 per cent. (Sonja Iskov/2maj)*

RIGHT: *All Western European countries will, in the comming decades, experience an ever increasing part of their population being made up of aged people. If the pace of immigration to Western Europe does not at least maintain its present level, then a relatively greater part of the foreign community will also consist of the elderly - in nursing homes. (UNHCR)*

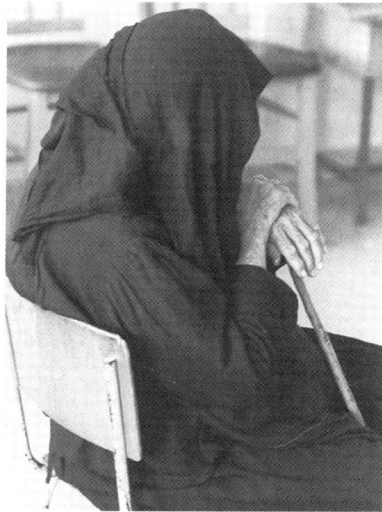

TOP: *The Maastricht Treaty was signed on 7th February 1992. This agreement with its "nine points of common interest" was the first attempt to introduce what might charitably be called a common policy on refugees and immigrants. Among the reservations that Denmark was to express at a later date were the points concerning refugees and immigration. The then Danish Foreign Minister, Uffe Ellemann Jensen, and the then Danish Minister of Taxation, Anders Fogh Rasmussen, are seen here signing the Treaty on behalf of Denmark. (EU Commission)*

BOTTOM: *A border barrier between Germany and the Netherlands is being sawn away. The politicians of Western Europe want such old-fashioned barriers to be consigned to museums after 1998. The 13 EU countries on the European continent along with Norway and Iceland are to remove all internal border controls in accordance with the terms of the Schengen Agreement. This will give rise to many problems.*

- *High level of immigration:* until the year 2010 there would be an annual
  intake of 500,000 from Eastern Europe while the intake from the Third
  World would rise in linear fashion from 500,000 in 1985 to 1.5 million
  by 2010, after which the intake would be set at 1.5 million per year.

These three scenarios all work with levels of immigration that are well
within the bounds of reality, particularly when viewed in relation to actual developments in this area over the past few years. Whether immigration turns out to be relatively low-key or intense, the level will be reflected in the results of the model which will be more or less pronounced in relation to what is shown by the tables.

Assumption 6.

Degrees of integration are expressed in purely technical terms whereby
the immigrants start at zero integration upon arrival to a point where
they belong to the "native" category. The model assumes yearly rates of
integration starting at zero per cent (very low degree of integration) rising to ten per cent (very rapid rate of integration). If, for instance, a
group of immigrants has a yearly integration rate of ten per cent, this
means that, after 25 years, 90 per cent of that group will be fully integrated and, in terms of the model, become Western Europeans. A five
per cent annual integration rate means that approximately 70 per cent
of a given group will be fully integrated after 30 years.

It is expected that the rate of integration for Eastern Europeans in all
scenarios will be ten per cent each year, which is a realistic assumption
of relatively rapid integration. It is further assumed that their children
will be fully integrated. However, in the case of immigrants from the
Third World, it is assumed that there will be three groups which will be
integrated at different paces – the immigrants proper, second-generation immigrants and third-generation immigrants. The model operates
with three levels of integration:

- *Low level of integration:* no integration in the case of immigrants and
  a rate of five per cent a year for their children. Their children, i.e.
  third-generation immigrants, are considered to be natives.
- *High level of integration:* Five per cent annual integration rate for immigrants and ten per cent for their children. Third-generation immigrants are fully integrated.
- *Low level of integration; also in the case of the children:* no integration in
  the case of the immigrants and a five per cent annual integration rate

for their children. Furthermore, there is a ten per cent annual integration rate for both third-generation immigrants from the Third World and second-generation immigrants from Eastern Europe.

On the basis of the above six assumptions, the following six distinct scenarios can be drawn up:

Scenario 1: low immigration and low integration.
Scenario 2: medium immigration and low integration.
Scenario 3: medium immigration and high integration.
Scenario 4: high immigration and low integration.
Scenario 5: high immigration and high integration.
Scenario 6: high immigration and low integration, also of offspring.

6.3 Integration more important than immigration

Table 6.3 shows demographic development in Western Europe until the year 2050 under these six different scenarios.

In the case of low immigration levels and low integration levels, the population drops from the year 2010 onwards; a decline which, as Table 6.4 shows, means a rapidly ageing continent.

Scenarios 2 and 3, where there are medium rates of immigration, the population may be seen to grow, though only at the beginning of the pe-

Table 6.3. Total population size by scenario (million)

Year	Scenario 1 Low migration Low integration	Scenario 2 Medium migration Low integration	Scenario 3 Medium migration High integration	Scenario 4 High migration Low integration	Scenario 5 High migration High integration	Scenario 6 High migration Low integration of offspring
1990	379	379	379	379	379	379
2000	398	398	398	402	401	402
2010	407	410	409	426	424	426
2020	406	416	414	450	447	450
2030	401	419	416	472	467	472
2040	389	417	413	490	483	490
2050	373	411	405	506	496	506

Source: Wolfgang Lutz and Christopher Prinz: "Modelling Future Immigration and Integration i Western Europe", in Russel King, ed.: *The New Geography of Western Migration*, Belhaven Press, London and New York 1993, chapter 5.

riod. At some point in time around 2030, the population will start to decline as immigration will not be able to compensate for the low birth rate.

In the case of high levels of immigration – Scenarios 4, 5 and 6 – it
can be seen that population would rise as a result of immigration and
the fact that the immigrants, over an extended period of time, would
have more children than the native Europeans.

However, if population growth is viewed in percentage terms, then it
will be seen to be declining in all the scenarios. This means that in any
event, at some point in time determined by whatever assumptions are
made, the population will start to decline. According to Scenario 1, this
will already happen in 2015. In Scenarios 2 and 3, with medium levels
of immigration, the decline will set in by the year 2025 and, in the last
three scenarios with high levels of immigration, the decline would set in
at a point after the middle of the next century.

In other words, immigration cannot in the long run stave off demographic shrinkage which is caused by low fertility rates in Western Europe. It is assumed that, sooner or later, the immigrants would adopt the
family patterns of the host country. Should they do so later rather than
sooner, this would only postpone the point in time at which the population would contract.

Tables 6.4 and 6.5 show how immigration will affect the lop-sided
age structure which the Western European countries can expect in the
coming decades.

Table 6.4. Proportion of elderly aged 65 years and over in Western Europe (%)

Year	Scenario 1 Low migration Low integration	Scenario 2 Medium migration Low integration	Scenario 3 Medium migration High integration	Scenario 4 High migration Low integration	Scenario 5 High migration High integration	Scenario 6 High migration Low integration of offspring
1990	14.4	14.4	14.4	14.4	14.4	14.4
2000	15.5	15.5	15.5	15.4	15.4	15.4
2010	17.1	17.0	17.1	16.4	16.5	16.4
2020	20.1	19.7	19.8	18.3	18.4	18.3
2030	24.6	23.6	23.8	21.3	21,5	21.3
2040	28.7	27.1	27.3	23.9	24.2	23.9
2050	30.3	28.1	28.4	24.5	26.0	24.5

Source: Wolfgang Lutz and Christopher Prinz: "Modelling Future Immigration and Integration i Western Europe", in Russel King, ed.: *The New Geography of Western Migration*, Belhaven Press, London and New York 1993, chapter 5.

Table 6.5. Proportion of elderly in the non-European immigrant population (%)

Year	Scenario 1 Low migration Low integration	Scenario 2 Medium migration Low integration	Scenario 3 Medium migration High integration	Scenario 4 High migration Low integration	Scenario 5 High migration High integration	Scenario 6 High migration Low integration of offspring
1990	2.0	2.0	2.0	2.0	2.0	2.0
2000	2.9	2.9	2.3	2.5	2.0	2.5
2010	5.6	5.0	3.3	3.6	2.2	3.6
2020	13.1	9.1	4.6	5.6	2.7	5.5
2030	29.6	15.6	6.1	9.1	3.6	8.8
2040	54.2	21.8	7.0	13.1	4.7	12.6
2050	73.5	24.0	7.2	16.8	5.7	15.9

Source: Wolfgang Lutz and Christopher Prinz: "Modelling Future Immigration and Integration i Western Europe", in Russel King, ed.: *The New Geography of Western Migration*, Belhaven Press, London and New York 1993, chapter 5.

It is quite clear that immigration will exert a direct influence on the composition of the population if the age distribution of the immigrants is different from that of the inhabitants of the host country.

As the majority of immigrants will be relatively young, this will have a positive effect in the short-term as the number of people of working age will grow. What will happen in the longer term is, however, less clear and dependent on several factors.

If the immigrants only have the same amount of children as the locals, this will not stop the development of an increasingly aged society as the immigrants themselves will grow old. If this should turn out to be the case, then a constant stream of immigration will be necessary in order to compensate for the negative population composition. If the immigrants are more prolific than the locals, then immigration will have a positive effect in raising the yearly total of births in any given country.

In the first instance, immigration helps to alleviate the contraction of the European population, as well as the age imbalance, under the very realistic assumption that the immigrants are younger than the population of the host country. In the longer term, however, they will be able to alleviate the problems only if they have more children than the locals. Otherwise the number of immigrants will have to rise from year to year.

From the six scenarios depicted in Tables 6.4 and 6.5, it can be seen that the age imbalance will come about whatever happens. According to Scenario 1, with low levels of immigration, the group of people over the age of 65 will constitute a little over 30 per cent of the population by 2050, whereas, in the case of high levels of immigration, they would "only" constitute about 25 per cent.

Therefore immigration cannot stave off the problem of the increasing age imbalance with ever more old people. This would require an ever-increasing rate of immigration on a vast scale. The group of Western Europeans who have few children and live longer is far too large for immigration to be able to change decisively the overall picture.

However, the age distribution among the immigrants would be strongly affected by whichever scenario was implemented. Table 6.5 shows that constant immigration from the Third World would mean there would be fewer old people among the immigrants than among the Europeans. It is only in Scenario 1, where there would be no more immigration after the year 2000 and the process of integration would be slow, that the immigrant group slowly dies out and, naturally, the further into the future you look, the older too this group becomes.

Table 6.6 shows how large the group of non-Europeans would be in the six different scenarios. Scenario 1 is not of much interest as the group eventually dwindles to zero as the original immigrants die out.

However, in the remaining five scenarios, the immigrants would constitute an ever growing part of the population. In Scenarios 4 and 6, where there is a high level of immigration and, respectively, a low rate of integration and also a low rate of integration in the case of the chil-

Table 6.6. Number of non-European in Western Europe (million)

Year	Scenario 1 Low migration Low integration	Scenario 2 Medium migration Low integration	Scenario 3 Medium migration High integration	Scenario 4 High migration Low integration	Scenario 5 High migration High integration	Scenario 6 High migration Low integration of offspring
1990	11.4	11.4	9.5	11.4	9.5	11.4
2000	18.6	18.6	11.7	22.1	14.8	22.1
2010	21.7	24.5	12.5	36.9	22.1	37.2
2020	19.5	28.9	12.9	54.4	29.9	55.5
2030	15.8	32.1	13.0	70.3	34.6	72.6
2040	12.0	34.3	13.1	83.4	37.1	87.2
2050	8.4	35.6	13.1	93.5	38.4	99.0

Source: Wolfgang Lutz and Christopher Prinz: "Modelling Future Immigration and Integration i Western Europe", in Russel King, ed.: *The New Geography of Western Migration*, Belhaven Press, London and New York 1993, chapter 5.

dren, it is apparent that this group would constitute almost 100 million people – about one fifth of the population of Western Europe.

The interesting thing about Table 6.6 is the comparison of the two results above with the results of Scenario 5, which also has a high level of immigration, but where the level of integration is correspondingly high. Here, the immigrants would only number 38 million or roughly the same number as in Scenario 2, with low levels of both immigration and integration.

What this means is that the size of the foreign share of the population is not so much determined by how many arrive as by how rapidly those who do are integrated.

Scenario 3, where the level of immigration is close to today's level, shows that towards the year 2050 the immigrant share of the population of Western Europe will grow to 3.2 per cent. This is only a slight increase in relation to the percentage predicted in 1985 of 2.4 per cent. Table 6.5 shows that, according to this scenario, only a tiny fraction of this share would consist of people over the age of 65. This fraction would only be 7.2 per cent which would, of course, be due to the fact that most of the foreign share of the population would have become Western European through the process of integration.

As to whether future immigration can alleviate on the one hand the decline of the population of Western Europe and an enormous imbalance in age distribution on the other, the following conclusions may be drawn:

Conclusion 1:
With respect to total population (Table 6.3) the low and medium immigration scenarios will result in declining population figures for Western Europe.

The reason for this, among other things, is that when the immigrants reach a certain level of integration, they will adopt local family patterns and have the same low number of children as the locals.

Assuming high levels of immigration, total population size could increase by 35 per cent over the next 60 years.

Conclusion 2:
Immigration would have a positive effect on the imbalance in the population age structure of Western Europe, mainly because the immigrants are, on average, younger than the locals on arrival. This, howev-

er, is only a short-term factor. In the long-term, it is doubtful whether immigration can have an effect on ageing Europe.

If the immigrants end up having the same number of children as the locals, then the age imbalance will increase unchecked. If they have more children than the locals, they would reduce the extent of the problem.

Whatever the outcome, the age distribution will inexorably move towards a much higher percentage of old people. If this is to be avoided, it would require a very high and constantly growing level of immigration.

Conclusion 3:

The process of integration is the decisive factor when it comes to the size of the foreign share of the population in the future. The degree of integration is a more significant factor than the actual number of immigrants.

7. A common policy on immigration

7.1 Europe without borders

It would seem as though Europe is reaching the end of a turbulent and chaotic period in the area of immigration. Immigration is on its way down; it has "levelled out" as the OECD puts it.[1] The countries of Central and Eastern Europe have reached political and economic stability, while the fragile peace process in former Yugoslavia could mean that the end of the civil war, which produced almost 3.7 million refugees, is finally in sight.[2] The nations of Europe have had a sorely needed and opportune breathing space.

It is sorely needed since most of the continent is engaged in the process of carrying out a highly complex and ambitious process of integration, the aim of which, among others, is to break down the national borders within the Union whilst building up an effective system of immigration control at the outer wall.

An eventual solution to the refugee and immigrant question is no longer merely a by-product of ever-increasing levels of political and economic integration. On the contrary many people, politicians and EU officials alike, are of the opinion that, in the light of the experience of recent years, a solution to the myriad problems in connection with refugees and immigrants does require a far greater degree of cooperation and harmonization between the member states. This would happen in areas where there would be many clashes with vital national interests such as cross-border police cooperation, transfer of border controls to other countries and the relinquishing of national sovereignty in the question of who and how many are allowed into the country.[3]

The major problem is that the individual countries have to implement an immigration policy at a time when they are abolishing controls on their common borders. That the process of European integration and the coordination of immigration are indeed closely connected can be seen in the fact that the first hesitant signs of actual cooperation manifested themselves with the setting up, in October 1986, of the so-called Ad Hoc Group on Immigration. The committee members were top civil servants and officials from the interior and justice ministries, and the committee was formed in precisely the period spanning the adoption of the Single European Act to its ratification in 1987.

It is evident that, in a Europe without borders, immigration control will play a central part. Hitherto, it has been the purview of the sovereign nation-state to decide who would be allowed to enter the country. All of a sudden, the individual countries now have to rely on other countries satisfactorily carrying out the necessary border controls.

Since the adoption of the Single European Act, integration has proceeded apace. The fact that the 12 erstwhile EC countries and, later on, the former EFTA countries in their agreement on the European Economic Area (EEA) failed to open up their borders and create a Europe with complete freedom of personal movement, as had otherwise been agreed, did not mean that this element of the project had been abandoned.

It just meant that the core members had to take a different route towards the gradual abolition of controls at common borders. The chosen route was through the Schengen Agreement. This cooperation clearly demonstrates the determination with which the nations of Western Europe are working their way towards a continent without internal borders. By mid-1996, 10 EU countries to the south of Denmark had signed the agreement abolishing border controls and, on 1st May 1996, the five Nordic countries joined the cooperation as observers.

At the time of writing, Italy, Austria and Greece were not full members of the agreement due to "practical transitional problems", while the five members of the Nordic Passport Union are formally to enter the cooperation in late 1998.

Within a few years, there will hardly be any visible inner borders left on the continent of Western Europe. Even Norway, where Union membership was turned down in a referendum, will be part of this process by virtue of its membership of the Nordic Passport Union. Britain and Ireland are the only countries still outside this cooperation.

In other words, cooperation on border control is, for the time being, taking place outside the boundaries of formal EU cooperation. However, it is up to the EU countries, along with Norway and Iceland through the EEA agreement, to implement a policy that ensures freedom of personal movement in accordance with the rules of the Single European Market.

Let us, for a moment, suppose that Western Europe, by means of the Schengen Agreement, manages to erect a common outer wall that effectively prevents all unwanted immigration. Then, there is still the problem of how to deal with the many non-Europeans already in Europe and those who will come in the future. In time, they will be able to cross freely all the non-existent borders. How will the Western European countries be able to implement, in practical terms, a policy which ensures freedom of mobility for the many along with restrictions on the few?

It appeared, during the summer of 1996, that European politicians imagined that this problem would be solved by means of increased internal supervision in the member states. For instance, all foreigners were to be able to provide proof of identity upon demand and workplaces would be subject to checks, and an Algerian girl from Paris visiting Denmark would have to report to the authorities within three days of crossing the non-operative border, see section 7.4 in Chapter 7.

There are many reasons why this situation is untenable. To start with, it provides a pretext for building up an extensive system of control and supervision. This begs the question of whether the citizens of Europe are prepared to accept increased supervision. Evidently the British are not. They prefer effective checks and control at the borders which mean that once people, whether British or foreign, are let in there are no identity cards, no obligation to provide proof of identity upon demand nor any kind of central registration system.

The other point is that it gives rise to discrimination against the non-nationals who have never been seen in a "country" without borders. This does not just apply to third-country citizens vis-à-vis true Europeans with EU citizenships, but also between those who live in a country which is relatively restrictive in the area of granting citizenship and those who live in a less restrictive country.

This inequality does exist today, but how can discrimination be avoided once the borders are opened? There is also the question of whether the citizens of Europe are prepared to accept such discrimination.

The situation would be analogous to that of a Frenchman emigrating to the USA, settling in Arizona, and then not being able to move on to California or Texas should, for instance, job opportunities be better there. The Frenchman would have to stay in Arizona and live on social security.

The above instance is somewhat far-fetched as anyone emigrating to the USA would be free to move around the whole country, just as anyone with a French residence permit is free to settle in Paris or Bordeaux. However, the comparison does throw the untenability of the situation into stark relief when the Western European nations on the one hand maintain the right of individual nations to decide who they let in or not and, on the other, remove all controls at the borders of the selfsame nations.

In reality, this system of supervision would work on mainly racist premises since those who resembled the local Europeans would rarely be challenged to produce proof of identity. The opposite would be the case for those with a different colour of skin or of foreign appearance, irrespective of whether they were Europeans born and bred or had just arrived on the continent. The British Institute of Race Relations has the following to say about this: "…racism does not distinguish between individuals of various ethnic origins or between a citizen, a refugee or an immigrant. In practice, appearance is the passport of those belonging to ethnic minorities."[4]

A further point is that the question of freedom of movement for labour in a Europe without borders has to be seen in the context of building up the European Monetary Union (EMU) which, according to the set timetable, is to become reality in 1999.

If such a monetary union is to work efficiently, one decisive precondition is that labour is mobile and can move around unimpeded within the EMU area. Should this not be the case, then any imbalance in one of the member states will lead to rising unemployment as the economy will no longer be able to be stimulated by the devaluation of the, by then, non-existent national currency. Therefore increased mobility between the regions of Europe is an important condition for the EMU to work as intended.

Although many measures have been adopted in order to promote the mobility of EU citizens, actual migration between EU member states is still at extremely modest levels. The experience gained from the Nordic Passport Union since 1954 would indicate that migration between relatively similar countries only takes place on a limited scale.

In view of this, it is reasonable to assume that citizens of third countries are the most mobile as they, in the nature of things, do not have the same historical links as the natives with any given area or country. Thus, the many special regulations for third country citizens actually act as a brake on the required mobility.

7.2 Conventions

The coincidence in timing of the wish to remove the common physical borders in Western Europe with that to reduce the rapidly growing flow of immigration has meant that the first moves taken to coordinate the immigration policies of the EU member states came across as the first steps on the road to building "Fortress Europe".

All the initial moves sought to restrict immigration. There were those who were quite happy with them as such, whereas others thought that these new restrictions were necessary above all to ensure that all the countries effectively enacted the same policy. The risk was that immigration would take place in those countries with the least stringent regulations and, with the lack of national border controls, other member countries would be affected just as they were trying to fully open their borders.

Since all the member states had introduced moratoriums on immigration many years ago, the main thrust of this effort was aimed at the rising number of asylum-seekers.

The Dublin Convention was signed by the then EC members in the summer of 1990, although Denmark did not sign until the following year. The main feature of the treaty was that refugees were entitled to have their cases reviewed by one EU country – but only by one.

The Convention does not seek to harmonize national regulations governing the granting of political asylum, which remain a national concern. The Convention does, however, prevent asylum seekers travelling from one EU member state to another in order to have their cases reviewed in several countries. Their cases are thus dealt with in the first EU country they reach.

The Convention also provides for the creation of a computerized finger-print archive, EURODAC, for asylum seekers. However, the countries are hesitant about implementing this. For the time being, the EU countries have merely established that the EURODAC system is technically operational on the basis of a consultant's report. They do not, however, wish to implement it fully before "all the juridical, technical and financial aspects have been clarified". Although the project has thus been postponed, the national ministers have still granted a working-group a mandate to draw up a draft for a convention text.

Just because the system is not officially operational does not mean that, in practice, fingerprints are not taken. Most of the countries fingerprint asylum seekers as a matter of routine, though they have still not reached the stage of exchanging data.

The Dublin Convention has been ratified by all participants in 1997 though, in practice, the signatories have, long before then, been generally behaving as though the Convention has been formally in place. Although there are disagreements between the countries on some of the points adopted, there is a clear tendency for harmonization to occur through practical application.

In 1989, work started on creating another convention whose purpose was to adapt immigration policy to a Europe without borders – the External Borders Convention. However, this convention was never passed due to the long-standing conflict between Britain and Spain over the status of Gibraltar. It is clear that Britain does not wish to take any part in the abolition of border controls. Nonetheless, the other EU countries are still working on finalizing the convention, probably in the hopes that Britain and Spain can eventually resolve their differences over Gibraltar.

The purpose of the External Borders Convention is to strengthen the control of the EU's outer borders. Besides more rigorous border controls, the draft text contains sections on, among other things, the criminal liability of transport companies that take passengers without the necessary travel documents, a common visa policy and the setting-up of a database containing information on unwanted third-country citizens.

Neither of these two conventions is a traditional EU directive; they are intergovernmental agreements drawn up between EU member states. In practice this means that, for instance, none of the cases can be tried at the European Court of Justice, nor can the Commission take any initiatives in this area.[5]

Towards the end of 1992, two more resolutions were passed. The first, known as the London resolution, is about the so-called safe third-country or country of first asylum from which an asylum seeker may have travelled to the EU, and to which they may be returned without their case being reviewed at all. The second deals with "manifestly unfounded applications" where the member states were of the opinion that a rising percentage of applicants did not require protection in terms of the Geneva Convention. That being so, these applications could be more speedily dealt with than normal asylum applications.

Both resolutions have been subject to violent criticism from many quarters, including the UNHCR and Amnesty International. Critics point out, among other things, that it is often impossible to draw clear distinctions between the various groups of refugees and that there would often be great uncertainty as to whether a given country was safe or not. The fact that the resolutions were the result of negotiations behind closed doors, without the participation of parliamentarians or any preceding public debate, has also drawn strong criticism.[6]

The motivation behind these conventions and resolutions is to ensure that no member state enacts or enforces particularly liberal legislation in this area as this would have an impact on all the other members when border controls are relaxed. The purpose of these initiatives is to reinforce Western Europe during the process of removing the EU countries' internal borders.

This reasoning, however, has strengthened the hand of those forces which want to introduce a very restrictive asylum policy as each country has tightened its regulations in this area, citing the common European interest as their main motivation.

Already in 1991, the Ad Hoc Group on Immigration had the following to say: "...if the harmonization process were initiated without defending basic principles, harmonization may be carried out at the lowest level. Assuming that immigration into member states must remain limited, it is above all the restrictive opinions which could dominate."[7]

7.3 The Maastricht Treaty

With the adoption of the Maastricht Treaty in December 1991 and its coming into force in November 1993, the EU countries moved a step further towards recognizing that the common problems could not be solved only by securing the outer borders. In October 1993, the Commission produced a working-document which contained, among other things, four basic factors that the member states would have to take into consideration.[8]

- The Commission pointed out the dangers involved if a negative image of asylum seekers were to be generated, which resulted in the general public then taking the view that the process of applying for political asylum was used principally as a short cut to immigration by people who were really economic migrants.
- The member states had to face the fact that all the talk about the halt on immigration reflected political wishful thinking and rhetoric rather than fact. Any public trust there might have been in national immigration policies had crumbled as everyone could plainly see that immigration continued through family reunification and, later on, via the asylum system.
- There was a pressing need to get to grips with illegal immigration in order to ensure that the integration process of legal immigrants was not jeopardized.
- The question of immigration had to be included in the foreign policy of the Union, primarily through a policy of active cooperation with the home countries in the hope of reducing the future potential for migration.

The Maastricht Treaty, therefore, did take the immigration question into account at various levels. The question of which third-country's nationals have to apply for entry visas to the EU was placed firmly in the Union's remit. This means that, since 1st January 1996, a two-thirds majority has been able to decide which countries' citizens require visas to enter the EU.

All other areas were still kept intergovernmental. The asylum and immigration policies were included in the Maastricht Treaty on the pretext that the member states agreed that the following nine areas were to be dealt with as being "of common interest". These were (1) Asylum policy, (2) Crossing of the external borders, (3) Immigration policy (conditions of entry, conditions of residence, including family reunion and illegal residence), (4) Combating drug addiction, (5) Combating fraud on an international scale, (6) Judicial cooperation in civil matters, (7) Judicial cooperation in criminal matters, (8) Customs cooperation and (9) Police cooperation.

The Maastricht Treaty is therefore the first attempt to implement what could justifiably be called a collective and coordinated EU refugee and immigration policy, although not at the same level as in traditional immigrant nations such as the USA, Canada, Australia and Israel. However, it is evident that the treaty expresses the desire of certain countries to work towards a common policy in this otherwise complex and politically sensitive area.

These nine points do not constitute actual EU cooperation but cooperation between states, intergovernmental cooperation. In practical terms, this is of decisive importance since unanimity is required if the countries are to implement a given course of action or set of measures, and any modifications to adopted plans have to be approved by all the national parliaments.

A central element in this difficult and complex process of cooperation is in the area of the police. Most countries are very wary of surrendering any sovereignty in this particular area, although they can all see the necessity of increased cross-border cooperation after the internal border controls are scrapped. If there is no increase in police cooperation, then all types of international crime, organized or otherwise, will have far too easy a time of it.

In July 1995, the Europol Convention was passed and the EU countries have since been busy working out and approving the practical details of the articles of implementation which should finally lead to proposals for national legislation and ratification by national parliaments. Until this happens Europol's precursor, the Europol Drugs Unit, EDU, has been operational since 1993 with its headquarters in The Hague. There is already some degree of cross-border police cooperation, although it will take a few years before all the rules and regulations are in place.

The EDU consists primarily of the cooperation between member states' crime squads. This is evident from the types of task that they tackle together which range from combating international terrorism to the struggle against drug trafficking. The EDU is facing a task of daunting proportions at a time when international crime is becoming as integrated throughout Europe as are the economies of the nation-states. Therefore many countries, with Germany in the lead, are pressing for this cooperation to become truly effective. There are only about 100 people working full-time for the EDU today: by comparison, the FBI has over 10,000 staff.

In principle, Europol has nothing to do with the other area of cross-border police work taking place between the Schengen signatories as this cooperation primarily relates to the operations of the uniformed police.

7.4 The Schengen Convention

In 1985 West Germany, France, the Netherlands, Belgium and Luxembourg signed the so-called Schengen Agreement, according to which the signatories were to gradually abolish their internal border controls. The chief purpose of this agreement was to gain experience in dismantling border controls which the then EEC countries could apply to the broader process of creating the Single European Market to be established by 1992, and which involved freedom of movement for individuals.

During the ensuing five years, the five signatories worked to extend the scope of, and to supplement, the 1985 Agreement. So, by the summer of 1990, the Schengen Convention was ready for signing. As mentioned earlier, all the EU countries, except for Britain and Ireland, but including Norway and Iceland, were shortly to become full participants in this cooperation. This cooperation in the future will link up the two large border-free areas of the continent, the Nordic Passport Union and the EU area on the European mainland.

The Schengen Convention also lies outside the formal EU cooperation which requires unanimity to take any decisions. The Convention largely covers the same areas of "common interest" mentioned above which are contained in the Maastricht Treaty.

The big question is why did the countries create this Convention when many of the same topics are dealt with in the Third Pillar of the Maastricht Treaty. According to both the EU commission and the European parliament, it is most desirable that the Schengen cooperation be superseded as soon as possible by genuine EU cooperation, see Section 7.5 of this Chapter.[9]

In the meantime, what is the impact of this Convention on refugees and immigrants?

In terms of future refugees, the Schengen Convention must be seen in connection with the Dublin Convention which only allows refugees to have their cases reviewed in one country. The main substance of the Dublin Convention is thus to be found in the Schengen Convention. The consequences of these two conventions are, firstly, that any given signatory leaves it up to the discretion of other signatories to decide whether a refugee fulfils the Geneva Convention's requirement to prove persecution. Refusal in one country means refusal in all the countries who have signed either of the two conventions.[10]

Secondly, the combination of a common visa policy and a database, where all those considered to be undesirable in the Schengen area are registered, constitutes an important element in building up a "common asylum policy". Thirdly, it means that this common policy will be implemented in the most restrictive fashion in order to prevent any single member letting more people into the border-free Schengen area than the other countries had agreed to.[11]

The Schengen Convention will also mean a reduction of the possibilities of entering Western Europe for all other third-country citizens. Previously, persons not welcome in a certain country would only be denied entry to just that particular country. Now, those same people would have to satisfy the criteria of all the signatory countries in order to get in. This is why the Convention can only lead to further controls, not fewer, as any traveller has now to satisfy the requirements of all the signatories and not just those of the country of arrival.[12]

The Schengen Convention does allow for an individual country to grant a residence permit on humanitarian grounds to a person who is considered undesirable elsewhere in the Schengen area. However, the residence permit is only valid in the country which issued it.

All foreigners are, in principle, free to travel anywhere in the Schengen area though the freedom is, in fact, relative in that whoever has a visa for just one country has to stay within its borders. This anomaly should be rectified on the day when the common visa policy becomes reality.

Another limitation as mentioned earlier is the requirement for a foreigner, crossing what should now be historical borders, to report to the authorities within three working days of arrival.

The Schengen Convention states in Paragraph 1 of the Convention's Article 22 the following: "Aliens who have legally entered the territory of one of the Contracting Parties shall be obliged to declare themselves, in accordance with the conditions laid down by each Contracting Party, to the competent authorities of the Contracting Party whose territory they enter. Such may be made, at each Contracting Party's choice, either on entry or within three working days of entry, in the territory of the Contracting Party into which they enter."[13]

Paragraph 2 of Article 22 further states that foreigners residing in Schengen area countries are to be subject to supervision and control. It reads: "Aliens resident in the territory of one of the Contracting Parties who enter the territory of another Contracting Party shall be required to declare themselves pursuant to Paragraph 1."[14]

The notion that the barriers to the freedom of personal movement are being removed belongs to the realm of myth. True, controls at the borders are pretty much a thing of the past, but the same controls and supervision are simply carried out elsewhere. The barriers between countries have not been removed in that the existing borders between the various nation-states and their legal systems are as much part of living reality as they ever were.[15]

The Schengen Convention does not grant anyone freedom of movement between the countries. All it does is remove the controls at the borders. Freedom of personal movement is guaranteed by the rules of the Single European Market which enable EU member state citizens to travel wherever they want within the Union.[16]

Thus, all the refugees and immigrants in Western Europe who have not obtained citizenship are adversely affected by the Convention as they are not allowed to travel betweeen EU member states. This prohibition remains in force after the implementation of the Schengen Convention, which means that the problem discussed in Chapter 2, and which both the EU Commission and the ILO already in 1990[17] pointed out as being a matter which the countries would have to solve, is just as unresolved today as it was then.[18]

These people have obtained one advantage, however, in that they may now travel to other countries for a period of three months provided they report to the authorities and, as mentioned earlier, do not take up employment or set up their own businesses. This limitation does not apply to foreigners and their children if they are married to an EU citizen. In some areas, special agreements have been made concerning, for instance, Turkish labour.[19]

The Schengen Convention does not, therefore, bring about any substantial changes, either in relation to the refugees and immigrants of today or to those of tomorrow because the juridical borders remain intact. An instance of this is that the rule which states that non-EU citizens do not have the same legal rights as EU citizens remains intact and unmodified.

One of the most noticeable consequences will probably be that it will become ever more difficult to obtain political asylum in Western Europe, while those who are allowed to enter in the future will be able to visit friends and relatives in another Schengen signatory country for a period of up to three months, but not seek employment. The supervisory mechanisms, along with their methods, which will ensure that the visitors stick to the straight and narrow, will respectively grow and intensify in future when such people are no longer stopped at the borders.

7.5 The Amsterdam Treaty

On the 16th and 17th June 1997, at the Amsterdam summit, EU heads of state and government agreed to take a further step towards a European Union without internal borders but with effective controls on the common outer border.

The Amsterdam Treaty is a continuation of, as well as a step in the effective implementation of the Maastricht Treaty; it contains the gradual introduction over a period of ten years of something which could almost be labelled a common policy on refugees and immigration.

Only partly because several areas are still kept outside actual EU cooperation and not all the EU member states are participating in this scheme on equal terms.

The Amsterdam Treaty contains two major points in terms of this book's subject area. The first one being that the member states took the logical step of incorporating most of the Schengen Convention into the EU Treaty in the form of a protocol to the Treaty. Thus did cooperation on freedom of movement within the EU area become a truly supranational concern, as opposed to an intergovernmental matter it had been hitherto.

The second major point is the transfer of some of the nine areas of cooperation from the Third Pillar to the First Pillar in accordance with the Maastricht Treaty.

The following five areas have been transferred from the Third Pillar to the First Pillar: Asylum policy, Crossing of the external borders, Immigration policy (conditions of entry, conditions of residence, including family reunion and illegal residence), Judicial cooperation in civil matters and Customs cooperation.

The main premise of this cooperation, for the first five years, is that the decisions have to be reached in unanimity. After this initial period, the member states may then decide – still unanimously – to reach future decisions on the basis of a qualified majority. Should this decision not be made after the first five years, the change from unanimity to qualified majority as a basis for future decisions will automatically take place after a further three year period. A final safety catch has been provided, in that the automatic switch from unanimity to qualified majority as a basis for decision making, eight years after the signing of the Amsterdam Treaty, may only take place if a qualified majority decides to let it go ahead.

The last four areas of cooperation, set down in the Maastricht Treaty, will remain in the intergovernmental Third Pillar. These are: Combating drug addiction, Combating fraud on an international scale, Judicial cooperation in criminal matters and Police cooperation.

Cooperation in those areas which cannot – wholly or in part – be transferred to actual EU cooperation will be augmented by, among other things, the drawing up of framework agreements.

This entire area is further complicated by the fact that the United Kingdom, Ireland and Denmark all have special agreements throughout the entirety of this legal area.

7.6 The countries bordering the Mediterranean

Although the countries of Western Europe are engaged in heroic labours in an attempt to stem immigration, there is a widespread understanding that the worst of migratory pressure is yet to come. In fact, it is looming over the not-so-distant horizon.

Rapid population growth in many of the countries bordering on Europe, mind-numbingly huge differences between the standards of living of Western Europe and the vast majority of Third World inhabitants, faster and cheaper transport and communications and the potent combination of all these factors tends to indicate that, in the long term, the problem will have to be solved in the countries from where the migration originates. This is commonly called "addressing root causes" in international reports.

As discussed in Chapter 5, there is enormous migratory potential in many of the countries bordering Europe, mainly in those on the southern and eastern shores of the Mediterranean. Another element in this picture is the fact that, until the late 1980s, the countries of North Africa were not considered or seen as security risks in Western Europe. The situation changed drastically in 1988 after the outbreak of the severe crisis in Algeria. The collapse of the Soviet Union soon afterwards meant that the countries on both northern and southern Mediterranean shores feared that the rest of Europe would then focus exclusively on Central and Eastern Europe.[20]

And indeed for a short period of time, the southern EU member states did find themselves in a minority as the rest of Europe oriented its politics and policies to the East. However, at the Essen Summit held at the end of 1994, the EU countries decided on an "appropriate balance in the geographic distribution of Community expenditure and commitments."[21] This revision of priorities was concretely expressed by the holding of a conference in Barcelona in November 1995, among whose participants, besides the 15 EU member states, were 11 Mediterranean nations and the Palestinian Authority. One of the resolutions adopted at this conference was that in future there was to be a much higher degree of political and economic integration between these two geographic entities. According to the plan, the EU would sign cooperation agreements with individual countries. To date, such agreements have been reached with Tunisia, Morocco and Israel. In the longer-term, the intention is to create a free-trade area encompassing all the countries in the region by the year 2010.

On the same occasion, money was made available for this Euro-Mediterranean partnership. This was approximately the same amount that the Union spent in Eastern and Central Europe – around four billion ECU, along with a similar amount of money in the form of favourable loans.

This series of initiatives has to be seen in the light of the necessity to create stability in this area by means of economic development, partly between the countries themselves and partly between the whole area and the EU. The cornerstones of this strategy are improved trading conditions, foreign investment and massive and better targeted development aid.

These political and economic efforts have to be seen in the context of the EU's wish to curtail demographic growth by means of enhanced economic development, thus reducing the future need to migrate.

It is uncertain whether this strategy will succeed or not. In the short term, economic development will probably enhance the migratory potential in that raised standards of living might mean that more people will be able to afford to travel and be encouraged to do so. In the long term, however, it is probable that, should these countries undergo sustained and substantial economic growth, the urge to leave the homeland will be much reduced.

Past experience has shown that, when a given country's economy reaches a higher level, emigration tends to fall and, in some instances, is replaced by immigration.

For example, emigration from Spain has largely come to a halt over the past fifteen years, during which period most Spaniards have returned. Today, Spain attracts immigrants from the Third World and similar tendencies are visible in the cases of Italy, Greece, Portugal, Poland, South Korea, Taiwan, Malaysia and Chile.

All the above countries are instances of how high rates of economic growth over several years do stop emigration; although this does not mean that two countries have to be at the same level of economic development and growth to prevent migration.

Just how evenly matched two countries have to be in economic terms in order to prevent migration is very much a moot point and depends on a series of other factors, just as circumstances vary from country to country. However, empirical surveys suggest that when the ratio of difference between income levels is at about 1 to 3, the economic incentive to move becomes so small that emigration begins to fall. Other surveys suggest that the ratio which makes the difference is 1 to 4, so there is great uncertainty in this area.[22]

It means that a strategy to reduce emigration through economic development is absolutely necessary and, in the long run, the only viable solution. At the same time, these measures provide the European politicians with an excuse to enforce the present extremely restrictive policies towards immigration. The tough measures are a necessary evil until such time as the migratory flow stops, as it has elsewhere in the world.

Whether combining the strategies of no immigration and economic aid will work, and to what extent, is anyone's guess. There are two areas in which this policy is clearly flawed, the first being that, nowadays, western development aid is falling.

The second is that immigration itself provides effective support to the economies of the home countries in the form of money sent to the families back home by the immigrants. It is known that many of the foreigners in Europe transfer considerable sums of money to their families. This is not only a direct economic boost to the families of the immigrant workers, but also to the exchequers of the home countries in that these considerable transfers end up increasing national foreign currency reserves, thus easing the balance of payments deficit with which most of these countries have to contend. These deficits are set to increase as these countries undergo the hoped-for process of economic development planned for them.

It is evident that the sums of money sent home by the immigrants do indeed play a decisive role from the fact that, in global terms, these sums exceed all the development aid paid out in the same period.[23] Surveys have been carried out in individual countries to find out just how significant these transfers are and the results indicate that in many countries they are of crucial importance.

Even today, about five per cent of the Portuguese GNP is made up of sums sent home by migrant workers.[24] At the close of the 1980s, three-quarters of the Turkish balance of payments deficit was covered by sums of money sent home whereas, back in the era before the moratorium of 1973, these sums amounted to 64 per cent of total Turkish exports. This percentage had, however, fallen to a little under 20 by the end of the 1980s.[25]

Surveys also show that it is not only the poor countries that benefit from these transfers; the countries of Western Europe do so as well. For instance, in 1993, Turkish immigrants in Germany sent almost four billion GDM back to Turkey. These sums contributed greatly to the Turkish ability to import German products, and thus contributed in turn to increasing production and employment in the country to which they had emigrated.[26]

A similar great dependence on money sent back home by workers abroad can be seen in the three North African countries targeted by the EU strategy of reducing migration through economic growth and development.

In 1994, a report produced by the EU Commission on conditions in the Maghreb countries revealed that, in Morocco and Tunisia, the contribution to the national economies made by migrant workers sending money home was greater than the combined sum of aid already received and foreign investment.

This particular instance is a graphic illustration of the decisive importance of the sums transferred back home to the national economies, Moroccans abroad sent home almost two billion US Dollars a year at the start of the 1990s, whereas development aid and foreign investment amounted to 1.5 billion US Dollars. The sums transferred by Moroccans abroad amount to about eight per cent of the Moroccan GNP. In the case of Tunisia, they amount to between four and five per cent of the GNP.[27]

In view of the economic situation of these countries, emigration is thus of vital importance to them. Surveys show that the sums sent home are largest during the first years of emigration; later on, the migrants settle down, have families and become ever more integrated. At this point, the sums transferred home begin to decline.[28]

When viewed in relation to the EU countries' policy towards the countries bordering the Mediterranean, it would be a decided setback if all migration from these countries were to be stopped as it would thus work against the policy which the EU states are relying on, the very intent of which is precisely to reduce migration from these countries in the long-term.

A complete halt to immigration would therefore hit the North African countries in one of their most vulnerable spots, their catastrophic lack of foreign currency. Present development in trade between the EU and the Mediterranean countries is overwhelmingly in the EU's favour. In 1994, the EU had a surplus in its trade with these countries of the order of over nine billion ECU.[29]

Or, couched in other terms, if the migration from the countries of North Africa were to be stopped, it would sharply reduce the ability of those countries to pay for imports. As most of these come from the EU, a halt on migration would adversely affect employment levels in Western Europe.

What we have here is an economic circuit in which migration from the poor countries bordering the Mediterranean is an important economic element which contributes positively to both EU and home economies.

Were migration from North Africa to be completely closed off and, consequently, the money transfers to the home countries as well, then the EU countries would face an even greater financial burden if their policy of reducing migration through economic development were to have the slightest chance of succeeding.

7.7 The Eastern borders

The great unknown faced by the Western European refugee and immigration policy consists of future developments in the ex-Communist countries where the picture is indeed most unclear.

The war that took place in ex-Yugoslavia has been one of the major reasons for the chaotic refugee situation in recent years. In all, 3.7 million people became refugees. Although the vast majority of them remained in the area, over 700,000 managed to escape to Western Europe, especially to Germany.[30] The peace agreement of November 1995 gave rise to hopes that not only would the stream of refugees cease, but that many of the refugees would go home more or less of their own free will.

Development in Central and Eastern Europe has been reasonably stable in recent years when the average level of wealth for the Eastern countries was found to be 30 per cent of the EU average. If the realistic premise of an average annual economic growth rate of 2.5 per cent above that of the EU countries should hold, then this percentage will rise to 35 per cent by the year 2000 and, by 2015, the wealth level of Central and Eastern Europe will have grown to half that of the EU countries[31].

Of course, such projections can be spoiled by a multitude of unforeseen events caused, for instance, by internal stresses brought about by rising inequality, also at the regional level. Other possible factors which could upset the present state of relative stability include massive migratory waves from the East and environmental disasters.

However, migratory pressure from the East will, in all probability, be relatively limited. The average standard of living, which stands at 30 per cent of the EU average, has, according to some research, already reached the level at which large scale migration stops. Therefore it is hoped that migratory pressure from this part of the world will be on a relatively manageable scale, especially if combined with other measures in fields such as trade, investment and development aid.

Meanwhile, agreements have been made with the countries bordering the EU whereby they accept that those refugees in transit to Western Europe via their territory are sent back. Already in the spring of 1993, Germany signed deals with Poland and the Czech Republic under which refugees arriving from these two countries, characterized as "safe countries", would be sent back across the German border. During the same period, Romania and Hungary were classified as "persecution free" countries to which asylum seekers could safely be returned.[32]

Thus, the problems of the EU countries are passed on to those countries of Central and Eastern Europe which have been designated as being "safe". These countries will, in the short term, accept those asylum seekers which the West rejects in return for financial aid to cope with the consequent problems. In this way, in 1993 and 1994, Poland received 125 million GDM to run refugee camps and buy surveillance equipment for its borders. Similar deals have been made with other Eastern and Central European countries.[33]

In addition to this, Germany allows in a certain number of workers with two or three year contracts as fixed-term contract labour. This particular arrangement has been reached with all the Central and Eastern European countries including Russia and Turkey. It is independent of both the moratorium on immigration and the general trend of development in the German labour market. Around 32,000 people were working under those conditions at the start of 1995, and there were just over 5,000 people between the ages of 18 and 40 who were in Germany as trainees who had come from all the ex-Communist countries, though mainly from Poland, Russia and Hungary.[34]

So primarily through German initiatives, the EU countries have established a buffer zone against the future refugee threat with the greatest potential in terms of numbers and unpredictability – the threat from the former Soviet Union. This area is characterized, among other things, by the following factors which could all contribute to extensive migration in the future:[35]

- According to the last population census taken in 1989 in the then Soviet Union, between 54 and 65 million people resided outside their home republic within the Soviet Union; of these, over 25 million Russians lived outside what is now the Russian Federation. Over 10 million Russians live in the new Central Asian republics where an Islamic variety of nationalism is making headway; and the Russians living in the Baltic republics of Latvia and Estonia now find themselves in a very awkward position due to ethnically-based citizenship laws passed soon after independence.
- In the southern part of the former Soviet Union there have been military conflicts in Georgia, Armenia, Moldova, Azerbaijan and Chechenia. None of these conflicts have been finally resolved and have already left large refugee problems in their wake.
- In all, there are 61 million people residing in areas where they form an ethnic minority.
- Over 22 million people in the Ukraine, Belarus and Russia live in areas where potential ecological and technological disasters could trigger off massive migratory waves.

Future developments in the former Soviet Union are thus extremely uncertain and there is simply no way of predicting whether Western Europe will be affected by future waves of migration from these areas. The
UNHCR appraised the situation very precisely when it said that it had
"...the objective premises for social disintegration and conflict on a
massive scale which, in turn, could lead to large scale population displacements".[36]

7.8 Should the EU adopt a policy on immigration?

There is a clear need for an EU immigration policy as such. The freedom of personal movement means that developments in one country
will soon spread to the others, and not just directly through increased
immigration where immigrants might travel on to and take up residence
in another country.

It would also be indirectly in terms of the effect which immigration
would have on the labour market. For instance, cheap Polish labour in
Germany could adversely affect the competitiveness of French companies not only in France and Germany, but thoughout the entire EU
area. The social and political consequences of immigration in one country would also be able to spread further afield, for example through the
extensive network which exists between radical right-wing parties in
Europe.

As this book has made plain, it is extremely difficult to harmonize
policy in this particular area. The reasons for this include different historical traditions, geographical locations, political climates, numbers of
immigrants already resident, demographic conditions and cultural contrasts. All these factors belong to the list of ingredients which make an
actual harmonization of policy virtually impossible within the foreseeable future.

However, the countries are under mounting pressure to bring national refugee and immigration policies into line, partly due to the general on-going process of integration which brings countries ever closer
but, and more to the point, also due to the opening up of internal borders. If the countries are not able to agree and reach a common view on
the rights of immigrants so that they too may travel around Europe
unimpeded, it is not hard to envisage a future Euro-police state marked
by a degree of suspicion and supervision unimaginable nowadays.

Demographic development, in the years to come, also requires a greater degree of harmonization in that certain geographic areas will soon suffer labour shortages. Since the implementation of the freedom of movement for labour, the individual countries no longer have the option of importing the necessary labour as they did in the early 1970s. After all, the new recruits could then travel to another EU country. Although immigrants cannot travel freely within Europe at this time, in the long run, it will not be possible to maintain this discrimination between the majority who can and the minority who cannot.

In 1997, the situation is such that there was intense intergovermental cooperation in the refugee and immigration area so that, through this example of practical politics, a process of more or less de facto harmonization is beginning to emerge. The signing of the Amsterdam Treaty ensures that this intergovernmental cooperation will, in the course of the next ten years, develop into actual EU cooperation.

At the same time, cooperation at the outer borders is becoming ever more effective by virtue of the Schengen Convention. Short-term policy as a result is clear. There is increased control and supervision of whatever immigration there happens to be, which in turn is to be kept at as low a level as possible.

However, is this a viable policy in the long-term? Does Western Europe really need an immigration policy similar to those of the USA, Canada and Australia? These questions can be approached in two ways.

Firstly, does Western Europe need immigration in the future and, if so, what kind of immigration? Secondly, will the countries of Western Europe be able to harmonize in precisely those areas affected by and brought into play by an actual immigration policy? This means will they be able, among other things, to cooperate on the nine areas of "common interest" described earlier?

It is precisely those areas which will be the test and measure of how rapidly the process of European integration will progress....or not, because an actual immigration policy with a fixed annual intake of people into the EU area would only be feasible if the immigrants were on an equal footing with EU citizens. Continuing the present policy whereby only those with European citizenships have rights throughout the Union while immigrants do not, and abolishing the internal borders at the same time, is an untenable proposition in the long run.

However, such equality between immigrants and locals is not likely to come about in the near future, which makes the adoption and enactment of an actual immigration policy just as unlikely. For instance, how would an annual quota of a million immigrants be introduced? Which EU member state would grant them residence permits? Where would they obtain welfare benefits, should they need them?

The structure of EU cooperation makes the drawing up, let alone the enactment, of an actual immigration policy virtually impossible. It will only be possible on the day when everyone can freely move throughout the Union, and when a much larger amount of public expenditure is channelled through the common budget. If the latter condition is not fulfilled, then the countries will not accept the freedom of movement for immigrants as they might be perceived as a potential burden on national welfare budgets. For instance, if Northern Italy set up quotas for immigrants due to labour shortages and, later on, these immigrants were to go to Germany to claim various kinds of welfare benefits; it would be impossible to get political and popular support for this.

However, as mentioned in Chapter 6, there are weighty demographic reasons for immigration becoming a necessity in the near future, as the following will make clear.

To start with, there is already a considerable volume of immigration taking place. The most reliable recent estimates put legal and illegal immigration at a total annual rate of around 1.5 million people, or 0.4 per cent of the total population of the EU countries as opposed to 0.5 per cent of the US population.[37] When considering these figures, however, the great degree of statistical uncertainty must be taken into account along with the fact that the EU also had 600,000 people emigrating in 1994, which is a considerable rate of emigration. So, when all is said and done, the net immigration to the EU countries is less than 0.3 per cent of the total population.

The other point to make is that the eventual shortage of labour will probably be alleviated by the slow integration of the Central and Eastern European countries where unemployment is relatively high. The long-term plan is that these countries will be gradually integrated into the EU. Then, the Western European members will receive the necessary addition of labour as, over the years, these newly-joined member countries are gradually drawn into the Single European Market and its regulations on the free movement of labour. The Central and Eastern European workforces are relatively highly educated and highly skilled, which is a decisive factor for future migrations as Western European demand for labour will be at its highest in highly skilled areas.

There is, therefore, no single, simple answer to the question of whether Western Europe should adopt a policy on immigration or not. What can be said at this stage is that such a policy is not a likely proposition in the near future, irrespective of whether the need for such a policy is either present or pressing.

In the short-term, the policy of the EU countries will be marked by an increased level of efficiency in the control and supervision of outsiders entering Union territory. The policy towards refugees will be harmonized further to the extent where actual practice will be replaced by a common EU policy.

This enhancement of the mechanisms of control and supervision will, in all probability, continue to grow in the years to come, partly due to dwindling internal border controls but, more importantly, also due to the massive labour surplus in the Third World. This surplus far exceeds the capacity of the Western European labour markets to absorb, irrespective of which immigration policy is eventually adopted and enacted.

This circumstance means that Western Europe must effectively apply that part of the immigration policy that consists in reducing the need for emigration. The aim of improving conditions for people in the Third World, especially those living around the Mediterranean, through trade, development aid and investment must be given top priority.

Still, the question remains whether migrations can be prevented in a world where the differences between rich and poor continue to be so incredibly great and when, at the same time, people all over the globe are being brought ever closer by transport and communications networks that are not subject to any man-made limitation.

As it says at Heathrow Airport, where 50 million people are in transit every year, "Nowhere on earth is more than 18 hours away from here."

Notes

Notes for chapter 1.

1: *Asylum applications in participating states 1983-1995*, IGC, Geneva, March 1996.

2: *The State of the World's Refugees 1995*, UNHCR, Oxford University Press, New York 1995. p. 198.

3: Enzensberger, Hans Magnus: *Den Store Vandring - 33 markeringer*, Gyldendal, Copenhagen 1993. p. 10.

4: *Asylum Applications in participating states 1983-1995*, IGC, Geneva, March 1996.

5: *Migration Statistics 1995*, Office for Official Publications of the European Communities, Luxembourg 1995. p.4.

6: *Statistics in Focus - Population and social conditions*, no. 1, Eurostat, Luxembourg 1996. p. 4., *The State of the World's Refugees 1995*, UNHCR, Oxford University Press, New York 1995. p. 12, and *World Population Monitoring*, United Nations, New York 1996.

7: *Asylum applications in participating states 1983-1995*, IGC, Geneva, March 1996 and *Monthly Asylum Applications as Reported by IGC Participating States 1992-1996*, IGC, Geneva, 22nd July 1996 and 30th of April 1997.

8: See Table 2.2, section 2.4. p. 35

9: *Illegal Aliens: A Preliminary Study*, IGC, Geneva, June 1995. p. 6.

10: Henrik Olesen: *Population movements within Europe: Migration, Visa and Asylum Policies*, speech delivered at the Wilton Park Conference, 23rd June 1995. p. 4.

11: *On Immigrants and Asylum Policy*, Communiqué from the Commission to the European Council and European Parliament, Commission of the European Communities, Brussels, 23rd February 1994. p. 49.

12: World Development Report 1993, The World Bank 1993. p.199.

13: *Trends in International Migration - Annual Report 1994*, 1995 Edition, OECD, Paris 1995. p. 21.

14: *Statistics in focus - population and social conditions*, Eurostat, Luxembourg, 1996.

15: *Older People in Europe: Social and Economic Policies - The 1993 Report of the European Observatory*, Commission of the European Communities, 1993. p.68.
16: Jean Bourgeois Pichat: "From the 20th to the 21st century: Europe and its Population after the year 2000", in *Population*, vol. 44, no.1, Institut National d'études Démographiques, Paris, September 1989. p. 57.

Notes for chapter 2.

1: Dorthe Nøhr Pedersen: "Hvis de kan jodle, bliver ventetiden kortere!" in *Tidsskriftet Grus*, no. 40, Aalborg 1993. p. 53.
2: Dorthe Nøhr Pedersen: "Hvis de kan jodle, bliver ventetiden kortere!" in *Tidsskriftet Grus*, no. 40, Aalborg 1993. p. 53.
3: Peter Stalker: *The Work of Strangers*, International Labour Office, Geneva 1994. p. 63.
4: The Jewish Agency, *Information*, 14th-15th March 1992.
5: *Trends in International Migration - Annual Report 1994*, OECD, Paris 1995. p. 194.
6: *International Migration Bulletin*, no. 7, November 1995, United Nations, Geneva, 1995. p. 5.
7: *Statistics in Focus - Population and social conditions*, no. 3, 1995, Eurostat, Luxembourg 1995. p. 7.
8: *Trends in International Migration - Annual Report 1994*, OECD, Paris 1995. p. 194.
9: Peter Stalker: *The Work of Strangers*, International Labour Office, Geneva 1994. p. 62.
10: *Trends in International Migration - Annual Report 1994*, OECD, Paris 1995. p. 194.
11: *Statistics in Focus - Population and social conditions*, no. 3, 1995, Eurostat, Luxembourg 1995. p. 3.
12: *Demographic Yearbook/Annuaire Démographique, 1989*, United Nations, NewYork 1991. p. 95.
13: *Migration Statistics 1995*, Office for Official Publications of the European Communities, Luxembourg 1995. pgs. 4 and 5.
14: Sarah Collinson: *Europe and International Migration*, Pinter Publishers, London and NewYork 1993. p. 115.
15: *Trends in International Migration - Annual Report 1994*, OECD, Paris 1995. p. 11.
16: Astri Suhrke and Svein Gjerdåker, eds.: *Dagens Folkevandringer - berører de oss?*, Chr. Michelsens Institutt/Cappelen, Oslo 1993. p. 88.

17: Sarah Collinson: *Europe and International Migration*, Pinter Publishers, London and NewYork 1993. p. 117.

18: Dorthe Nøhr Pedersen: "Hvis de kan jodle, bliver ventetiden kortere!" in *Tidsskriftet Grus*, no. 40, Aalborg 1993. p. 55.

19: Peter Stalker: *The Work of Strangers*, International Labour Office, Geneva 1994. p. 64.

20: Dorthe Nøhr Pedersen: "Hvis de kan jodle, bliver ventetiden kortere!" in *Tidsskriftet Grus*, no. 40, Aalborg 1993. p. 55.

21: James F. Hollifield: *Immigrants, Markets and States*, Harvard University Press, London 1992. Ch. 8.

22: Dorthe Nør Pedersen: "Hvis de kan jodle, bliver ventetiden kortere!" in *Tidsskriftet Grus*, no. 40, Aalborg 1993. p. 61.

23: James F. Hollifield: *Immigrants, Markets and States*, Harvard University Press, London 1992. Ch. 8.

24: James F. Hollifield: *Immigrants. Markets and States*, Harvard University Press, London 1992. Ch. 8.

25: Two years later – 13th of august 1997 – Wilson Kipketer was the first person to beat Sebastian Coe's 16-year-old world record of 800 meters.

26: "Befolkning og valg", *Statistical News*, Statistics Denmark, no. 5 Copenhagen 1996.

27: Astri Suhrke and Svein Gjerdåker, eds.: *Dagens Folkevandringer - berører de oss?*, Chr. Michelsens Institutt/Cappelen, Oslo 1993. p. 34.

28: Astri Suhrke and Svein Gjerdåker, eds.: *Dagens Folkevandringer - berører de oss?*, Chr. Michelsens Institutt/Cappelen, Oslo 1993. p. 42.

29: *Statistical Yearbook and Vital Statistics*, Statistics Denmark, Copenhagen 1992.

30: *Migration Statistics 1995*, Office for Official Publications of the European Communities, Luxembourg 1995. p. 14.

31: Henrik Olesen: *Migration ...into the 21st Century*, IGC, Geneva, 23rd May 1995. p. 1.

32: Peter Stalker: *The Work of Strangers*, International Labour Office, Geneva 1994. p. 17.

33: *Migration Statistics 1995*, Office for Official Publications of the European Communities, Luxembourg 1995. p. 4.

34: The figures for net immigration have been derived from the difference between the population size on 1st January and 31st December of the same given year, minus the difference between the number of deaths and births, and, finally, the figures are corrected with the input from e.g. population censuses. It is for these reasons that the net immgration figures may be at variance with those of other tables, where, according to Eurostat, the immigration figures tend to be more reliable than emigration figures, which are often underestimated. *Statistics in Focus - Population and social conditions*, Eurostat, no. 3, 1995. p. 2.

35: *Migration Statistics 1995*, Office for Official Publications of the European Communities, Luxembourg 1995. p. 4.

36: *Migration Statistics 1995*, Office for Official Publications of the European Communities, Luxembourg 1995. p. 4.

37: *Migration Statistics 1995*, Office for Official Publications of the European Communities, Luxembourg 1995. p. 14.

38: *Migration Statistics 1995*, Office for Official Publications of the European Communities, Luxembourg 1995 and 1996.

39: Henrik Olesen: *Population movements within Europe: Migration, visa and asylum policies*, IGC, Geneva, July 1995. p. 4.

40: IGC, Geneva, December 1995 and July 1997.

41: *Monthly Asylum Applications as Reported by IGC Participating States 1992-1996*, IGC, Geneva, July 1997.

42: Astri Suhrke: "Den vanskelige migrasjonen - vandring i en verden med barrierer", in *Dagens folkevandringer - berører de oss?*, Astri Suhrke and Svein Gjerdåker, eds., Chr. Michelsens Institutt/Cappelen, Oslo 1993. p. 35.

43: Henrik Olesen: *Organizing Diversity, Migration Policy and Practice.* Speech delivered at conference at Berg en Dal, the Netherlands, 8th-12th November, 1995.

44: *The State of the World's Refugees - In Search of Solutions*, UNHCR, Oxford University Press, New York 1995. p. 198.

Notes for chapter 3.

1: Glyn Ford, ed.: *Fascist Europe - The Rise of Racism and Xenophobia*, Pluto Press, London 1992. p. XV.

2: Glyn Ford, ed.: *Fascist Europe - The Rise of Racism and Xenophobia*, Pluto Press, London 1992. p. X.

3: *Progress Report, Migration, Development and Trade*, IGC, Geneva, 6 January 1994. p. 1.

4: Peter Stalker: *The Work of Strangers*, International Labour Office, Geneva 1994. p. 195.

5: Giacomo Luciani, ed.: *Migration Policies in Europe and the United States*, Kluwer Academic Publishers, Dordrecht 1993. p. 53.

6: Daniel Cohn-Bendit: "Europe and its borders: The case for a common immigration policy.", in *Towards a European Immigration Policy*, The Philip Morris Institute for Public Policy Research, October 1993. p. 25.

7: *The State of World Population 1992*, UNFPA, New York 1992. p. 20.

8: Finn Stepputat: *Efter nødhjælpen - fra katastrofe til udvikling?*, CUF Notat, Copenhagen, September 1994. Ch. 2.

9: Finn Stepputat: *Efter nødhjælpen - fra katastrofe til udvikling?*, CUF Notat, Copenhagen, September 1994. p. 13.

10: *Politiken*, 23rd April 1995.

11: Finn Stepputat: *Efter nødhjælpen - fra katastrofe til udvikling?*, CUF Notat, Copenhagen, September 1994. p. 8.

12: *The New York Times*, 14th December 1990.

13: Giles Merrit: *Østeuropa og Sovjetunionen - Frihedens udfordringer*, Schultz, Copenhagen 1991. p. 4.

14: Giacomo Luciani, ed.: *Migration Policies in Europe and the United States*, Kluwer Academic Publishers, Dordrecht 1993. p. 20 and V. Grecic: "East-West Migration and its Possible Influence on North-South Migration", in *International Migration*, vol. XXIX, no. 2, June 1991. p. 243.

15: Richard Layard, Oliver Blanchard, Rudiger Dornbusch, Paul Krugman: *East-West migration - The Alternatives*, The United Nations University, 1992. p. 6.

16: *Statistics in Focus - Population and social conditions*, Eurostat, no. 1 1996, Luxemburg 1996. p.5.

17: Richard Layard, Oliver Blanchard, Rudiger Dornbusch, Paul Krugman: *East-West Migration - The Alternatives*, The United Nations University, 1992. p. 6.

18: *Ugebrevet Mandag Morgen*, no. 16, 30th April 1990.

19: *Europe*, no. 10, The European Commission, October 1995.

20: Peter Wendt: Valutasamarbejdet: sammenbrud eller nybrud?, in *Økonomi og Politik*, no. 3, Jurist- og Økonomforbundets Forlag, Copenhagen 1993. p. 30.

21: Peter Wendt: Valutasamarbejdet: sammenbrud eller nybrud?, in *Økonomi og Politik*, no. 3, Jurist- og Økonomforbundets Forlag, Copenhagen 1993. p. 35.

22: Glyn Ford, ed.: *Fascist Europe, The Rise of Racism and Xenophobia,* Pluto Press, London 1992. p. XXI.

23: *Ugebrevet Mandag Morgen,* no. 12, 21st March 1994.

24: *OECD Economic Outlook,* December 1994, Paris 1994. Annex, Table 22.

25: *OECD "Samfund I Forandring",* OECD's International Futures Programme, Paris 1994.

26: *Ugebrevet Mandag Morgen,* no. 21, 1st June 1993.

27: OECD *Economic Outlook,* June 1993, Paris 1993. p. XI.

28: *Ugebrevet Mandag Morgen,* no. 20, 24th May 1994.

29: *OECD Economic Outlook,* December 1994, Paris 1994. Annex, Table 1.

30: Lars Dencik: "Reflexions on Xenophobia and Exile in Contemporary Modernity", in *Rescue - 43 - Xenophobia and Exile,* Munksgaard, Copenhagen 1993. p. 97.

31: Peter Stalker: *The Work of Strangers,* International Labour Office, Geneva 1994. p. 36.

32: *Børsens Nyhedsmagasin,* Special Edition, September 1988.

33: *Ugebrevet Mandag Morgen,* no. 37, 29th October 1990.

34: *Oxford Analytica,* 24th February, Oxford, 1992.

35: Philip Martin: "The Migration Issue", in *The new Geography of European Migrations,* ed. Russell King, Belhaven Press, London 1993, p. 9.

36: Hans Kornø Rasmussen: *Befolkningseksplosionen,* Save the Children, Copenhagen 1993. p. 22.

37: Poul Christian Matthiessen: "Verden på vandring mod Europa" in *Tema Spot,* no. 1, 1992. p. 2.

38: Hans Kornø Rasmussen: *Befolkningseksplosionen,* Save the Children, Copenhagen 1993. p. 34.

39: *Population,* vol. 5, Institut National d'Études Démographiques, Paris 1993. p. 251.

40: Sarah Collinson: *Europe and International Migration,* Pinters Publishers, London and New York 1993. p. 88.

41: *Population,* vol. 5, Institut National d'Études Démographiques, Paris 1993. p. 255.

Notes for chapter 4.

1: Laurids S. Lauridsen: "Masseimmigration fra syd - en tikkende bombe?" in *Den Ny Verden* 3, Copenhagen 1993. p. 114.

2: Sarah Collinson: *Europe and International Migration*, Pinters Publishers, London and New York 1993. p. 31.

3: Göran Rystad: "History and the Future of International Migration", in *International Migration Review*, vol. XXVI, no. 4, Winter 1992. p. 1171.

4: Herbert Giersch, ed.: *Economic Aspects of International Migration*, Springer Verlag, Berlin - Heidelberg 1994. p. 4.

5: Peter Stalker: *The Work of Strangers*, International Labour Office, Geneva 1994. p. 4.

6: Herbert Giersch, ed.: *Economic Aspects of International Migration*, Springer Verlag, Berlin - Heidelberg 1994. p. 4.

7: Peter Stalker: *The Work of Strangers*, International Labour Office, Geneva 1994. p. 11.

8: Peter Stalker: *The Work of Strangers*, International Labour Office, Geneva 1994. p. 12 and Sarah Collinson: *Europe and International Migration*, Pinters Publishers, London and New York 1993, p. 32.

9: Peter Stalker: *The Work of Strangers*, International Labour Office, Geneva 1994. p. 13.

10: Paul Harrison: "*Inside the Third World - the anatomy of poverty*", Penguin Books, London 1987. p. 218.

11: Sarah Collinson: *Europe and International Migration*, Pinters Publishers, London and New York 1993. p. 35.

12: Giacomo Luciani, ed.: *Migration Policies in Europe and the United States*, Kluwer Academic Publishers, Dordrecht 1993. p. 56 and Peter Stalker: *The Work of Strangers*, International Labour Office, Geneva 1994. p. 14.

13: Herbert Giersch, ed.: *Economic Aspects of International Migration*, Springer Verlag, Berlin -Heidelberg 1994. p. 10.

14: Herbert Giersch, ed.: *Economic Aspects of International Migration*, Springer Verlag, Berlin - Heidelberg 1994. p. 7.

15: Russell King: "European International Migration 1945-90: a statistical and geographical overview", in *Mass Migration in Europe*, Russell King, ed., Belhaven Press, London 1993. p. 20.

16: Russell King: "European International Migration 1945-90: a statistical and geographical overview", in *Mass Migration in Europe*, Russell King, ed., Belhaven Press, London 1993. p. 20.

17: Giacomo Luciani, ed.: *Migration Policies in Europe and the United States*, Kluwer Academic Publishers, Dordrecht 1993. p.58.
18: Herbert Giersch, ed.: *Economic Aspects of International Migration*, Springer Verlag, Berlin - Heidelberg 1994. p. 5.
19: Giacomo Luciani, ed.: *Migration Policies in Europe and the United States*, Kluwer Academic Publishers, Dordrecht 1993. p. 57.
20: Sarah Collinson: *Europe and International Migration*, Pinters Publishers, London and New York 1993. p. 49.
21: Giacomo Luciani, ed.: *Migration Policies in Europe and the United States*, Kluwer Academic Publishers, Dordrecht 1993. p. 58.
22: Russell King: "European International Migration 1945-90: a statistical and geographical overview", in *Mass Migration in Europe*, Russell King, ed., Belhaven Press, London 1993. p. 20.
23: Trygve Bølstad, Øivind Fjeldstad and Dag Lerrand: *Jordas Fordrevne - Flyktninger i 90-åra*, Universitetsforlaget, Oslo 1995. p. 119.
24: Sarah Collinson: *Europe and International Migration*, Pinters Publishers, London and New York 1993. p. 49.
25: Jean Louis Rallu and Alain Blum: "European population", in *European Population*, vol. 2, Institut National d'Études Démographiques, Paris, October 1991. p. 16.
26: Trygve Bølstad, Øivind Fjeldstad and Dag Lerrand: *Jordas Fordrevne - Flyktninger i 90-åra*, Universitetsforlaget, Oslo 1995. p. 121.
27: Sarah Collinson: *Europe and Intenational Migration*, Pinters Publishers, London and New York 1993. p. 42, and Trygve Bølstad, Øivind Fjeldstad and Dag Lerrand: *Jordas Fordrevne - Flyktninger i 90-åra*, Universitetsforlaget, Oslo 1995. p. 123.
28: Peter Stalker: *The Work of Strangers*, International Labour Office, Geneva 1994. p. 16.
29: Göran Rystad: "History and the Future of International Migration", in *International Migration Review*, vol. XXVI, no. 4, Winter 1992. p. 1177.
30: Trygve Bølstad, Øivind Fjeldstad and Dag Lerrand: *Jordas Fordrevne - Flyktninger i 90-åra*, Universitetsforlaget, Oslo 1995. p. 121.
31: Trygve Bølstad, Øivind Fjeldstad and Dag Lerrand: *Jordas Fordrevne - Flyktninger i 90-åra*, Universitetsforlaget, Oslo 1995. p. 123.
32: Peter Stalker: *The Work of Strangers*, International Labour Office, Geneva 1994. p. 18.

33: Peter Stalker: *The Work of Strangers*, International Labour Office, Geneva 1994. p. 17.

34: Göran Rystad: "History and the Future of International Migration", in *International Migration Review*, vol. XXVI, no. 4, Winter 1992. p. 1185, and Robin Cohen: *The New Helots*, Gower Publishing Company, Vermont 1987. p. 118.

35: Giacomo Luciani, ed.: *Migration Policies in Europe and the United States*, Kluwer Publishers, Dordrecht 1993. p. 128, and Svend Aage Hansen and Ingrid Henriksen: *Dansk Socialhistorie 1940 - 83: Velfærdsstaten*, Gyldendal, Copenhagen 1984. p. 169 and 301.

36: Peter Stalker: *The Work of Strangers*, International Labour Office, Geneva 1994. p. 17.

37: Peter Stalker: *The Work of Strangers*, International Labour Office, Geneva 1994. p. 17.

38: Robin Cohen: *The New Helots*, Gower Publishing Company, Vermont 1987. p. 124.

39: Sarah Collinson: *Europe and International Migration*, Pinters Publishers, London and New York 1993. p. 47.

40: Robin Cohen: *The New Helots*, Gower Publishing Company, Vermont 1987. p. 125.

41: Giacomo Luciani, ed.: *Migration Policies in Europe and the United States*, Kluwer Academic Publishers, Dordrecht 1993. p. 129.

42: Robin Cohen: *The New Helots*, Gower Publishing Company, Vermont 1987. p. 132.

43: Göran Rystad: "History and the Future of International Migration", in *International Migration Review*, vol. XXVI, no. 4, Winter 1992. p. 1177.

44: Robin Cohen: *The New Helots*, Gower Publishing Company, Vermont 1987. p. 133.

45: Philip Martin: "The migration issue", in the *New Geography of European Migrations*, Russell King, ed., Belhaven Press, London and New York 1993. p. 7.

46: Göran Rystad: "History and the Future of International Migration", in *International Migration Review*, vol. XXVI, no. 4, Winter 1992. p. 1179.

47: Göran Rystad: "History and the Future of International Migration", in *Intenational Migration Review*, vol. XXVI, no. 4, Winter 1992. p. 1184, and Jan Ekberg and Lars Andersson: *Invandring, sysselsättning och ekonomiska effekter*, Report to the Expert Study Group for Public Economy, Department of Finance, Stockholm 1995. p. 186.

48: Trygve Bølstad, Øivind Fjeldstad and Dag Lerrand: *Jordas Fordrevne - Flyktninger i 90-åra*, Universitetsforlaget, Oslo 1995. p. 124.
49: Sarah Collinson: *Europe and International Migration*, Pinters Publishers, London and New York 1993. p. 53.
50: Philip Martin: "The Migration Issue", in the *New Geography of European Migrations*, Russell King, ed., Belhaven Press, London and New York 1993. p. 9.
51: Hans Kornø Rasmussen: "U-landene og de internationale metalmarkeder", in *Den Nye Verden*, no. 2, Copenhagen 1977. p. 58, and *OECD Economic Outlook*, Paris June 1993. p. 201.
52: Sarah Collinson: *Europe and International Migration*, Pinters Publishers, London and New York 1993. p. 54.
53: Robin Cohen: *The New Helots*, Gower Publishing Company, Vermont 1987. p. 220.
54: Giacomo Luciani, ed.: *Migration Policies in Europe and the United States*, Kluwer Academic Publishers, Dordrecht 1993. p. 133.
55: Grethe Brochmann: "Der sitter tre mann på en flåte...", in *Dagens folkevandringer - berører de oss?* Astri Suhrke and Svein Gjerdåker, eds. Chr. Michelsens Institutt/Cappelen, Oslo 1993. p. 85.
56: Peter Stalker: *The Work of Strangers*, International Labour Office, Geneva 1994. p. 141.
57: Peter Stalker: *The Work of Strangers*, International Labour Office, Geneva 1994. p. 55.
58: Julian L. Simon: "On the Economic Consequences of Immigration", in *Economic Aspects of International Migration*, Herbert Giersch, ed., Springer Verlag, Berlin - Heidelberg 1994. p. 139.
59: Peter Stalker: *The Work of Strangers*, International Labour Office, Geneva 1994. p. 142.
60: James F. Hollifield: *Immigrants, Markets and States*, Harvard University Press, London 1992. p. 92.
61: James F. Hollifield: *Immigrants, Markets and States*, Harvard University Press, London 1992. p. 96.
62: James F. Hollifield: *Immigrants, Markets and States*, Harvard University Press, London 1992. p. 84.
63: Carsten Svane Hansen: *Tal dansk din hund*, Kirkernes Race-program-Systime, Copenhagen 1992. p. 20.
64: James F. Hollifield: *Immigrants, Markets and States*, Harvard University Press, London 1992. p. 86.
65: Jan Ekberg and Lars Andersson: *Invandring, sysselsättning och ekonomiska effekter*, Report to the Expert Study Group for Public Economy, Department of Finance, Stockholm 1995. p. 186.

66: Russell King: "European international migration 1945-90: a statistical and geographical overview", in *Mass Migration in Europe*, Russell King, ed., Belhaven Press, London 1993. p. 34.

67: Trygve Bølstad, Øivind Fjeldstad and Dag Lerrand: *Jordas Fordrevne - Flyktninger i 90-åra*, Universitetsforlaget, Oslo 1995. p. 14.

68: Jonas Widgren: "Asylum Seekers in Europe in the Context of South-North Movements", in *International Migration Review*, vol. XXIII, no. 3, Fall 1989. p. 601.

69: "Statistik om indvandrere og flygtninge 1995", in *Dokumentation om Indvandrere*, Mellemfolkeligt Samvirke 1995. p. 18.

70: Jonas Widgren: "Asylum Seekers in Europe in the Context of South-North Movements", in *International Migration Review*, vol. XXIII, no. 3, Fall 1989. p. 600.

71: Jonas Widgren: "Asylum Seekers in Europe in the Context of South-North Movements", in *International Migration Review*, vol. XXIII, no. 3, Fall 1989. p. 600.

72: Jonas Widgren: "Asylum Seekers in Europe in the Context of South-North Movements", in *International Migration Review*, vol. XXIII, no. 3, Fall 1989. p. 600.

73: Russell King: "European international migration 1945-90: a statistical and geographical overview", in *Mass Migration in Europe*, Russell King, ed., Belhaven Press, London 1993. p. 34.

74: Jonas Widgren: "Asylum Seekers in Europe in the Context of South-North Movements", in *International Migration Review*, vol. XXIII, no. 3, Fall 1989. p. 601.

75: *Statistics in Focus - Population and Social Conditions*, no. 1, Eurostat, Luxembourg 1996. p. 5.

76: *The State of the World's Refugees 1995*, UNHCR, Oxford University Press, New York 1995. p. 198, and Laurids S. Lauridsen: "Masseimmigration fra syd - en tikkende bombe?", in *Den Nye Verden* no. 3, Copenhagen 1993. p. 117.

77: *Statistics in Focus - Population and Social Conditions*, no. 1, Eurostat, Luxembourg 1996, and *The State of the World's Refugees 1995*, UNHCR, Oxford University Press, New York 1995. p. 12.

Notes for chapter 5.

1: *Business Today*, Den Danske Bank, 5th January 1996.

2: Peter Birch Sørensen, *Information*, 4th January 1996.

3: *International Direct Investment, Policies and Trends in the 1980s*, OECD, Paris 1993. p.13.

4: Giacomo Luciani, ed.: *Migration Policies in Europe and the United States*, Kluwer Academic Publishers, Dordrecht 1993. p. 69, and *Annual Yearbook of Statistics 1994*, World Tourist Organization 1995.

5: Peter Stalker: *The Work of Strangers*, International Labour Office, Geneva 1994. p. 63.

6: John Salt: "The Future of International Labour Migration", in *International Migration Review*, vol. XXVI, no. 4, Winter 1992. p. 1078, and *Trends in International Migration - Annual Report 1994*, 1995 edition, OECD, Paris 1995. p. 40.

7: *Trends in International Migration - Annual Report 1994*, 1995 edition, OECD, Paris 1995. p. 21.

8: John Salt: "The Future of International Labour Migration", in *Internatinal Migration Review*, vol. XXVI, no. 4, Winter 1992. p. 1085.

9: Peter Birch Sørensen, *Information*, 4th January 1996.

10: Esben Dalsgaard: "Kan velfærdsstaten opretholdes?", in *Velfærdsstatens Fremtid*, Copenhagen Business School Press, Copenhagen 1996. p. 109.

11: IGC, 8th-12th November, Geneva 1995.

12: Alan Walker, Jens Alber and Anne-Marie Guillemard: *Older People in Europe: Social and Economic Policies - The 1993 Report of the European Observatory*, Commission of the European Communities, Brussels 1993. p. 70.

13: *OECD Economic Outlook*, June 1993, Paris 1993. p. 9.

14: Hans Kornø Rasmussen: *Befolkningseksplosionen*, Save the Children, Copenhagen 1993. p. 7.

15: Hans Kornø Rasmussen: *Befolkningseksplosionen*, Save the Children, Copenhagen 1993 .p. 23.

16: *Population Issues*, Briefing Kit 1992, UNFPA, New York 1992. p. 2.

17: Carl Haub: "New UN Projections Show Uncertainty of Future World", in *Population Today*, vol. 20, no. 2, Population Reference Bureau, Inc., February 1992. p. 7.

18: Jean Bourgeois-Pichat: "From the 20th to the 21st Century: Europe and its Population after the Year 2000", in *Population*, vol. 44, no. 1, Institut National d'Études Démographiques, Paris, September 1989. p. 57.

19: Jørgen Bech Simonsen: "Den arabiske verden I 1990'erne - nye tendenser ?", in *Middelhavet - et sikkerhedsproblem ?* , Europæisk Politik, Special Edition, November 1995. p. 32.

20: *Ugebrevet Mandag Morgen*, no. 23, 12th June 1995.

21: Mihály Simai: *Global Employment - An International Investigation into the Future of Work - volume 1*, United Nations University - World Institute for Development Economics Research, Zed Books Ltd., London and New Jersey 1994. p. 205.

22: Poul Christian Matthiessen: "Verden på vandring mod Europa", in *Tema-spot*, no. 1, 1992. p.2.

23: *Investing in Health*, World Development Report 1993, World Bank, Oxford University Press, New York 1993. p. 199.

24: *A Population Perspective on Development: The Middle East and North Africa*, The World Bank, August 1994. p. 10.

25: *A Population Perspective on Development: The Middle East and North Africa*, The World Bank, August 1994. p. 15.

26: *Maghreb Countries 1994 - Country Profile*, Statistisches Bundesamt and Eurostat, Brussels and Luxembourg 1994. p. 37.

27: *Maghreb Countries 1994 - Country Profile*, Statistisches Bundesamt and Eurostat, Brussels and Luxembourg 1994. p. 37.

28: Herbert Giersch, ed.: *Economic Aspects of International Migration*, Springer Verlag, Berlin- Heidelberg 1994. p. 10.

29: Bernhard Heitger: "Migration in the World Economy of 1870 - 1914", in *Weltwirtschaftliches Archiv*, vol. 129, no. 3, Journal of the Kiel Institute of World Economics 1993. p. 610.

30: Bernhard Heitger: "Migration in the World Economy of 1870 - 1914", in *Weltwirtschaftliches Archiv*, vol. 129, no. 3, Journal of the Kiel Institute of World Economics 1993. p. 610.

31: Peter Stalker: *The Work of Strangers*, International Labour Office, Geneva 1994. p. 21.

32: Paul Harrison: *Inside the Third World*, Penguin Books, London 1987. p. 220.

33: Partha Dasgupta: "The Population Problem: Theory and Evidence", in the *Journal of Economic Literature*, vol. XXXIII, no. 4, December 1995. p. 1881.

34: J.F. Bongaarts and R. Lesthaege: "The Proximate Determinants of Fertility", in *Population Growth and Reproduction in Sub-Saharan Africa - A World Bank Symposium* by G.T.F. Acsadi, G. Johnson-Scsadi and R.A. Bulatao, Washington 1990. pgs. 133-143. As well as an interview given by the demographer Thomas Mortensen of the IGC, Geneva, 2nd June 1996.

35: *Human Development Report 1992*, UNDP, Oxford University Press 1992. p. 34.

36: *The State of the World Population 1992*, UNFPA, New York 1992. Advance Press Copy. p. 2.

37: Gorm Rye Olsen: "Den nødvendige politiks umulighed", in *Mid-*

delhavet - et sikkerhedsproblem?, Europæisk Politik, Special Edition, November 1995. p. 18.

38: *Maghreb Countries 1994 - Country profile*, Statistisches Bundesamt and Eurostat, Brussels and Luxembourg 1994. p. 52.

39: *A Population Perspective on Development: The Middle East and North Africa*, the World Bank, August 1994. p. 8.

40: Peter Stalker: *The Work of Strangers*, International Labour Office, Geneva 1994. p. 28, and Gorm Rye Olsen: "Den nødvendige politiks mulighed", in *Middelhavet et sikkerhedsproblem?*, Europæisk Politik, Special Edition, November 1995. p. 23.

41: Peter Stalker: *The Work of Strangers*, International Labour Office, Geneva 1994, p. 31.

42: Peter Stalker: *The Work of Strangers*, International Labour Office, Geneva 1994. p. 32.

43: Hans Kornø Rasmussen: *Befolkningseksplosionen*, Save the Children, Copenhagen 1993. p. 79.

44: *Trafficking of Migrants*, IGC, Geneva, December 1995, p. 2.

45: Peter Stalker: *The Work of Strangers*, International Labour Office, Geneva 1994. p. 33.

46: *On Immigration and Asylum Policies*, Communiqué from the Commission to the European Council and the European Parliament, The Commission of European Communities, Brussels, 23 February 1994.

47: *Illegal Aliens: A Preliminary Study*, IGC, Geneva, June 1995. p. 5.

48: Gorm Rye Olsen: "Den nødvendige politiks mulighed", in *Middelhavet - et sikkerhedsproblem?* Europæisk Politik, Special Edition, November 1995. p. 5.

49: Henrik Olesen: *Population movements within Europe: Migration, Visa and Asylum policies*, speech given at the Wilton Park Conference on the 23rd of June 1995. p. 4.

50: *Illegal Aliens: A Preliminary Study*, IGC, Geneva, June 1995. p. 6.

51: *On Immigration and Asylum Policies,* Communiqué from the Commission to the European Council and the European Parliament, Commission of the European Communities, Brussels, 23rd of February 1994.

52: *Trafficking of Migrants*, IGC, Geneva, 11th December 1995. p. 2.

53: *Trafficking of Migrants*, IGC, Geneva, 11th December 1995. p. 2.

54: Henrik Olesen: *Population movements within Europe: Migration, Visa and Asylum Policies*, speech delivered at the Wilton Park Conference, 23rd June 1995.

55: *Illegal Aliens: A Preliminary Study*, IGC, Geneva, June 1996. p. 10.

56: H. W. Overbeek: "Globalization and the restructuring of the European Labour Market: The Role of Migration", in *Global Employment*, ed. Mihály Simai, vol. 1, Zed Books Ltd, London and New Jersey 1995. p. 211.

57: *The State of the World's Refugees 1995*, UNHCR, Oxford University Press, New York 1995. p. 20, and Trygve Bølstad, Øivind Fjeldstad and Dag Leraand: *Jordas Fordrevne - Flyktninger i 90-åra*, Universitetsforlaget, Oslo 1995. p. 14.

58: *Statistics in Focus - Population and social conditions*, no. 1, Eurostat, Luxembourg 1996. p. 4.

59: *Monthly Asylum Applications as Reported by IGC Participating States 1992-1996*, IGC, Geneva, 22 July 1996.

Notes for chapter 6.

1: *Statistics in Focus - population and Social Conditions 1996*, European Community Statistical Office, Luxembourg 1996.

2: *European Population*, no. 2 , 1991, Institut National d'Études Démographiques, Paris 1991. p. 13.

3: *Older People in Europe: Social and Economic Policies - the 1993 Report of the European Observatory*, Commission of the European Communities, 1993. p. 14.

4: *Older People in Europe: Social and Economic Policies - the 1993 Report of the European Observatory*, Commission of the European Communities, 1993. p. 14.

5: *Older People in Europe: Social and Economic Policies - the 1993 Report of the European Observatory*, Commission of the European Communities, 1993. p. 68.

6: *Older People in Europe: Social and Economic Policies - the 1993 Report of the European Observatory*, Commission of the European Communities, 1993. p. 96.

7: "Aging Populations and National Budgets", in *The OECD Observer*, no. 197, Paris, December 1995/ January 1996. p. 33.

8: *Older People in Europe: Social and Economic Policies - The 1993 Report of the European Observatory*, Commission of the European Communities, 1993. p. 104.

9: Richard Layard, Olivier Blanchard, Rudiger Dornbusch and Paul Krugman: *East-West Migration - The Alternatives*, The United Nations University 1992. p. 8, and Solon Ardittis, ed.: *The Politics of East-West Migration*, The Macmillan Press, London 1994. p. 233.

10: Wolfgang Lutz and Christopher Prinz: "Modelling future immigration and integration in Western Europe", in *The New Geography of European Migrations*, ed. Russell King, Belhaven Press, London and New York 1993. Chapter 5.

11: Joop de Beer and Willem van Hoorn: *New long-term national population scenarios for the countries of the European Economic Area: Principal assumptions and main outcomes*, Statistics Nederlands, Paper for Second Users Meeting on Demographic Projections, Brussels, 25th April 1996. p. 7.

Notes for chapter 7.

1: *Trends in International Migration - Annual Report 1994*, OECD, Paris 1995. p. 11.

2: *The State of the World's Refugees 1995*, UNHCR, Oxford University Press, New York 1995. p. 12.

3: *The Independent*, 14th September 1992.

4: Bashy Quraishy: *EU - Det tabte paradis*, Etnisk Debatforum, Copenhagen 1995. p. 28.

5: Anne la Cour Vågen: "Status i det europæiske samarbejde om asyl- og flygtningepolitik", in *EU og udlændingepolitik*, The Danish European Movement, Copenhagen 1994. p. 9.

6: Anne la Cour Vågen: "Status i det europæiske samarbejde om asyl- og flygtningepolitik", in *EU og udlændingepolitik*, The Danish European Movement, Copenhagen 1994. p. 12.

7: Solon Ardittis: *The Politics of East-West Migration*, St Martin Press, The Macmillan Press Ltd., London 1994. p. 222.

8: Adrian Fortescue: "Defining a European immigration policy", in *Towards a European Immigrant* Policy, The Philip Morris Institute, Brussels, October 1993. p. 38.

9: European Parliament: *No. 27: Briefing on The 1996 Intergovernmental Conference and the Schengen Convention*, Luxembourg, 30th January 1996. p. 4.

10: J. J. Bolten: "From Schengen to Dublin: the new frontiers of refugee law", in *Schengen - Internationalization of central chapters of the law on aliens, refugees, privacy, security and the police* by W.E.J. Tjeenk Willink, ed. J.D.M. Stenbergen - Kluwer law and taxation, Utrecht 1991. pgs. 26 and 28.

11: J. J. Bolten: "From Schengen to Dublin: the new frontiers of refugee law", in *Schengen -Internationalization of central chapters of the law on aliens, refugees, privacy, security and the police* by W.E.J. Tjeenk Willink, ed. J.D.M. Stenbergen - Kluwer law and taxation, Utrecht 1991. p. 32.

12: H. Meijers: "Schengen: Introduction", in *Schengen - Internationalization of the central chapters of the law on aliens, refugees, privacy, security and the police* by W.E.J. Tjeenk Willink, ed. J.D.M. Stenbergen - Kluwer law and taxation, Utrecht 1991. p. 32.

13: *Schengen Convention as of 19th June 1990*, Article 22, paragraph 1.

14: *Schengen Convention as of 19th June 1990*, Article 22, paragraph 2.

15: J. J. Bolten: "From Schengen to Dublin: The new frontiers of refugee law" in *Schengen - Internationalization of central chapters of the law on aliens, refugees, privacy, security and the police* by W.E.J. Tjenk Willink, ed. J.D.M. Stenbergen - Kluwer law and taxation, Utrecht 1991. p. 11.

16: T. Hoogenboom: "Free Movement of non-EC nationals, Schengen and beyond", in *Schengen - Internationalization of central chapters of the law on aliens, refugees, privacy, security and the police* by W. E.J. Tjeenk Willink, ed. J.D.M. Stenbergen - Kluwer law and taxation, Utrecht 1991. p. 81.

17: W. R. Böhning and J. Werquin: *Some Economic, Social and Human Rights Considerations Concerning the Future Status of third Country Nationals in the Single European Market*, International Labour Office, Geneva, April 1990.

18: Quote from a meeting of 3rd June 1996 with the Chief for the *Migration Employment Branch*, W. Roger Böhning of the ILO, Geneva.

19: T. Hoogenboom: "Free movement of non-EC nationals, Schengen and beyond", in *Schengen - Internationalization of central chapters of the law on aliens, refugees, privacy, security and police* by W.E. J. Tjeenk Willink, ed. J.D.M. Stenbergen - Kluwer law and taxation, Utrecht 1991. p. 76.

20: Ulla Holm: "Nordafrika og Europa: Kollisionskurs eller partnerskab?", in *Middelhavet - et sikkerhedsproblem?* Europæisk Politik, November 1995. p. 9.

21: Gorm Rye Olsen: "Bruxelles vender så småt blikket mod Syd", in *Information*, 22nd December, 1994.

22: Henrik Olesen: *Migration... into the 21st century*, IGC, Geneva, 23rd May 1995. p. 7.

23: Ninna Nyberg Sørensen: *Globale drømme - Migration og udvikling i et transnationalt perspektiv*, in CUF Notat, November 1995. p. 21.

24: *Trends in International Migration - Annual Report 1994*, OECD, Paris 1995. p. 114.

25: Sarah Collinson: *Europe and International Migration*, Pinter Publishers, London and New York 1993. p. 74.

26: Martin Frey and Ulrich Mammey: "Germany", in *Impact of migration in the receiving countries*, ed. L. A. Kosinski, CICRED and IOM, Geneva 1996. p. 107.

27: *Country Profile - Maghreb Countries 1994*, Statistisches Bundesamt and Eurostat, Luxembourg 1994. pgs. 190-198.

28: Martin Frey and Ulrich Mammey: "Germany", in *Impact of migration in the receiving countries*, ed. L. A. Kosinski, CICRED and IOM, Geneva 1996. p. 107.

29: *Supplement - Det grænseløse Europa*, Eurostat, monthly newsletter, April 1996.

30: *Statistics in Focus - Population and social conditions*, no. 1, Eurostat, Luxembourg 1996. p. 4, and *The State of the World's Refugees 1995*, UNHCR, Oxford University Press, New York 1995. p. 12.

31: *EU's udvidelse mod øst*, Ministry of Economy, February 1996. p. 96.

32: Dorthe Nøhr Pedersen: "Hvis de kan jodle, bliver ventetiden kortere!" in *Tidsskriftet Grus*, Aalborg 1993.p. 60.

33: Solon Ardittis: *The Politics of East-West Migration*, The Macmillan Press, London 1994. p. 230.

34: Martin Frey and Ulrich Mammey: "Germany", in *Impact of migration in the receiving countries*, CICRED and IOM, Geneva 1996. p. 7.

35: *Response of international organizations to the humanitarian problems and population displacements in the former Soviet Union*, IGC, Geneva, April 1994. p. 1.

36: *Response of international organizations to the humanitarian problems and population displacements in the former Soviet Union, IGC*, Geneva, April 1994. p. 2.

37: Henrik Olesen: *Migration... into the 21st Century*, IGC, Geneva, 23rd May 1995. p.1, and the Reflection Group on Managing Migration in the Wider Europe, working paper, IGC, Geneva 1997.

Bibliography

Appleyard, Reginald, "Migration and Development: Myth and Reality", in *International Migration review*, vol. XXIII, no. 3, Fall 1989.

Ardittis, Solon, ed., *The Politics of East-West Migration*, The Macmillan Press, London 1994.

Beer, Joop de and Willem van Hoorn, *New long-term national population scenarios for the countries of the European Economic Area: Principal assumptions and main outcomes*, Statistics Nederlands, Paper for Second Users Meeting on Demographic Projections, Brussels, 25th April 1996.

Böhning, W.R. and J. Werquin, *Some Economic, Social and Human Rights Considerations Concerning the Future Status of Third-Country Nationals in the Single European Market*, International Labour Office, Geneva, April 1990.

Böhning, W.R. and M.-L. Schloeter-Paredes, *Aid in place of Migration*, ILO, Geneva 1994.

Bolten, J.J., "From Schengen to Dublin: The new frontiers of refugee law", in J.D.M. Stenbergen, ed., *Schengen – Internationalization of central chapters of the law on aliens, refugees, privacy, security and the police*, W.E.J. Tjeenk Willink -Kluwer law and taxation, Utrecht 1991.

Bongaarts, J.F. og Lesthaeghe, R., "The Proximate Determinants of Fertility", in Acsadi, G.T.F., G. Johnson-Scsadi and R.A. Bulatao, *Population Growth and Reproduction in Sub-Saharan Africa – A World Bank Symposium*, Washington 1990.

Borjas, George, J., "The Economics of Immigration", in *Journal of Economic Literature*, vol. XXXII, no. 4, December 1994.

Bourgeois-Pichat, Jean, "From the 20th to the 21st Century: Europe and its Population after the Year 2000", in *Population*, vol. 44, no. 1, Institut National d'Études Démographiques, Paris, September 1989.

Breuilly, John, *Nationalism and the State. Second Edition*, Manchester University Press, 1993.

Brochmann, Grete, "Der sitter tre menn på en flåte...", in Astri Suhrke og Svein Gjerdåker, eds., *Dagens folkevandringer - berører de oss?*, Chr. Michelsens Institutt/Cappelen, Oslo 1993.

Bødtcher, Anne la Cour, Jane Hughes, Vagn Klim Larsen, *Legal and Social Conditions for Asylum Seekers and refugees in selected European Countries*, Danish Refugee Council, February 1993.

Bølstad, Trygve, Øivind Fjeldstad, Dag Leraand, *Jordas Fordrevne – Flyktninger i 90-åra*, Universitetsforlaget, Oslo 1995.

Børsens Nyhedsmagasin, special issue, september 1988.

Castles, Stephen and Godula Kosack, *Immigrant Workers and Class Structure in Western Europe*, Oxford University Press, 1985.

Castles, Stephen & Mark J. Miller, *The Age of Migration*, The Macmillan Press Ltd, London 1993.

CIS-Conference, *Forced to Move by War or Circumstance*, Geneva 1996.

Cohen, Robin, *The New Helots*, Gower Publishing Company, Vermont 1987.

Cohn-Bendit, Daniel, "Europe and its borders: The case for a common immigration policy", in *Towards a European Immigration Policy*, The Philip Morris Institute, Brussels, October 1993.

Collinson, Sarah, *Europe and International Migration*, Pinter Publishers, London and New York 1993.

Commission of the European Communities, *Immigration of citizens from third countries into the southern Member States of the European Community*, Luxembourg 1991.

Commission of the European Communities, *Older People in Europe: Social and Economic Policies – The 1993 Report of the European Observatory*, 1993.

Commission of the European Communities, *On Immigration and Asylum Politicies*, Brussels, 23rd February 1994.

Council of Europe, *Evolving mobility and current legislative disposition: how well do they match up?* Strasbourg, 17th–18th June 1997.

Cross, Malcolm, ed., *Ethnic minorities and industrial change in Europe and North America*, Cambridge University Press, 1992.

Dalgaard, Esben, "Kan velfærdsstaten opretholdes?", in *Velfærdsstatens Fremtid*, Handelshøjskolens Forlag, Copenhagen 1996.

Dasgupta, Partha, "The Population Problem: Theory and Evidence", i *Journal of Economic Literature*, vol. XXXIII, no. 4, December 1995.

Dencik, Lars, "Reflexions on Xenophobia and Exile in Contemporary Modernity", in *Rescue – 43 – Xenophobia and Exile*, Munksgaard, Copenhagen 1993.

Den Danske Bank, *Business Today*, 5th January 1996.

Ekberg, Jan and Lars Andersson, *Invandring, sysselsättning och ekonomiska effekter*, Report for the Expert Group on Public Economy, Department of Finance, Stockholm 1995.

European Commission, *The demographic situation in the European Union*, 1994 report, Luxembourg 1995.

European Commision, *Europa*, no. 10, October 1995.

European Parliament, *No. 27: Briefing on The 1996 Intergovernmental Conference and the Schengen Convention*, Luxembourg, 30th January 1996.

Eurostat, *Statistics in Focus – Population and Social Conditions*, no. 1, Luxembourg 1996.

Eurostat, *Statistics in Focus – Population and Social Conditions*, no. 3, Luxembourg 1995.

Eurostat, *Supplement – Det grænseløse Europa*, Monthly Newsletter, April 1996.

Faini, Riccardo and Alessandra Venturini, "Trade, aid and migrations", in *European Economic Review*, vol. 37, April 1993.

Fernandez, John. P., *The Diversity Advantage*, Lexington Books, New York 1993.

Fielding, Anthony, "Mass migration and economic restructuring", in Russel King, ed., *Mass Migration in Europe*, Belhaven Press, London 1993.

Ford, Glyn, ed., *Fascist Europe – The Rise of Racism and Xenophobia*, Pluto Press, London 1992.

Fortescue, Adrian, "Defining a European immigration policy", in *Towards a European Immigration Policy*, The Philip Morris Institute, Brussels, October 1993.

Frey, Martin and Ulrich Mammey, "Germany", in L.A. Kosinski, ed., *Impact of migration in the receiving countries*, CICRED and IOM, Geneva 1996.

Giersch, Herbert, ed., *Economic Aspects of International Migration*, Springer-Verlag, Berlin-Heidelberg 1994.

Golini, Antonio and Rita Bisio, "North-South links: Level of development and migration status report from different regions of the world", in *European Population*, vol. 2, Institut National d'Études Démographiques, Paris 1991.

Gordon, Ian, ed., *European Factor Mobility*, The Macmillan Press Ltd, London 1989.

Grecic, V., "East-West Migration and its Possible Influence on South-North Migration", in *International Migration*, vol. XXIX, no. 2, June 1991.

Hammer, Ole, *25 års arbejde i det fremmede*, Mellemfolkeligt Samvirke, Copenhagen 1995.

Hansen, Carsten Svane, *Tal dansk din hund* og *Rejs hjem din hund*, Kirkernes Raceprogram, Systime, Copenhagen 1992.

Hansen, Hans O., *Some demographic impacts of the current regional population development and ethnic heterogeneity in Denmark*, Paper prepared for European Population Conference, Institute of Statistics, Copenhagen University, June 1995.

Hansen, Svend Aage og Ingrid Henriksen, *Dansk socialhistorie 1940-83: Velfærdsstaten*, Gyldendal, Copenhagen 1984.

Harrison, Paul, *Inside the Third World – the anatomy of poverty*, Penguin Books, London 1987.

Haub, Carl, "New UN Projections Show Uncertainty of Future World", in *Population Today*, vol. 20, no. 2, Population Reference Bureau, Inc., February 1992.

Heitger, Bernhard, "Migration in the World Economy of 1870 -1914", in *Weltwirtschaftliches Archiv*, vol. 129, no. 3, Journal of the Kiel Institute of World Economics 1993.

Hollifield, James F., *Immigrants, Markets and States*, Harvard University Press, London 1992.

Holm, Ulla, "Nordafrika og Europa: Kollisionskurs eller partnerskab?", in *Middelhavet – et sikkerhedsproblem?*, Europæisk Politik, November 1995.

Hoogenboom, T., "Free movement of non-EC nationals, Schengen and beyond", in J.D.M. Stenbergen, ed., *Schengen – Internationalization of central chapters of the law on aliens, refugees, privacy, security and the police*, W.E.J. Tjeenk Willink -Kluwer law and taxation, Utrecht 1991.

IGC, *Asylum applications in participating states 1983-1995*, Geneva, March 1996.

IGC, *Illegal Aliens: A Preliminary Study*, Geneva, June 1995.

IGC, *Monthly Asylum Applications as Reported by IGC Participating States 1992-1996*, Geneva, 22nd July 1996.

IGC, *Progress Report, Migration, Development and Trade*, Geneva, 6th January 1994.

IGC, *Response of international organizations to the humanitarian problems & population displacements in the former Soviet Union*, Geneva, April 1994.

IGC, *Summary Description of Asylum Procedures in States in Europe, North America and Australia*, Geneva, October 1995.

IGC, *Summary Description of Legislation on Aliens Trafficking in States in Europe, North America and Australia*, Geneva, December 1995.

ILO, IOM and UNHCR, *Migrants, Refugees and International Cooperation*, International Conference on Population and Development, 1994.

International Migration, "Ninth IOM Seminar on Migration: South-North migration", vol. XXIX, no. 2, June 1991.

Joly, Daniéle, *Refugees – Asylum in Europe*, Minority Rights Publications, London 1992.

Kane, Hal, *The Hour of Departure: Forces that Create Refugees and Migrants*, Worldwatch Paper 125, Washington, June 1995.

King, Russel, "European International Migration 1945-90: a statistical and geographical overview", in Russel King, ed., *Mass Migration in Europe*, Belhaven Press, London 1993.

Kritz, Mary, Lin Lean Lim and Hania Zlotnik, eds., *International Migration Systems. A Global Approach*, Clarendon Press, Oxford 1992.

Kubat, Daniel, ed., *The Politics of Migration Policies. Settlement and Integration. The First World into the 1990s*, Center for Migration Studies, New York 1993.

Lauridsen, Laurids S., "Masseimmigration fra syd – en tikkende bombe?", in *Den Ny Verden* 3, Copenhagen 1993.

Layard, Richard, Oliver Blanchard, Rudiger Dornbusch, Paul Krugman, *East-West Migration – The Alternatives*, The United Nations University, 1992.

Luciani, Giacomo, ed., *Migration Policies in Europe and the United States*, Kluwer Academic Publishers, Dordrecht 1993.

Lutz, Wolfgang and Christopher Prinz, "Modelling future immigration and integration in Western Europe", in Russel King, ed., *The New Geography of European Migrations*, Belhaven Press, London and New York 1993.

Martin, Philip, "The migration issue", in Russel King, ed., *The New Geography of European Migrations*, Belhaven Press, London and New York 1993.

Matthiessen, Poul Christian, "Verden på vandring mod Europa", in *Tema-spot*, no. 1, 1992.

Meijers, H., "Schengen: Introduction", in J.D.M. Stenbergen, ed., *Schengen – Internationalization of central chapters of the law on aliens, refugees, privacy, security and the police*, W.E.J. Tjeenk Willink – Kluwer law and taxation, Utrecht 1991.

Mellemfolkeligt Samvirke, "Statistik om indvandrere og flygtninge 1995", in *Dokumentation om Indvandrere*, no. 1, 1995.

Merrit, Giles, *Østeuropa og Sovjetunionen – frihedens udfordringer*, Schultz, Copenhagen 1991.

Ministry of Economy, *EU's udvidelse mod øst*, February 1996.

Molle, Willem and Aad Van Mourik, "International Movements of Labour under Conditions of Economic Integration: The Case of Western Europe", in *Journal of Common Market Studies*, vol. XXVI, no. 3, March 1988.

Monnier, Alain and C. de Guibert-Lantoine, "The demographic situation of Europe and the developing countries overseas: an annual report", in *Population*, vol. 5, Institut National d'Études Démographiques, Paris 1993.

Montanari, Armando and Antonio Cortese, "South to North migration in a Mediterranean perspective", in Russel King, ed., *Mass Migration in Europe*, Belhaven Press, London 1993.

Öberg, Sture, "Europe in the context of world population trends" ,in Russel King, ed., *Mass Migration in Europe*, Belhaven Press, London 1993.

OECD, *International Direct Investment, Policies and Trends in the 1980s*, Paris 1993.

OECD, *Migration – The Demographic Aspects*, Paris 1991.

OECD, *OECD Economic Outlook*, Paris, June 1993 and December 1994.

OECD, *The Changing Course of International Migration*, Paris 1993.

OECD, *Trends in International Migration – Annual Report 1994*, 1995 edition, Paris 1995.

Office for Official Publications of the European Communities, *Asylum-Seekers and Refugees – a Statistical Report*, vol. 1: EC Member States, Luxembourg 1994.

Office for Official Publications of the European Communities, *Migration Statistics*, Luxembourg 1995.

Olsen, Gorm Rye, "Den nødvendige politiks umulighed", in *Middelhavet et sikkerhedsproblem?*, Europæisk Politik, special issue, November 1995.

Olesen, Henrik, *Migration... into the 21st Century*, IGC, Geneva 23th May 1995.

Olesen, Henrik, *Organizing Diversity, Migration Policy and Practice.* Speech at conference at Berg en Dal, the Netherlands, 8th-12th November 1995.

Olesen, Henrik, *Population movements within Europe: Migration, Visa and Asylum Policies.* Speech at Wilton Park Conference, 23rd June 1995.

Overbeek, H. W., "Globalization and the restructuring of the European Labour Market: The Role of Migration", in Mihály Simai, ed., *Global Employment*, vol. 1, Zed Books Ltd, London and New Jersey 1995.

Oxford Analytica, February 24, Oxford 1992.

Pedersen, Dorthe Nøhr, "Hvis de kan jodle, bliver ventetiden kortere!", in *Tidsskriftet Grus*, no. 40, Aalborg 1993.

Population Reference Bureau, Inc., "Population Today", vol. 20, no. 2, February 1992.

Quraishy, Bashy, *EU – Det tabte paradis*, Etnisk Debatforum, Copenhagen 1995.

Rallu, Jean-Louis, Alain Blum, "European Population", in *European Population*, vol. 2, Institut National d'Études Démographiques, Paris, October 1991.

Rasmussen, Hans Kornø, *Befolkningseksplosionen*, Save the Children, Copenhagen 1993.

Rystad, Göran, "History and the Future of International Migration", in *International Migration Review*, vol. XXVI, no. 4, Winter 1992.

Salt, John, "The Future of International Labor Migration", in *International Migration Review*, vol. XXVI, no. 4, Winter 1992.

Salt, John, "The geographical impact of migration in Europe: lessons for Europe from the New World", in Russel King, ed., *The New geography of European Migrations*, Belhaven Press, London and New York 1993.

Schengen-Convention of 19th June 1990.

Simai, Mihály, *Global Employment – An International Investigation into the Future of Work – volume 1*, United Nations University – World Institute for Development Economics Research, Zed Books Ltd, London and New Jersey 1994.

Simon, Julian L., "On the Economic Consequences if Immigration", in

Herbert Giersch, ed., *Economic Aspects of International Migration*, Springer-Verlag, Berlin-Heidelberg 1994.

Simonsen, Jørgen Bæk, "Den arabiske verden i 1990'erne – nye tendenser?", in *Middelhavet – et sikkerhedsproblem?*, Europæisk Politik, special issue, November 1995.

Sørensen, Ninna Nyberg, *Globale drømme – Migration og udvikling i et transnationalt perspektiv*, CUF Notat, November 1995.

Stalker, Peter, *The Work of Strangers*, International Labour Office, Geneva 1994.

Statistics Denmark, *Vital Statistics* and *Statistical Yearbook*, Copenhagen 1992.

Statistics Denmark, *Statistical News*, "Befolkning og valg", no. 5, Copenhagen 1996.

Statistisches Bundesamt and Eurostat, *Maghreb countries 1994 - Country profile*, Brussels and Luxembourg 1994.

Stepputat, Finn, *Efter nødhjælpen – fra katastrofe til udvikling?*, CUF Notat, Copenhagen, September 1994.

Suhrke, Astri and Svein Gjerdåker, eds., *Dagens folkevandringer – berører de oss?*, Chr. Michelsens Institutt/Cappelen, Oslo 1993.

The Legal Affairs Commitee, Notes on Schengen Convention and Europol af 29th April 1996. (App. 789)

The OECD Observer, "Aging Populations and National Budgets", no. 197, Paris, December 1995/January 1996.

The World Bank, *A Population Perspective on Development: The Middle East and North Africa*, August 1994.

The World Bank, *Investing in Health*, World Development Report 1993, Oxford University Press, New York 1993.

Ugebrevet Mandag Morgen, no. 16 and no. 37 in 1990, no. 21 in 1993, no. 12 and no. 20 in 1994 and no. 23 in 1995.

UNDP, *Human Develoment Report 1992*, UNDP, Oxford University Press 1992.

UNFPA, *Population Issues*, Briefing Kit 1992, New York 1992.

UNFPA, *The State of the World Population 1992*, New York 1992. Advance Press Copy.

UNFPA, *The State of the World Population 1993*, New York 1993.

UNHCR, *The State of the World's Refugees 1995*, Oxford University Press, New York 1995.

UNHCR, *UNHCR and its Partners in Europe*, Geneva 1995.

United Nations, *Demographic Yearbook/Annuaire démographique 1989*, New York 1991.

United Nations, *International Migration Bulletin*, no. 7, Geneva, 1995.

United Nations, *World Population Monitoring 1993 – With a Special Report on Refugees*, New York 1996.

Vågen, Anne la Cour, "Status i det europæiske samarbejde om asyl- og flygtningepolitik", in *EU og udlændingepolitik*, The Danish European Movement, Copenhagen 1994.

Walker, Alan, Jens Alber and Anne-Marie Guillemard, *Older People in Europe: Social and Economic Policies – The 1993 Report of the European Observatory*, Commission of the European Communities, Brussels 1993.

Webber, Frances, *Crimes of arrival: Immigrants and Asylum-seekers in the New Europe*, A Statewatch publication, London 1995.

Wendt, Peter, "Valutasamarbejdet: Sammenbrud eller nybrud?", in *Økonomi og Politik*, no. 3, Jurist- og Økonomforbundets Forlag, Copenhagen 1993.

Widgren, Jonas, "Asylum Seekers in Europe in the Context of South-North Movements", in *International Migration Review*, vol. XXIII, no. 3, Fall 1989.

Wilpert, Czarina, "From One Generation to Another...", in Czarina Wilpert, ed., *Entering the Working World*, European Science Foundation, 1988.

World Tourist Organization, *Annual Yearbook of Statistics 1994*, 1995.

Wæver, Ole, Barry Buzan, Morten Kelstrup and Pierre Lemaitre, *Identity, Migration and the New Security Agenda in Europe*, Pinter Publishers Ltd, London 1993.

Zimmermann, Klaus F., "Tackling the European Migration Problem", in *The Journal of Economic Perspectives*, vol. 9, no. 2, Spring 1995.

Zolberg, Aristide R., "The Next Waves: Migration Theory for a Changing World", in *International Migration Review*, vol. XXIII, no. 3, Fall 1989.

Index